John Bunyan was a major figure in seve
one deeply embroiled in the religious up.
considers all his major texts, including *The Pilgrim's Progress* and his autobiography *Grace Abounding*. The essays, by leading Bunyan scholars, place these
and his other works in the context of seventeenth-century history and literature.
They discuss such key issues as the publication of dissenting works, the history of
the book, gender, the relationship between literature and religion, between literature and early-modern radicalism, and the reception of seventeenth-century
texts. Other chapters assess Bunyan's importance for the development of allegory,
life-writing, the early novel and children's literature. This *Companion* provides a
comprehensive and accessible introduction to an author with an assured and
central place in English literature.

A complete list of books in the series is at the back of this book

THE CAMBRIDGE
COMPANION TO
BUNYAN

EDITED BY
ANNE DUNAN-PAGE

CAMBRIDGE UNIVERSITY PRESS
Cambridge, New York, Melbourne, Madrid, Cape Town, Singapore,
São Paulo, Delhi, Dubai, Tokyo

Cambridge University Press
The Edinburgh Building, Cambridge CB2 8RU, UK

Published in the United States of America by Cambridge University Press, New York

www.cambridge.org
Information on this title: www.cambridge.org/9780521733083

First published 2010

Printed in the United Kingdom at the University Press, Cambridge

A catalogue record for this publication is available from the British Library

Library of Congress Cataloguing in Publication data
The Cambridge companion to Bunyan / edited by Anne Dunan-Page.
p.   cm. – (Cambridge companions to literature)
Includes bibliographical references and index.
ISBN 978-0-521-51526-9 – ISBN 978-0-521-73308-3 (pbk.)
1. Bunyan, John, 1628–1688 – Criticism and interpretation.   2. Christianity and
literature – England – History – 17th century.   3. Christian literature, English – History and
criticism.   4. Dissenters, Religious, in literature.   5. Puritan movements in
literature.   6. Bunyan, John, 1628–1688 – Appreciation.   7. Bunyan, John,
1628–1688 – Influence.
I. Dunan-Page, Anne.   II. Title.   III. Series.
PR3332.C36   2010
828'.407–dc22
2009054023

ISBN 978-0-521-51526-9 Hardback
ISBN 978-0-521-73308-3 Paperback

CONTENTS

CONTRIBUTORS

VERA J. CAMDEN is Professor of English at Kent State University, Training and Supervising Analyst at the Cleveland Psychoanalytic Center and Clinical Assistant Professor of Psychiatry at Case Western Reserve University. She is co-editor of *American Imago*. Her most recent publications include ' "The Language of Tenderness and Passion" or, Sex in Paradise', *New Literary History* (Autumn 2007), *Trauma and Transformation: The Political Progress of John Bunyan* (ed.) (2008) and ' "The Past is a Foreign Country": The Uses of Literature in the Psychoanalytic Process', in Peter Rudnytsky and Rita Charon (eds.), *Psychoanalysis and Narrative Medicine* (2008).

MICHAEL DAVIES is Senior Lecturer in English at the University of Liverpool. He has research interests in English literature of the Renaissance and Restoration periods, focusing especially on the literary and religious cultures of seventeenth-century England. He has published essays on a range of writers, from William Shakespeare to William Cowper, and is the author of *Graceful Reading: Theology and Narrative in the Works of John Bunyan* (2002).

ANNE DUNAN-PAGE is Professor of early-modern British studies at the Université de Provence, Aix-Marseille I (France). She works on various aspects of religious dissent, focusing on seventeenth-century separatists and the Huguenots. She is the author of *Grace Overwhelming: John Bunyan, 'The Pilgrim's Progress' and the Extremes of the Baptist Mind* (2006), and has edited *The Religious Culture of the Huguenots, 1660–1750* (2006), *Les Huguenots dans les Îles Britanniques de la Renaissance aux Lumières* (with Marie-Christine Munoz, 2008) and *Roger L'Estrange and the Making of Restoration Culture* (with Beth Lynch, 2008).

ISABEL HOFMEYR is Professor of African literature at the University of the Witwatersrand in Johannesburg, South Africa. She has published widely on South African and African literary and cultural history. Her first monograph, *We Spend our Years as a Tale that is Told: Oral Historical Narrative in a South African Chiefdom* (1994), was shortlisted for the Hersovits Prize. Her monograph, *The*

Portable Bunyan: A Transnational History of 'The Pilgrim's Progress' won the 2007 Richard L. Greaves Award, The International John Bunyan Society.

N. H. KEEBLE is Professor of English studies and Senior Deputy Principal at the University of Stirling, Scotland. His publications include *Richard Baxter: Puritan Man of Letters* (1982), *The Literary Culture of Nonconformity in Later Seventeenth-Century England* (1987), *The Restoration: England in the 1660s* (2002) and a two-volume *Calendar of the Correspondence of Richard Baxter* (with Geoffrey F. Nuttall, 1991). He has edited *John Bunyan: Conventicle and Parnassus – Tercentenary Essays* (1988), *The Cultural Identity of Seventeenth-Century Woman: A Reader* (1994), *The Cambridge Companion to Writing of the English Revolution* (2001), *John Bunyan: Reading Dissenting Writing* (2003), Bunyan's *The Pilgrim's Progress* (1984) and texts by Richard Baxter, Lucy Hutchinson, Andrew Marvell and Daniel Defoe. He is a volume editor for the forthcoming *Oxford Complete Works of John Milton*.

EMMA MASON is Senior Lecturer in the Department of English and Comparative Literary Studies at Warwick University and is a specialist in nineteenth-century poetry and religion. She is the author of *Women Poets of the Nineteenth Century* (2006), *Nineteenth-Century Religion and Literature* (with Mark Knight, 2006) and *The Cambridge Introduction to Wordsworth* (2009); and co-editor of *The Blackwell Companion to the Bible in English Literature* (2009) and *The Oxford Handbook to the Reception History of the Bible* (2010).

SHANNON MURRAY teaches early-modern and children's literature at the University of Prince Edward Island, Canada. She is the founder and editor of *The Recorder: A Publication of the International John Bunyan Society* (1993–9). She writes on adaptations of *The Pilgrim's Progress* for children, on the Polish children's writer Janusz Korczak and on learning communities and teaching for creativity in higher education. She is a Canadian 3M National Teaching Fellow for excellence and leadership in university teaching and a published children's writer.

W. R. OWENS is Professor of English literature at The Open University. His research interests are in seventeenth- and early eighteenth-century English literature, textual scholarship and book history. He is Director of the AHRC-funded project 'The Reading Experience Database' (www.open.ac.uk/Arts/RED). A past President of the International John Bunyan Society, he has published extensively on Bunyan, and has edited two volumes of *Miscellaneous Works* (1994), and editions of *Grace Abounding to the Chief of Sinners* and *The Pilgrim's Progress* (1987, 2003 respectively). Together with P. N. Furbank he has written four books and many articles on Daniel Defoe, and they are the General Editors of *The Works of Daniel Defoe* (44 volumes, in progress, 2000–).

ROGER POOLEY teaches English at Keele University. His books include *English Prose of the Seventeenth Century* (1993) and a new edition of *The Pilgrim's Progress* (2008). He has published a number of articles and chapters on Bunyan and seventeenth-century literature. He is currently President of the International John Bunyan Society (2007–10).

STUART SIM is Professor of critical theory in the English Department, University of Sunderland. He is the author of numerous publications on the fiction of the long eighteenth century and contemporary critical theory. A joint-editor and founder-member of the journal *Bunyan Studies*, he was elected a Fellow of the English Association in 2002. Recent works include *The Eighteenth-Century Novel and Contemporary Social Issues* (2008), and he has edited, with W. R. Owens, *Reception, Appropriation, Recollection: Bunyan's 'Pilgrim's Progress'* (2007).

NIGEL SMITH is Professor of English at Princeton University. He is the author of *Perfection Proclaimed: Language and Literature in English Radical Religion, 1640–1660* (1989), *Literature and Revolution in England, 1640–1660* (1994) and *Is Milton Better than Shakespeare?* (2008), as well as articles on Shakespeare, Donne, Herbert, Milton and Bunyan, and on such topics as atheism, vegetarianism and Socinianism. He has edited the *Ranter Tracts* (1983), the *Journal of George Fox* (1998), the *Poems of Andrew Marvell* (2003) and co-edited *The Oxford Handbook of Milton* (2009).

DAVID WALKER is Principal Lecturer and Head of English and creative writing at Northumbria University. Co-author (with Stuart Sim) of *Bunyan and Authority: The Rhetoric of Dissent and the Legitimation Crisis in Seventeenth-Century England* (2000), he has published articles on Bunyan's non-fiction in *Prose Studies* and *Bunyan Studies*. He is reviews editor for *Bunyan Studies* and currently writing a book on memories of the sixteenth-century Reformation in mid to later seventeenth-century literature.

NOTE ON THE TEXT

Early-modern texts cited in this *Companion* can be consulted via Early English Books Online (EEBO). Unless stated otherwise, the place of publication is London. Spelling and punctuation have not been modernised. Dates are given in Old Style with the year beginning on 1 January.

Page references to Bunyan's works appear in parentheses within the text. The titles of his non-fiction works have been shortened. The dating of all the works follows Richard L. Greaves's chronology in *Glimpses of Glory: John Bunyan and English Dissent* (Stanford University Press, 2002), pp. 637–41.

ABBREVIATIONS

Bunyan's works

B&G	*A Book for Boys and Girls*, ed. Graham Midgley, in *The Miscellaneous Works of John Bunyan* (Oxford: Clarendon Press, 1980), VI:183–269
Bunyan, *Works*	*The Works of that Eminent Servant of Christ, Mr John Bunyan*, ed. Charles Doe (1692)
GA	*Grace Abounding to the Chief of Sinners*, ed. Roger Sharrock (Oxford: Clarendon Press, 1962)
HW	*The Holy War*, ed. Roger Sharrock and James F. Forrest (Oxford: Clarendon Press, 1980)
LDB	*The Life and Death of Mr Badman*, ed. Roger Sharrock and James F. Forrest (Oxford: Clarendon Press, 1988)
MW	*The Miscellaneous Works of John Bunyan*, gen. ed. Roger Sharrock, 13 vols. (Oxford: Clarendon Press, 1976–1994)
P'sP	*The Pilgrim's Progress*, ed. James Blanton Wharey; 2nd edn, rev. Roger Sharrock (Oxford: Clarendon Press, 1960)

Critical works

Brown, *Bunyan*	John Brown, *John Bunyan 1628–1688: His Life, Times, and Work*, 1885, 2nd edn, rev. Frank M. Harrison (London: The Hultbert Publishing Company, 1928)

Greaves, *Glimpses*	Richard L. Greaves, *Glimpses of Glory: John Bunyan and English Dissent* (Stanford University Press, 2002)
Hill, *Turbulent*	Christopher Hill, *A Turbulent, Seditious, and Factious People: John Bunyan and his Church, 1628–1688* (1988; Oxford University Press, 1989)
Keeble (ed.), *Conventicle*	N. H. Keeble (ed.), *John Bunyan: Conventicle and Parnassus – Tercentenary Essays* (Oxford: Clarendon Press, 1988)

Reference works

Oxford DNB	H. C. G. Matthew and Brian Harrison (eds.), *Oxford Dictionary of National Biography*, 60 vols. (Oxford University Press, 2004)

Journals

BQ	*Baptist Quarterly*
BS	*Bunyan Studies: John Bunyan and his Times*
ELH	*English Literary History*
ELR	*English Literary Renaissance*
PMLA	*Publications of the Modern Language Association of America*
RES	*Review of English Studies*
SEL	*Studies in English Literature, 1500–1900*
SP	*Studies in Philology*

CHRONOLOGY

1628 Born in Elstow, near Bedford (Bedfordshire), the son of Thomas Bunyan (a brazier) and his second wife Margaret Bentley. Assassination of George Villiers, Duke of Buckingham. Petition of Right.

1629 Dissolution of Parliament and beginning of Charles I's personal rule (to 1640).

1633 George Herbert's *The Temple* and John Donne's *Poems*. William Laud appointed Archbishop of Canterbury.

1640 Summoning of the Long Parliament

1642 Beginning of the First Civil War. Closing of the theatres. Thomas Browne's *Religio Medici* (first authorised edition, 1643).

1643 The Westminter Assembly of Divines begins meeting (to 1649).

1644 John Milton's *Areopagitica*. Death of Bunyan's mother and sister. His father marries his third wife within a few months. Bunyan joins the Parliamentary forces in Newport Pagnell (Buckinghamshire), in the garrison of Sir Samuel Luke (company of Richard Cokayne).

1645 Formation of the New Model Army. Battle of Naseby. Birth of Bunyan's half-brother Charles, who dies shortly afterwards.

1646 End of the First Civil War. Episcopacy abolished. Bunyan volunteers for service in Ireland (but does not serve).

1647 The Army Debates at Putney concerning democracy and the constitution. Bunyan is demobilised and he returns to his father's house in Elstow.

1648   Second Civil War (to 1649). Colonel Pride's purge of the Long Parliament to secure a majority for bringing the King to trial, creating the 'Rump' Parliament.

1649   Trial and execution of Charles I. Monarchy and the House of Lords abolished. Commonwealth proclaimed. Bunyan marries his first wife, whose name is not recorded (four children born of the union). She brings as a dowry Arthur Dent's *The Plaine Mans Path-way to Heaven* (1601) and Lewis Bayly's *The Practise of Pietie* (1612?).

1650   Birth of Bunyan's first child Mary, who is blind. Spiritual awakening after an encounter with 'three or four poor women'. Starts meeting with the separatist congregation of John Gifford in Bedford.

1651   Thomas Hobbes's *Leviathan*.

1652   First Anglo-Dutch War (to 1654).

1653   Cromwell becomes Lord Protector. Margaret Cavendish's *Poems, and Fancies*.

1655   Moves from Elstow to Bedford. Admitted a full member of the Bedford congregation, possibly after accepting baptism by total immersion. Begins to preach. Death of John Gifford, succeeded by John Burton.

1656   Margaret Cavendish's *Natures Pictures*. Bunyan's first printed work, *Some Gospel-truths Opened*, against the Quakers.

1657   First Fifth-Monarchist rising in London led by Thomas Venner. Cromwell refuses the crown. *A Vindication ... of Some Gospel-Truths Opened*.

1658   Death of Oliver Cromwell. Richard Cromwell becomes Lord Protector. Richard Allestree's *The Whole Duty of Man*. Death of Bunyan's first wife. *A Few Sighs from Hell*, one of his most popular non-fiction works.

1659   Collapse of Richard Cromwell's Protectorate and restoration of the Rump Parliament. Bunyan marries his second wife, Elizabeth (three children born of the union). Supposed at this date to have written a tract in support of a woman accusing Quakers of witchcraft. His right to preach is challenged by Thomas Smith, keeper of Cambridge University Library and Professor of Arabic. *The*

Doctrine of the Law and Grace Unfolded, Bunyan's exposition of his doctrinal principles.

1660   Collapse of the Commonwealth and restoration of the full Long Parliament which votes to restore monarchy and for its own dissolution. Declaration of Breda. Charles II returns to England. Reopening of the theatres with actresses on stage. Founding members of the Royal Society begin meeting. Samuel Pepys begins his *Diary* (which he continues until 1669). Death of the Bedford congregation's minister, John Burton. William Wheeler is offered the pastorate, but declines. Bunyan arrested for illegal preaching in the hamlet of Lower Samsell (Bedfordshire). His wife Elizabeth gives premature birth to an infant who dies shortly afterwards.

1661   Venner's second Fifth-Monarchist rising in London. Corporation Act requiring all municipal officers to swear the oaths of allegiance, supremacy and non-resistance. *Mirabilis Annus, Or The Year of Prodigies and Wonders* (Second Part, 1662). Bunyan prosecuted under a 1593 Elizabethan Act and sentenced (remains in prison until 1672). Proceedings later published as *A Relation of the Imprisonment of Mr John Bunyan* (1765), usually reprinted with *Grace Abounding*. Publication of his first poem, *Profitable Meditations*.

1662   Quaker Act. Ejection of Puritan ministers who refuse to conform as required by the Act of Uniformity re-establishing the episcopal Church of England (24 August). Licensing Act. Charles II marries Catherine of Braganza. *I Will Pray with the Spirit* (?).

1663   Shakespeare's Third Folio. Samuel Butler's *Hudibras* (Second Part, 1664; Third Part, 1678). Roger L'Estrange appointed Surveyor of the Press. Samuel Fenne and John Whitman elected co-pastors of the Bedford congregation. *Prison-Meditations*, Bunyan's second verse collection, *Christian Behaviour*, a conduct book and *A Mapp Shewing the Order & Causes of Salvation & Damnation* (?).

1664   First Conventicle Act. Lucy Hutchinson begins writing the *Memoirs of the Life of Colonel Hutchinson* (first published 1806).

1665   Five Mile Act. Bubonic plague. Second Anglo-Dutch War (to 1667). *The Holy City, The Resurrection of the Dead* (?); *One Thing is Needful* (?) and *Ebal and Gerizzim* (?), two verse collections.

1666   Great Fire of London. Margaret Cavendish's *Observations upon Experimental Philosophy. To which is added ... A New Blazing World. Grace Abounding to the Chief of Sinners*, Bunyan's spiritual autobiography.

1667   Milton's *Paradise Lost*. John Dryden's *Annus Mirabilis*. Thomas Sprat's *History of the Royal Society. Poems* of Katherine Philips (the 'matchless Orinda'). Fall of Charles II's first minister, Edward Hyde, Earl of Clarendon.

1668   John Dryden created Poet Laureate. Bunyan probably begins writing *The Pilgrim's Progress* while still imprisoned.

1669   *The Holy City.*

1670   Second Conventicle Act. Treaty of Dover secretly concluded between Charles II and Louis XIV, committing Charles to return England to Roman Catholicism. Samuel Parker's *A Discourse of Ecclesiastical Politie*. Twenty-eight members of the Bedford congregation are arrested at an illegal conventicle.

1671   John Milton's *Paradise Regain'd* and *Samson Agonistes*.

1672   Andrew Marvell's *The Rehearsal Transpros'd* (Second Part, 1673). Bunyan elected pastor of the Bedford congregation (January). Declaration of Indulgence (March). Third Anglo-Dutch War (to 1674). Bunyan released from prison and applies for a licence to preach as a Congregationalist at the house of Josiah Ruffhead, a cordwinder. Controversy with the Anglican Edward Fowler and the 'closed-communion' Baptists recorded respectively in *A Defence of the Doctrine of Justification, by Faith in Jesus Christ* and *A Confession of my Faith* (followed by *Differences in Judgment upon Water-Baptism, no Bar to Communion*).

1673   Declaration of Indulgence withdrawn. Anti-Catholic Test Act. Charles II's brother and heir, James, Duke of York, refuses to take the sacrament at Easter and marries the Italian Catholic Mary of Modena, raising the prospect of a Roman Catholic ruling dynasty. *The Barren Fig-Tree*. Bunyan pursues his controversy with the Baptists with *Peaceable Principles And True*.

1674   Death of John Milton. Bunyan causes a scandal by riding on horseback with a young maid, Agnes Beaumont. Her *Narrative of the Persecution of Agnes Beaumont* will be published in 1760.

1675   Charles II cancels the licences formerly issued in accordance with the Declaration of Indulgence. Rebuilding of St Paul's Cathedral by Christopher Wren begins (completed 1711). Bunyan goes into hiding for a few months, possibly finding refuge with London Congregationalists. *Instruction for the Ignorant*, a catechism, and *Light for Them that Sit in Darkness*.

1676   George Etherege, *The Man of Mode*. Bishop Henry Compton's census of religious nonconformity. Death of Bunyan's father. Beginning of his second imprisonment (December 1676 to June 1677). Released, probably thanks to the intervention of John Owen. *The Strait Gate, Saved by Grace*.

1677   Andrew Marvell's *An Account of the Growth of Popery, and Arbitrary Government*. Aphra Behn, *The Rover*. William of Orange marries Mary, daughter of the Duke of York and his wife, the late Ann Hyde, daughter of Clarendon.

1678   Popish Plot. Death of Andrew Marvell. First Part of *The Pilgrim's Progress* published by Nathaniel Ponder. *Come, & Welcome, to Jesus Christ*, one of Bunyan's most popular non-fiction works.

1679   Death of Thomas Hobbes. Fall of the first minister, Sir Thomas Osborne, Earl of Danby. Beginning of the 'Exclusion Crisis' (to 1681). Lapse of the Licensing Act. *A Treatise of the Fear of God*.

1680   Death of John Wilmot, Earl of Rochester, and publication of his *Poems*. *The Life and Death of Mr Badman*.

1681   Andrew Marvell's *Miscellaneous Poems*. John Dryden's *Absalom and Achitophel*. The opposition leader Anthony Ashley Cooper, Earl of Shaftesbury, imprisoned and later released when a London Grand Jury issues a verdict of *ignoramus*.

1682   Spurious 'second' part of *The Pilgrim's Progress* by the General Baptist Thomas Sherman. *The Holy War, The Greatness of the Soul*.

1683   Rye House Plot. Foundation of the Ashmolean Museum. *A Case of Conscience Resolved* against separate women assemblies.

1684   Suicide of the apostate John Child, once a member of the Bedford congregation. Aphra Behn's *Love-Letters Between a Noble-Man and his Sister* (Second Part, 1685, Third Part, 1687). Authentic Second Part of *The Pilgrim's Progress, A Holy Life, Seasonable Counsel, A Caution to Stir Up Against Sin*.

1685   Death of Charles II. Accession of James II. Unsuccessful rebellion of Charles II's illegitimate son, James, Duke of Monmouth. Revocation of the Edict of Nantes. Licensing Act renewed for seven years. Aphra Behn's *Miscellany*. Montaigne's *Essays* translated by Charles Cotton. *Questions about the Nature and Perpetuity of the Seventh-Day-Sabbath* against the Sabbatarians worshipping on Saturdays, *A Discourse upon the Pharisee and the Publicane*.

1686   *A Book for Boys and Girls: Or, Country Rhimes for Children*.

1687   James's Declaration of Indulgence suspending the Test and Corporation Acts. John Dryden's *The Hind and the Panther*, Isaac Newton's *Principia Mathematica*.

1688   Aphra Behn's *Oroonoko*. Mary of Modena gives birth to a son. Reissue of the Declaration of Indulgence. Trial and acquittal of the 'Seven Bishops' who opposed the Declaration. William of Orange lands at Brixham (Torbay, Devon). James flees to France. Bunyan dies in London, 31 August, at the house of the grocer John Strudwick, in Holborn. Interred in Strudwick's tomb in the dissenting cemetery of Bunhill Fields. *Solomon's Temple Spiritualiz'd, A Discourse of ... the House of God, The Water of Life, The Advocateship of Jesus Christ, Good News for the Vilest of Men*. Posthumous publication of *An Exhortation to Peace and Unity* and Bunyan's deathbed sayings, both spurious.

1689   Death of Aphra Behn. Crown offered to William and Mary. Declaration of Rights. Toleration Act. John Locke's first *Letter Concerning Toleration* (a second and third follow in 1690 and 1692), *Two Treatises on Government* (dated 1690). Posthumous publication of Bunyan's *Last Sermon* and *The Acceptable Sacrifice*.

1690   John Locke's *Essay Concerning Human Understanding*.

1692   Death of Elizabeth Bunyan. Bunyan's friend Charles Doe publishes *The Works of That Eminent Servant of Christ, Mr John Bunyan* in folio, including twelve previously unpublished pieces (*An Exposition on ... Genesis, Of Justification by an Imputed Righteousness, Paul's Departure and Crown, Of the Trinity and a Christian, Of the Law and a Christian, Israel's Hope Encouraged, The Desire of the Righteous Granted, The Saints Privilege and Profit, Christ a Compleat Saviour, The Saints Knowledge of*

Christ's Love, A Discourse of the House of the Forest of Lebanon, Of Antichrist, and His Ruine).

1694   George Fox's *Journal*.

1696   Richard Baxter's *Reliquiae Baxterianae* published by Matthew Sylvester.

1698   Charles Doe publishes *The Heavenly Foot-man*, possibly composed by Bunyan in late 1667 or early 1668, its central metaphor anticipating *The Pilgrim's Progress*.

ANNE DUNAN-PAGE

Introduction

In November 1817, *Ladies' Monthly Museum* informed its readers that 'the celebrated John Bunyan, author of the Pilgrim's Progress, at one period of his life, kept a public house in the neighbourhood of Turvey, in Bedfordshire, and, perhaps, in commemoration of the profession of his father, and his own in his youth, put up the sign of the Tinker of Turvey'.[1] It comes as a surprise to discover that the reputation of John Bunyan (1628–88), Puritan minister and author of a religious classic, could encompass the innkeeper's trade in the nineteenth century, often regarded as the era of his greatest fame as a spiritual writer. The story of Bunyan the taverner provides a welcome reminder that nothing can be taken for granted about this established and canonical author of the English-speaking world. To explore the Bunyan tradition is to encounter centuries of accumulated legend, polemic and prejudice that began to spread even during his lifetime, for Bunyan was accused of being a witch, a highwayman, a Jesuit, a gypsy and a whoremaster. Some even said he had murdered the father of Agnes Beaumont, falsely charged with being his mistress. Several of these accusations are recorded in his spiritual autobiography *Grace Abounding* (1666), and were evidently well known to him. They bury the traditional picture of Bunyan the stern and puritanical minister as surely as the image of the tinker of Turvey serving ale obscures the religious allegorist of *The Pilgrim's Progress* (1678).

Hence it is right that the works of this contentious figure are still widely read and taught. With this in mind, the present *Companion* has been designed to serve three major purposes for a broad constituency of readers. It explores how Bunyan's writings inspired readers, commentators and translators to reshape his legacy during three centuries, it provides up-to-date readings of Bunyan's major works, and it reassesses his place as one of the greatest early-modern authors, whose life and writings were embroiled in the upheavals of his time. This *Companion* is the first accessible collection of essays seeking to introduce Bunyan's life, works and posterity to students, scholars and the general reader in the light of the most recent scholarship.

After the Authorised Version of the Bible and the plays of Shakespeare, Bunyan's writings have been foremost among the major books of the Anglophone world. In the nineteenth century, ships left the port of London for the British imperial colonies freighted with as many copies of *The Pilgrim's Progress* (1678 and 1684) as the Bible. The pictures in the many illustrated editions shaped the imagination of generations, as revealed by literary works as diverse as George Eliot's *The Mill on the Floss* (1860) and M. R. James's *Oh, Whistle and I'll Come to you, my Lad* (1904) where the frightened narrator ponders the description of Apollyon coming over the field to meet Christian in *The Pilgrim's Progress*, a passage 'which catches most people's fancy at some time of their childhood', according to James.[2] Despite such horrors, the most devout or diligent pupils in Victorian Sunday schools were rewarded with copies of *The Pilgrim's Progress*, whence the many nineteenth-century editions now to be found in second-hand bookshops with florid and gilded bookplates announcing 'First Prize for Scripture Knowledge' or 'Prize for Regular Attendance'. Many were family gifts and are sometimes supplied with manuscript admonitions from the giver such as 'mark, read and inwardly digest'. (George Eliot's account of Maggie Tulliver's reading suggests that the attraction for many young devotees lay mostly in the adventures of the pilgrims, rather than in the teachings, not to mention the opportunity to colour the line-drawings.) Spreading Bunyan's message orally also mattered. In 1862, Archdeacon Jones from Liverpool recalled that he had 'read [*The Pilgrim's Progress*] publicly, with a running commentary, to a large Sunday evening congregation in [his] National Schoolroom', the assembly listening to the recital with 'fixed attention and deep interest'.[3] Schoolmasters with a special commitment to *The Pilgrim's Progress* as an extra-curricular means to educate the minds and spirits of the young can be traced in oral tradition to at least the 1950s, but perhaps no further.

If no readers celebrated Bunyan's life and works better than the Victorians, no Victorian embodied this better than George Offor (1767–1864). Offor was a critic and patron of the arts who published Bunyan's works in the 1850s, an edition not superseded until the Oxford Bunyan was completed in 1994 under the general editorship of Roger Sharrock.[4] An avid collector, Offor claimed to possess (in addition to copies of Bunyan's works by the thousand) an iron pencase made by the author, his buckles, two pocket knives, his apple scoop, a seal and his box of scales and weights, all of which were lost in the fire that destroyed Sotheby's auction-rooms prior to the sale of his collection in June 1865. Not everything disappeared in that blaze, however. The Bunyan Museum in central Bedford remains a true *cabinet de curiosités* for all Bunyan enthusiasts, showing how assiduously relics of Bunyan have been treasured or (as is often the way with relics) manufactured. There one may see Bunyan's pulpit, his chair, his flute (supposedly cut from the leg of a chair while in prison) and the jug that was used to carry broth to him in prison or his Sunday dinner in the meeting-house, according to a different account. There is also a chest adorned with representations of musical instruments. All these things rub shoulders in the Museum with copies of *The Pilgrim's Progress*, translated into hundreds of languages in the course of three centuries. Compared to Bunyan, who is associated with so many and varied mementoes in addition to his literary works, Shakespeare seems almost to have vanished from the earth without trace.

As this hoard of memorabilia suggests, Bunyan was ubiquitous in nineteenth-century culture. Wallpapers, picture-puzzles and board-games depicted characters and scenes from his works, and a whole attic of material was released by canny merchants that included busts, medallions, statues, prints and facsimiles.[5] The term 'Bunyaniana' was coined to refer to this unprecedented body of artefacts. Bunyan enthusiasts and collectors formed a formidable network of correspondents through the pages of *Notes & Queries* and *The Times* advertisements. This interest did not subside in the early twentieth century. British soldiers in the trenches of 1914–18 used material from *The Pilgrim's Progress*, notably the Slough of Despond and the Valley of the Shadow of Death, to express the inexpressible in letters and other writings which reveal the importance of the book to an entire generation on the verge of both Modernism and their own City of Destruction.[6] In later decades, an opera by Vaughan Williams and writings by C. S. Lewis, Iain Sinclair, Samuel Beckett and Peter Ackroyd (to look no further) show the long-lasting influence of Bunyan's most famous works. American presidents from Abraham Lincoln to J. F. Kennedy have proclaimed their life-long attachment to him. As Isabel Hofmeyr shows in the last chapter of this *Companion*, Bunyan's name was even mentioned in the wake of Barack Obama's presidential election in 2008.

This wave of interest, with some readers praising Bunyan for his religious principles, some for his literary merits and most of them for both, obscures some very inauspicious beginnings. As Neil Keeble shows in chapter 1, it was a challenge for the son of a Bedfordshire tinker with little education to make his mark in the world of books, and perhaps no other decades than the 1640s and 1650s could have nurtured and authorised Bunyan's intrusion into the public sphere. However, Bunyan was not praised in his own day as a writer of literature in any sense of that word now immediately familiar, and his fame suffered in the eighteenth century when polite taste shunned the vulgarity of the tinker while admiring the faith and energy of the evangelical preacher.

Only during the Romantic revival was Bunyan's racy and homely genius rediscovered and popularised.

'That John Bunyan was a tinker, a poor man, and a lay preacher has been generally known, but insufficiently pondered.'[7] That might have been the case in 1934 when William York Tindall wrote his socially oriented study of the author's life and works, but in recent years Bunyan the 'poor' man, the radical champion of the oppressed, has attracted much attention, notably in Christopher Hill's work of 1988 (*A Turbulent, Seditious, and Factious People: John Bunyan and his Church, 1628–1688*) which remained the standard biographical account, together with John Brown's Victorian biography, until the publication of Richard Greaves's *Glimpses of Glory* in 2002.[8] The material is rich, for Bunyan's life spanned the major historical events of the seventeenth century. He spent most of his years in and around Bedford and its prison, where he was held for a total of thirteen years for refusing to conform. He was evidently a talented, charismatic and at times a fearless preacher who was not prepared to compromise his nonconformist position for the sake of an easy life or accommodation with the authorities. He managed to attract the attention of prominent London nonconformists such as George Cockayne and John Owen, who were among his many admirers and invited him to preach in the capital. In 1678, and therefore already late in his career, he published *The Pilgrim's Progress* to instantaneous acclaim. Within a year there was a second and then a third edition, testifying to the flair of its editor, Nathaniel Ponder. An unwelcome measure of its success can be seen in the appearance of pirated editions, spurious sequels and imitations that embroiled Ponder in legal wranglings. Today, *The Pilgrim's Progress* is still Bunyan's best-loved work, for most people associate him with the fate of Christian the pilgrim, with the monster Apollyon (as did M. R. James) and with the pleasures of a Vanity Fair that Bunyan bequeathed to W. M. Thackeray. In the wake of a renewed interest in spiritual autobiographies and conversion narratives, *Grace Abounding* has also found many admirers.

These works are of outstanding interest and have continued to inspire debate. Pioneering work by scholars such as Stuart Sim, Michael Davies and the late Richard Greaves has reassessed the relationship between Bunyan's fiction and his Calvinism. They have provided subtle discussions of Bunyan's predestinarian theology, greatly modifying the stereotypical picture of the severe preacher condemning his hearers to eternal hell-fire.[9] These theological readings of Bunyan have gone hand in hand with an interest not only in Bunyan's spiritual conditions but also in his psychological state. Following William James's seminal *The Varieties of Religious Experience* (1902) and later works on Puritan spirituality such as John Stachniewski's

The Persecutory Imagination (1991), it is now widely recognised that Bunyan's oeuvre cannot be read without taking into account the internal conflicts that he termed despair or melancholy, and that we term depression.[10] In chapter 4, Vera J. Camden explores a new direction in psychoanalytical approaches to Bunyan's work.[11]

Yet an emphasis upon *The Pilgrim's Progress* and *Grace Abounding*, the two works that dominate the way Bunyan is read and taught today, necessarily narrows our sense of his scope. To these two books one should add *The Life and Death of Mr Badman* (1680), *The Holy War* (1682), the Second Part of *The Pilgrim's Progress* (1684) and scattered works of poetry from *Profitable Meditations*, a prison poem published in 1661, to his famous collection of verse for children, *A Book for Boys and Girls* (1686). Even this simple list can give some insight into Bunyan's literary and stylistic experiments. There is an autobiography, two strikingly different allegories (*The Pilgrim's Progress*, on the pilgrimage of the soul, and *The Holy War*, on the Fall and redemption of Mankind, couched in military terms); there is a proto-novel in dialogue (*The Life and Death of Mr Badman*) and a didactic verse collection that resembles books of emblems or occasional meditations (*A Book for Boys and Girls*).

Bunyan's fiction appeared at regular intervals for only eight years and does not represent a major proportion of his work. Of the fifty-eight writings that form the Bunyan canon as it is received today, five are larger works of fiction and seven are verse collections, leaving forty-six non-fiction writings. One of the challenges faced by this *Companion* is therefore to provide readings of the major fictional works in dialogue with Bunyan's other generic experiments. He produced extended sermons, a conduct book, a catechism, a map of salvation, a versified church-order, various pamphlets directed against the Quakers, the Seventh-Day men (who worshipped on Saturdays) and the Anglicans; there are also works on church discipline (most notably on the validity of adult baptism and the suitability of women's assemblies), works of practical or pastoral theology and a series of epistles later released as *A Relation of the Imprisonment of Mr John Bunyan* (1765). We have probably lost a pamphlet supporting accusations of witchcraft against the Quakers and two works, 'A Christian Dialogue' and a pocket concordance, were never published. To sample these writings in all their diversity is to find dreams, allegories, exempla, poems, letters, emblems, dialogues, hymns, marginalia, aphorisms, conversion narratives, judgement stories, millenarian and typological commentaries. Bunyan had an obvious appetite for words that the present chapters explore by foregrounding this unique body of prose and verse against key issues in current scholarship. These include the publication of dissenting works, the history of the book, questions of gender and psychoanalysis, the relationship between literature and religion, between literature and early-modern radicalism, and the 'reception, appropriation and recollection' of seventeenth-century texts, to paraphrase the title of a recent collective volume on Bunyan's afterlife.[12]

As a theologian, Bunyan was a Calvinist evangelist who accepted the doctrine of double-predestination. As Roger Pooley remarks, the journey Christian takes in *The Pilgrim's Progress* 'is not that of an Everyman figure, but of an elect Christian'.[13] Bunyan's world is peopled with Elect who reach heaven and Reprobates who are condemned to an eternity of suffering. Mr Badman never mends his ways, Ignorance is sent to Hell while in sight of the Celestial City and the Diabolonians in *The Holy War* are crucified in scenes that can still shock by their violence, whatever their theological intent.[14] Coleridge proclaimed that Bunyan's piety 'was baffled by his genius, and the Bunyan of Parnassus had the better of the Bunyan of the Conventicle', but this is to make a misguided distinction between theology and literature, as if Bunyan's Calvinism hindered the work of his Muse.[15]

Bunyan has often been considered within the context of seventeenth-century radical sectarianism, although he hardly fits the picture of a dissenting radical, if such a thing can even be defined. In print, he kept silent about the main political events of his day and never took an active part in any insurgency other than the Great Rebellion.[16] Recent interpretations of his works have shown how misguided it may be to assume that Bunyan never altered his spiritual or political positions in the course of his career, but they have also revealed how he may, in general, have been far more conservative than formerly supposed.[17] Presented in this light, Bunyan appears as a quiescent advocate of political non-resistance and religious orthodoxy, perhaps opposing the execution of Charles I and later favouring the policies of James II, who stigmatised the enthusiasm of the Quakers and Ranters as much as the pious moralism of the Anglican church.

At the heart of this *Companion* are readings of Bunyan's six major works of fiction that take into consideration the above issues, while being sensitive to questions of genre. We have assumed that readers may have an interest not only in dissenting literature in general but more specifically in seventeenth-century allegory, life-writing and early novels or children's literature, for which Bunyan's writings offer key points of entry. These chapters are framed by an introductory section on Bunyan's place within seventeenth-century culture, both literary and religious, and a section on aspects of his readership and reception. The volume does not give a complete panorama of Bunyan's varied and extensive writings, for that would be impossible in the space available; for the same reason, it cannot ackowledge every direction taken in the ever-growing corpus of Bunyan scholarship. We have attempted to present readings that avoid the complacency and hagiography of Whiggish criticism, and which are inspired instead by a desire to reflect upon one of the most fascinating literary achievements of the seventeenth century. It is one in which modern readers will find much to ponder and question.

Unlike his contemporary John Milton, John Bunyan never quite reached the status of Puritan bard. Some commentators found it hard to accept that a tinker could deliver what is arguably the finest allegory in the English language. Bunyan's pride in a poor education that pitched the Holy Spirit against human learning, his 'plain' style designed to appeal to the greatest number and his profound attachment to both a predestinarian theology and a congregational church ensured that the course of his fame rarely ran smooth with either readers or scholars.[18] Bunyan scholarship today is much indebted to those who have laboured to rediscover and reassess the Puritan and dissenting literatures of the Civil War and Restoration periods, moving them inwards from their marginal position in seventeenth-century culture.[19] All the following chapters draw upon this wave of innovative literary-historical work among seventeenth-century specialists worldwide. The Bunyan that emerges from them is neither the dangerous Anabaptist firebrand of seventeenth-century polemic nor the tolerant champion of tender consciences. He is not the supreme pastor who inspired the dissenting and missionary zeal of later centuries. He appears instead as a man barely enlightened, as we may now judge it, upon many subjects. A political conservative and an indifferent poet, he made enemies both within and without the dissenting community with his fiery temper and lack of poise. He was a witch-monger, sometimes a hypocrite towards women and an ardent believer in a theology not always associated today with tolerance. That is what makes him the writer he is. George Eliot, a most incisive observer of dissent, captured this as the true complexity of the man:

> The blessed work of helping the world forward, happily does not wait to be done by perfect men; and I should imagine that neither Luther nor John Bunyan, for example, would have satisfied the modern demand for an ideal hero, who believes nothing but what is true, feels nothing but what is exalted, and does nothing but what is graceful.[20]

Bunyan did indeed help the world forward by leaving some of the most poignant pages of seventeenth-century literature. Our purpose is to guide the reader to the many graceful – and not so graceful – aspects of his life, his works and his heritage.

NOTES

1. *The Ladies' Monthly Museum*, 1 November 1817, p. 249. An anonymous work called *The Tincker of Turvey* was published in 1630.

2. M.R. James, *Count Magnus and Other Ghost Stories*, ed. S.T. Joshi (Harmondsworth: Penguin, 2005), p. 87.
3. *The Whole Works of John Bunyan*, ed. George Offor, 3 vols. (1852–3; London, Glasgow and Edinburgh: Blackie, 1862), I:3, 'Opinions recommendatory of this edition'.
4. The Oxford Bunyan began with *The Pilgrim's Progress* in 1960, followed by three separate volumes, *Grace Abounding* in 1962, *The Holy War* in 1980 and *The Life and Death of Mr Badman* in 1988, continuing with Bunyan's other writings, which appeared in thirteen volumes between 1976 and 1994 under the general title *Miscellaneous Works*.
5. A good selection can be found in the late Victorian and Edwardian scrapbook of George Potter of Highgate, 'An Album Containing Material Relating to John Bunyan', now in the British Library (RB.31.C.52). The scrapbook was arranged thematically in 1892, with additions made in 1901, 1905 and 1907. The main themes are: Bunyan's portraits and frontispieces, Elstow and Bunyan's cottage, Bunyan in prison, meeting-houses and schools, Bunyan's tankard, his tomb and statue, his pulpit, his copy of Foxe's *Actes and Monuments*, his will, book reviews and articles, auction and sales catalogues.
6. Paul Fussell, *The Great War and Modern Memory* (1975; Oxford University Press, 2000), pp. 137–44.
7. William York Tindall, *John Bunyan: Mechanick Preacher* (New York: Columbia University Press, 1934), p. vii.
8. See Brown, *Bunyan*.
9. Stuart Sim, *Negotiations with Paradox: Narrative Practice and Narrative Form in Bunyan and Defoe* (Savage, Md.: Barnes and Noble, 1990); Michael Davies, *Graceful Reading: Theology and Narrative in the Works of John Bunyan* (Oxford University Press, 2002); Greaves, *Glimpses*.
10. See my *Grace Overwhelming: John Bunyan, 'The Pilgrim's Progress' and the Extremes of the Baptist Mind* (Bern: Peter Lang, 2006).
11. For psychoanalytical approaches, see for instance W.N. Evans, 'Notes on the Conversion of John Bunyan: A Study in English Puritanism', *International Journal of Psycho-Analysis*, 24 (1943), 176–85; Andrew W. Brink, 'Bunyan's *Pilgrim's Progress* and the Secular Reader: A Psychological Approach', *English Studies in Canada*, 1 (1975), 386–405; Ivan Leudar and Wes Sharrock, 'The Cases of John Bunyan, Part 1. Taine and Royce' and 'The Cases of John Bunyan, Part 2. James and Janet', *History of Psychiatry*, 13 (2002), 247–65, 401–17; John Sneep and Arlette Zinck, 'Learning to Read Salvation: Psychological and Spiritual Change in Bunyan's *Grace Abounding* and *The Pilgrim's Progress*', *Journal of Psychology and Christianity*, 24.2 (2005), 156–64.
12. W.R. Owens and Stuart Sim (eds.), *Reception, Appropriation, Recollection: Bunyan's 'Pilgrim's Progress'* (Bern: Peter Lang, 2007).
13. See below, p. 86.
14. On the darker side of Bunyan's œuvre, see Beth Lynch, *John Bunyan and the Language of Conviction* (Cambridge: D.S. Brewer, 2004).
15. Quoted in Roger Sharrock (ed.), *'The Pilgrim's Progress': A Casebook* (London and Basingstoke: Macmillan, 1976), p. 53.
16. Richard F. Hardin, 'Bunyan, Mr Ignorance, and the Quakers', *SP*, 69 (1972), 496–508; Dayton Haskin, 'The Pilgrim's Progress in the Context of Bunyan's

Dialogue with the Radicals', *Harvard Theological Review*, 77 (1984), 73–94; Ted L. Underwood, ' "It pleased me much to contend": John Bunyan as Controversialist', *Church History*, 57 (1988), 456–69.

17. Michael Mullett, *John Bunyan in Context* (Keele University Press, 1996); Vera J. Camden (ed.), *Trauma and Transformation: The Political Progress of John Bunyan* (Stanford University Press, 2008).

18. See Roger Pooley, 'Plain and Simple: Bunyan and Style', in Keeble (ed.), *Conventicle*, pp. 91–110.

19. Very selectively, see N. H. Keeble, *The Literary Culture of Nonconformity in Later Seventeenth-Century England* (Leicester University Press, 1987); Nigel Smith, *Perfection Proclaimed: Language and Literature in English Radical Religion, 1640–1660* (Oxford: Clarendon Press, 1989); David Norbrook, *Writing the English Republic: Poetry, Rhetoric and Politics, 1627–1660* (Cambridge University Press, 1999); Sharon Achinstein, *Literature and Dissent in Milton's England* (Cambridge University Press, 2003); Nicholas McDowell, *The English Radical Imagination: Culture, Religion, and Revolution, 1630–1660* (Oxford: Clarendon Press, 2003); Joad Raymond, *Pamphlets and Pamphleteering in Early Modern Britain* (Cambridge University Press, 2003).

20. George Eliot, *Scenes of Clerical Life* (1858), ed. Thomas A. Noble, Oxford World's Classics (1988; Oxford University Press, 2000), pp. 228–9.

PART I

John Bunyan in his
seventeenth-century context

I

N. H. KEEBLE

John Bunyan's literary life

Print and the English Revolution

Bunyan might be thought the most improbable of authors. In a hierarchical age, when cultural patronage was in the hands of the court, the universities, the established church and London social elites, the literary prospects for a poorly educated provincial sectarian preacher might appear dim, and yet this same Bedfordshire tinker, 'of a low and inconsiderable generation' from one of the 'meanest, and most despised of all the families in the Land' (*GA*, p. 5), wrote nearly sixty works and, with *The Pilgrim's Progress*, became the century's bestselling writer.[1] While, however, his success was exceptional, the fact of Bunyan's authorship was not quite as improbable as it might seem. His early literary career coincided with, and was shaped by, the unprecedented increase in press activity associated with the gathering momentum of the English Revolution. The political and religious tensions of the first half of the century were accompanied by, and articulated through, a proliferating press whose annual output rose from 625 titles in 1639 to 848 in 1640, over 2,000 in 1641 and over 3,666 in 1642, thereafter to continue at between one and two thousand annually until the Restoration.[2] A unique record of this productivity is preserved in the remarkable collection of broadsides, tracts, pamphlets and books assembled by the bookseller George Thomason, who, between 1640 and 1661, amassed 22,000 publications. Never before had so many people turned to writing, never before had so many seen their thoughts into print and never before had what they printed generated such extensive interest and public debate.[3]

Bunyan, mustered in the New Model Army in 1644 as he turned sixteen, came to maturity in the midst of this out-pouring of print.[4] Overwhelmingly religious and predominantly Puritan in character, it was the work of new kinds of writer. An increasing number of non-university men and, for effectively the first time, many women, were prompted to write, and to publish, by their Puritan experience. Writing in 1648, the minister Richard Baxter exclaimed in dismay that '*Every ignorant, empty braine (which usually hath the highest esteem of it selfe) hath the liberty of the Presse, whereby ... the number of bookes is grown so great that they begin with many to grow contemptible.'*[5] The revolutionary and radical ideas published in the tracts of Levellers, Anabaptists, Ranters and, later, Quakers, disclosed to Baxter's orderly temper a prospect of anarchy: in the oft-quoted words of Acts 17:6, 'a world turned upside down'.[6] Ministers and members of gathered churches, such as the Bedford open-communion Baptist church Bunyan joined in 1655,[7] and Quakers in particular, made repeated use of the press to disseminate their message, publishing broadsides, tracts, prophecies, personal testimonies, sermons, as well as polemical and controversial pieces, by authors from a wide range of socio-economic backgrounds. The result was a 'democritisation' of the press, a 'downwards dissemination of print', as radical Puritanism inspired in those such as Bunyan the confidence to access, and to participate in, a literary culture from which they had hitherto been excluded.[8]

Books anticipate readers. In a population of some 3 million in 1500 and 5.5 million in 1700, full literacy (that is, the ability both to read and to write) was possessed by perhaps 15 per cent of the population at the start of this period, and no more than 30 per cent at its close.[9] Puritanism, with what one historian has described as its 'obsession with the written word',[10] saw it as one of its tasks to increase this proportion so that believers might study the Bible and benefit from the wealth of religious works available: *'By all means let children be taught to read'*, parents were exhorted, *'if you are never so poor, and what ever shift you make.'*[11] To this end, Bunyan's *A Book for Boys and Girls* (1686) included an alphabet and numerical tables to help children learn to read and to count (*B&G*, pp. 194–6).

Puritan writers were especially anxious to reach the socially disadvantaged and marginalised who had never before been supposed capable of literary engagement. They addressed their texts to the 'vulgar', that is, the mass of the common people. For this market, Bunyan's publications were all cheaply produced and sold at the lowest prices. Three of them appear to have been broadsheets, probably for pasting on walls for ready and general availability to those who may not have been able to purchase them (*MW*, XII:xxv–xxvi). To reach such readers, breviates and chapbook versions of larger texts were frequently available, hawked for a few pennies – as of *The Pilgrim's Progress* in 1684.[12] Reading aloud to groups, lending, borrowing and bequeathing books, establishing public libraries: these and other expedients were much encouraged among the godly, facilitating the dissemination of texts among, and access to them by, the impoverished. Bunyan's first wife came from a poor family, but texts were not beyond its reach: she brought with her as dowry two of the century's bestsellers: Lewis Bayly's *Practise of Pietie* (1612?) and Arthur Dent's *Plaine Mans Path-way* (1601, see *GA*, p. 8).

This drive for readers was a key step in moving the patronage of literature away from privileged elites to a popular readership, a necessary prerequisite for the development of the novel in the next century. In so doing Puritanism revalued the act of reading. Puritan readers, whatever their background, were not to be unduly impressed by the fact of a book's publication, nor by the reputation of its author. They were, as Bunyan's pastor John Gifford taught, to take 'not up any truth upon trust, as from this or that or another man or men, but to cry mightily to God, that he would convince us of the reality thereof' (*GA*, p. 37). In the oft-quoted words of 1 Thessalonians 5:21, the godly were themselves to 'Prove all things, hold fast that which is good', to assess, weigh and analyse evidence before accepting an author's contentions. This individual responsibility to determine truth invested the act of reading with high seriousness: faith carried the obligation to be a critical and self-aware reader.[13] This is precisely the tenor of Bunyan's frequent injunctions to his readers carefully to weigh his arguments, and, persuaded, to act accordingly: '*read, and consider, and iudg*'; '*lay my Book, thy Head and Heart together*' (*MW*, VIII:51; *P'sP*, p. 7).

Bunyan and the press

An incentive to this sudden upsurge in press productivity was the collapse of pre-publication censorship following the sitting of the Long Parliament in November 1640 and the subsequent abolition of the Court of Star Chamber in August 1641. Since the time of Henry VIII print publishing had been regarded by governments as a threat to their authority and they hence sought to restrain and control the output of the press: the printing trade and pre-publication censorship developed together. Every legally published title required prior approval (that is, a licence to publish) from an appointed censor (generally an episcopalian cleric), which was not to be had for texts challenging either political or ecclesiastical authority. In addition, laws on defamation, libel, slander, sedition and treason were used to control the output of the press. Very substantial fines and terms of imprisonment, and even banishment or execution (such as Bunyan himself feared (*GA*, pp. 95–101)) were risked by printers who produced, booksellers who disseminated and authors who wrote unlicensed texts or texts judged to be subversive.[14] The Long Parliament, however, quickly found that it had no more liking for a free press than had earlier regimes, and by an ordinance of 14 June 1643 licensing of texts before publication was re-instituted. This was the immediate occasion of Milton's *Areopagitica: A Speech of Mr John Milton for the Liberty of Unlicensed Printing* (1644), which construed a free press, the availability of cheap print and pamphleteering as essential marks of a Christian commonwealth:

Where there is much desire to learn, there of necessity will be much arguing, much writing, many opinions; for opinion in good men is but knowledge in the making. Under these fantastic terrors of sect and schism, we wrong the earnest and zealous thirst after knowledge and understanding which God hath stirr'd up ... What some lament of, we rather should rejoyce at.[15]

Milton's plea wonderfully captures the disputatious ferment within which Bunyan grew to maturity, but it had no effect on governing elites, not during the Interregnum and certainly not at the Restoration, when the Licensing Act (1662) re-imposed the old press controls and the penal legislation of what came to be known as the 'Clarendon Code' sought to extirpate Puritan opinion through sustained persecution.[16] Writers adopted a number of expedients to circumvent the restraining authority of the censor. Heterodox works, such as Milton's theological treatise *De Doctrina Christiana*, and satirical works, such as Andrew Marvell's Restoration verse satires, might circulate in manuscript and not be put into print. *The Pilgrim's Progress*, begun probably in 1668 and completed in 1671, was shared with friends in this way before its publication in 1678 (*P'sP*, p. 2); the seven-year delay was perhaps due in part to apprehensions about its reception by the authorities.[17] Bunyan's much more directly inflammatory *Relation of His Imprisonment* remained in manuscript until 1765 (*GA*, pp. xxiii–xxv) and his contentious millenarian *Of Antichrist, and His Ruine*, with its praise of Tudor but not Stuart monarchs, its criticism of the established church and condemnation of Roman Catholicism when the heir to the throne was a known Catholic, its promotion of liberty of conscience and denunciation of persecutors, was published only posthumously in 1692 (e.g. *MW*, XIII:424–6, 441–2, 493–4, 497–8). This was one of fifteen (perhaps sixteen)[18] works in manuscript at Bunyan's death, their number suggesting he withheld works from the press rather than risk their publication; certainly, the censor was hardly likely to pass the explicit association of 'Absolute Monarchy' with the persecuting tyranny of Nimrod, the founder of Babel, 'the first great Seat of Oppressors' in Bunyan's *Exposition on the First Ten Chapters of Genesis* (*MW*, XII:267–9). These unpublished manuscripts were finally printed in the 1692 folio edition of Bunyan's works when, in the changed circumstances following the 'Glorious Revolution' of 1688 and the Toleration Act of 1689, it became 'lawful now to print the Works of Dissenters, though it was not so formerly' (Bunyan, *Works*, sig. 5T1v).[19]

In works that did reach print, a variety of rhetorical and allusive strategies might allow oblique and implicit expression of meanings that could be denied if need be. In fiction and allegory the relationship between imagined and contemporary worlds might be particularly suggestive: in *The Pilgrim's Progress*, is it worldliness in general, or Restoration London in particular, that is represented in Vanity Fair, and, if the latter, does Bunyan glance at Charles II in its lord, Beelzebub (*P'sP*, pp. 89–97)? By-ends' self-seeking materialism can be read as a hit at those who prospered through conformity to the established church (*P'sP*, p. 100). Indeed, the Restoration *beau monde* in general comes rather badly out of Bunyan: to be socially privileged, pre-occupied with forms of civility and fashion, with status and hierarchy, these are almost invariably signs of moral turpitude: Giant Despair owns a castle and a great estate barred to trespassers; By-ends is from '*Fair-speech*', 'a *Wealthy place*'; Mercy's suitor Mr Brisk is 'a man of some breeding' but merely 'pretended to Religion' (*P'sP*, pp. 98, 113, 226). In *The Life and Death of Mr Badman* (1680), what the protagonist takes to be 'neatness, handsomness, comeliness, cleanliness ... following of fashions' is condemned by Mr Wiseman as pride, and courtly Restoration female dress is denounced as a shameless inducement to licentiousness, 'with their naked shoulders, and Paps hanging out like a Cows bag' (*LDB*, pp. 121–2, 125). Bunyan finds it readily understandable that in the parable of Dives and Lazarus 'the ungodly [are] held forth under the notion of a rich man', for 'to see how the great ones of the world will go strutting up and down the streets sometimes, it makes me wonder'; by contrast, God's own people 'are most commonly of the poorer sort', 'for the most part, a poor, despised, contemptible people' (*MW*, 1:252, 253–4, 255).[20] Such socially subversive sentiments would hardly recommend themselves to the political authorities, and so Bunyan, like other authors, often avoided the censor altogether by resorting to unlicensed publication. Only eight first editions of the forty or so titles published during Bunyan's lifetime appear to have been properly licensed,[21] including the two parts of *The Pilgrim's Progress*, but neither *Mr Badman* nor *The Holy War* (1682), both of which might be readily construed as deeply critical of the social values and political practices of the Restoration. Indeed, in *The Holy War* Bunyan had a tilt at the licensing authorities themselves in the figure of Mr Filth, almost certainly a caricature of Roger L'Estrange, the Surveyor of the Press (*HW*, pp. 31–2, 257n).

Bunyan's works, like those of other Puritan authors, are hence to be read as oppositional texts produced at considerable risk to all involved. Nonconformist publishing was a collaborative enterprise requiring from printers, booksellers and other tradesmen a shared commitment with the author to challenge and outwit the agents of the state. These networks operating in Restoration London in defiance of the authorities included the publishers of Bunyan's works.[22] It is perhaps small wonder that no bookseller risked public association with Bunyan's *I Will Pray With the Spirit* (1662?): the imprint of this defiant rejection of the restored episcopal national church and of set forms of worship just when these were being re-imposed by the Act of Uniformity (1662) reads simply 'Printed for the Author' (*MW*, II:229, 233). Otherwise, Bunyan's publishers were identified on his title pages. In all, he contracted with thirteen publishers, but two stand out. From 1661 until 1679 the majority of his works were put out by Francis Smith, a Baptist and (later) licensed preacher who, despite a bewildering succession of arrests, examinations and imprisonments for publishing allegedly subversive works, survived to become a prominent Whig publisher during the Popish Plot and Exclusion Crisis. In 1678, Nathaniel Ponder, publisher of Andrew Marvell's prose satires (he was arrested in 1676 for his involvement in the production of *Mr Smirke*) and of the works of the leading Congregationalist John Owen, who may have referred Bunyan to him, published *The Pilgrim's Progress*, and thereafter, understandably, maintained his connection with Bunyan. These two were responsible for twenty-one and twenty-seven editions respectively of Bunyan's works during Bunyan's lifetime, twelve and eight of them first editions of Bunyan titles. Other works were taken by publishers with equally distinctive nonconformist lists, such as George Larkin, prosecuted in 1668 for his role in publishing satirical verse; Benjamin Alsop, who went into exile after fighting in Monmouth's army in 1685; and the Presbyterian and Whig Dorman Newman.[23]

'That Unworthy Servant of Christ'

In a 'Catalogue-Table of Mr Bunyan's Books' included in his 1692 folio edition of *The Works of that Eminent Servant of Christ, Mr John Bunyan, Late Minister of the Gospel, and Pastor of the Congregation at Bedford*, Charles Doe wrote of 'Sixty Pieces of his Labours, and he was Sixty Years of Age' (Bunyan, *Works*, sig. 5T1r).[24] Forty-two separate titles were first published from 1656 up to, and including, 1688, the year of Bunyan's death. In the following year, George Larkin published first editions of two other works, *The Acceptable Sacrifice* and, presumably from Bunyan's or an auditor's notes, his *Last Sermon* preached on 19 August 1688. Doe's 1692 collected edition included twelve works previously unpublished and in 1698 he issued *The Heavenly Foot-man*. Finally, the *Relation of My Imprisonment* appeared in 1765. This gives us fifty-eight works in all, sixteen of them posthumous.[25]

For Doe, as for the great majority of Bunyan's first readers, these '*many excellent Books*' were, as he wrote in *The Struggler*, a memoir of Bunyan and account of his own editorial labours included in the 1692 edition, '*Gospel-Books*' '*that have published to the World [God's] great Grace, and great Truths*' (*MW*, XII:456). It is as an exemplum of the power of divine grace to create a '*Gospel-Minister*' and '*a lawful Successor of the Apostles*' despite worldly and educational disadvantage that Doe lauds Bunyan as '*a second

Paul' whose writings are extensions in another medium of his evangelistic work (*MW*, XII:455), that is, didactic and edificatory works in the Puritan tradition. These included theological treatises, such as his Calvinist exposition of justification in *The Doctrine of the Law and Grace Unfolded* (1659); controversial divinity, such as the early pieces against the Quakers, *A Defence of the Doctrine of Justification* (1672) against the Latitudinarian episcopalian Edward Fowler, and disputes with other Baptists in defence of admitting into communion those who had not received adult baptism; Biblical commentary, such as his *Exposition of ... Genesis* (1692); practical theology, such as his *Christian Behaviour* (1663); and sermons and treatises developed from sermons. Bunyan's early readers did not distinguish as a separate category either *Grace Abounding* (1666) or the later allegorical works, and no more did Bunyan: their intention was still to encourage his reader to '*make thy Profession shine by a Conversation* [i.e. way of life] *according to the Gospel*' (*LDB*, p. 10). These, like all Bunyan's works, seek to transform lives.

Bunyan's literary career began with two anti-Quaker tracts, *Some Gospeltruths Opened* (1656) and its *Vindication* (1657). He is introduced and described on his first title page as 'that unworthy servant of Christ *John Bunnyan*, of Bedford, By the grace of God, Preacher of the Gospel of his dear Son' (*MW*, 1:5).[26] These, and Bunyan's third piece, the sermon *A Few Sighs from Hell* (1658), carried commendatory prefaces by ministerial colleagues which anticipated, and turned to advantage, the objection that Bunyan lacked the cultural resources to set up as a preacher or writer of books: 'Reader, in this book thou wilt not meet with high-flown aerie notions ... but the sound, plain, common ... truths of the Gospel' delivered 'not by humane art, but by the spirit of Christ' (*MW*, 1:10, 12). The claim of the apostle Paul to preach 'not with enticing words of man's wisdom, but in demonstration of the Spirit' (1 Corinthians 2:1–5), alluded to here, shaped Bunyan's self-construction as a writer whose authority lies not in academic distinction but in experiential authenticity and divine inspiration. He presents himself as an ill-educated and culturally impoverished writer solely dependent upon the Bible and divine illumination: he 'never endeavoured to, nor durst make use of other men's lines' for he 'found by experience, that what was taught me by the Word and Spirit of Christ, could be spoken, maintained, and stood to, by the soundest and best established Conscience' (*GA*, pp. 87–8). Unlike 'carnal Priests' who 'tickle the ears of their hearers with vain Philosophy', he 'never went to School to *Aristotle* or *Plato*' and '*has not writ at a venture, nor borrowed my Doctrine from Libraries. I depend upon the sayings of no man*'; instead, he offers the reader 'a parcel of plain, yet sound, true, and home sayings' drawn from '*the Scriptures of Truth, among the true sayings of God*' (*MW*, 1:345, II:16, VIII:51). Bunyan has not 'fished in other mens *Waters*, my Bible and Concordance are my only Library in my writings' (*MW*, VII:9). He does not clutter his margins with 'a Cloud of Sentences from the Learned FATHERS' because 'I have them not, nor have not read them': 'I prefer the BIBLE before them; and having that still with me, I count my self far better furnished than if I had (without it) all the Libraries of the two Universities' (*MW*, III:71–2). In short, 'A little from God is better than a great deal from men' (*MW*, XIII:332).

Bunyan was not in fact as ill-educated or poorly read as he maintains; he certainly did not 'loose that little I learned, even almost utterly' (*GA*, p. 5), and he may even have attended grammar school.[27] He had indeed done a spot of 'fishing in other mens *Waters*', notably in John Foxe's immensely influential martyrology *Actes and Monuments* (1563), in the expository matter in the Geneva Bible (1560), in an English translation of Luther's commentary on Galatians (*GA*, p. 40) and in a range of works of practical and controversial English theology.[28] Radical and sectarian Puritanism, noting the precedent of Jesus's poorly educated disciples, was generally distrustful of the association between ministerial authority and academic distinction. Doe, alluding to the confutation of Jewish leaders by Peter and John though 'unlearned and ignorant men' (Acts 4:13), pointed to Bunyan as evidence that those lacking 'School-Education' and *'unlearned'* might through divine grace minister more effectually than those with university degrees, citing with some glee Bunyan's refutation in oral debate of the *'hellish Logick'* of Thomas Smith, professor of Arabic at Cambridge (*MW*, XII:455–7).[29] Bunyan's self-presentation is to be understood in this context. His insistence on his lack of resources creates a persona trustworthy precisely because it relies on divinely guided personal experience. To those nonconformist readers with misgivings about recourse to the literary contrivances of fiction and allegory Bunyan's response is to appeal not to Classical and Renaissance theories of the efficacy of imaginative writing, still less to 'humane' art, but to the immediacy of divine inspiration through his account of the unpremeditated origin of *The Pilgrim's Progress*: having fallen *'suddenly into an Allegory'*, ideas multiplied *'Like sparks that from the coals of Fire do flie'* without, it seems, his own active intervention (*P'sP*, p. 1). This is a view of creativity that accords no credit to the skill of the writer: Bunyan is but an 'instrument' in 'the hand of Christ' (*GA*, p. 91).

The evidence for experiential (or, as the seventeenth-century term was, 'experimental') Christianity is necessarily autobiographical, and its expression straightforward, *'plain and simple'*; Bunyan deliberately eschews *'a stile much higher then this'* lest he falsify his experience through rhetorical embellishment (*GA*, p. 3). His *'own native Language'* (*P'sP*, p. 168) is, indeed, oral rather than literary in its mannerisms and directness. In the early works especially we find 'a total unselfconsciousness in regard to the function of the writer'.[30] Bunyan does refer to putting *'Pen to Paper'*, to taking his *'Pen in hand'* and to being 'moved ... to Write and Print this Little Book' (*MW*, IV:193, XI:7; *P'sP*, p. 1), but he will *'tell'* his readers of the dangers of sin and he promises to *'say'* more in a subsequent *'discourse'* (*MW*, I:245, 247).[31] Rather than construct a text for readers, Bunyan directly addresses auditors who find themselves caught up in a conversation. The writer/reader relationship is constructed as dialogic: 'If thou shouldest say ... To this I shall answer ...', 'But (you will say) ... I answer' (*MW*, II:16, 219). Bunyan's frequent exclamations, questions and self-reflexive interjections are locutory – 'I say therefore ...', 'let me tell you ...', 'Only let me say ...' , 'I told you before' (*MW*, II:14, 15, 285, VIII:125). Through colloquialisms, dialectal forms, proverbs, Bunyan seeks openly to convey in print, as he did in the pulpit, the immediacy of 'what I felt, what I smartingly did feel' (*GA*, p. 85).

'A Prisoner of Hope'

By 1660 Bunyan had four published titles to his name, but with his arrest in November 1660 and subsequent twelve-year imprisonment his output greatly increased and his literary persona gained sharper definition. Incarceration provided him with additional incentives to write. As Baxter, himself imprisoned for nonconformity, tellingly noted, *'Preachers* may be silenced or banished, when *Books* may be at hand.'[32] For Bunyan, separated from his people by prison, writing was the one way he could continue his ministry. *'Taken from you in presence'* and unable in person to *'perform that duty that from God doth lie upon me, to you-ward'*, through print he could yet address his congregation and the wider community (*GA*, p. 1). His precedent lay in the epistles St Paul had written from captivity in Rome, in Bunyan's time thought to include the epistles (1 Timothy and Hebrews) which provided him with the titles for *Grace Abounding* and *The Pilgrim's Progress*.[33]

Far from disguising Bunyan's circumstances, his 1660s texts explicitly locate themselves in jail, directly confronting their readers with the fact of his imprisonment. The title page of *Christian Behaviour* identifies its author as 'a Prisoner of *Hope*' (*MW*, III:5). *Prison-Meditations* (1663) is no poetic fancy but 'By JOHN BUNYAN, a Prisoner' (*MW*, VI:39). *The Holy City* (1665) originated 'Upon a certain *First day*, I being together with my Brethren, in our Prison-Chamber, they expected that, according to our Custom, something should be spoken out of the Word ... it being my turn to speak' (*MW*, III:69). *Grace Abounding* will relate what its author 'hath met with in Prison' and 'was written by his own hand there' (*GA*, p. xliv). The 'Denn' upon which the narrator happens as he 'walks through the wilderness of this world' at the opening of *The Pilgrim's Progress* is marginally glossed

'Gaol' and it is '*from* the Lions Dens', from the prison where '*I stick between the Teeth of the Lions in the Wilderness*', that Bunyan addresses his reader in the prefatory epistle to *Grace Abounding*. Lions signify here, as they do in *The Pilgrim's Progress*, the cruelties of persecution (*P'sP*, pp. 8, 45–6, 218–19; *GA*, p. 1). That he writes from prison enables Bunyan once again to associate his ministry with that of Paul. From the account in Acts 23–4 of the charges preferred by the Jews against Paul before Felix, Roman procurator of Judaea, Bunyan infers that '*an hypocritical people, will persecute the power of those truths in others, which themselves in words profess*', adding 'I am this day, and for this very thing persecuted by them' (*MW*, III:204).

By so insisting on the circumstances of his texts' production Bunyan associates their experiential authority with a validating tradition of Christian witness. Through Biblical instruction (notably Luke 6:22: 'Blessed are they that are persecuted for righteousness' sake, for theirs is the Kingdom of Heaven'), the historical persecutions of Christians recounted in Foxe's *Actes and Monuments* and their own experience, suffering became for Puritans a defining characteristic of Christian experience. Evangelist warns Christian and Faithful that they 'must through many tribulations enter into the Kingdom of Heaven' and that 'bonds and afflictions' await them (*P'sP*, p. 87). That 'the people of God are a suffering people' (*MW*, x:95) is the theme of *Seasonable Counsel: or, Advice to Sufferers* (1684). Through suffering, the Christian is tried and purified: 'Goals [*sic*] are Christ his Schools / In them we learn to dye' (*MW*, VI:45). Bunyan's authority to teach lies in the education he has received in this school.[34]

'The Author of *The Pilgrim's Progress*'

With the publication of *The Pilgrim's Progress* in 1678 and its immediate success Bunyan's sense of his literary self and of his relationship to his writings changed significantly. As he explained in its preface, he had had misgivings over the propriety of his allegorical method and publication was delayed while he sought advice from friends, for many of whom the book was either superficial or obscure, or both (*P'sP*, pp. 2–5). In the preface to Part II (1684), however, defensiveness and misgivings are replaced by a defiant assertiveness as Bunyan delightedly tells of the extraordinary success of Part I in Britain, in New England and across Europe. He is now sufficiently possessive about his texts to seek to discredit imitators, and sufficiently confident to point to his own distinctive style to confirm his authorial identity and the authenticity of this text (*P'sP*, pp. 168–71). In short, Bunyan's identity as a literary figure and the integrity of his creative output are now to be defended hardly less energetically than the Christian gospel.

There is hence a new kind of purposefulness and a new ambition in the later works. *Mr Badman* is explicitly designed to partner *The Pilgrim's Progress* (*'It came again into my mind to write, as then, of him that was going to Heaven, so now, of the Life and Death of the Ungodly'* (LDB, p. 1)), and Part II of *The Pilgrim's Progress* follows in its turn, building up a library of related allegorical works. This new sense of ambition is most evident in the multi-layered complexity of *The Holy War*, in an 'Advertisement' to which Bunyan is still more concerned to assert his own unaided authorship of *The Pilgrim's Progress* against those who allege that only through plagiarism could he have written it, but he does so with a quip that directs attention not to gospel truths nor to divine inspiration but to his own individual claim on original literary inventiveness: 'Witness my name, if Anagram'd to thee, / The Letters make, *Nu hony in a B*' (HW, p. 251).

The culmination of this process was Doe's complete edition of Bunyan's works, a publishing project designed to establish Bunyan as an author to set beside episcopalian preachers such as Isaac Barrow and John Tillotson, Presbyterian Puritans such as Richard Baxter, republicans and Whigs such as John Milton and Quakers such as George Fox, all of whom had folio editions in the 1690s.[35] Planned originally before his death, *'but an interested Book-seller opposed it'*, a preliminary announcement in 1690 was followed the next year by a fuller announcement from the publisher, William Marshall, and by a pamphlet in which Doe listed thirty reasons in support of the proposed two-volume edition to be funded by advance subscription from purchasers. In his *Reasons* Doe might insist on Bunyan's ministerial mission and character, addressing himself to *'Christian People'*, describing Bunyan as 'a very able and excellent Minister of the Gospel' and saluting him as 'an Apostle of our Age', but he did recognise that what was 'extraordinary' about Bunyan's case was that, unlike other 'good Ministers', he had 'writ much, which hath gone off well' (Bunyan, *Works*, sig. 5T1r), and (in *The Struggler*) that the success of *The Pilgrim's Progress*, in its 100,000 English copies (he estimated) and many translations, had made its author *'famous'* (MW, XII:456). Through this fame Bunyan now enjoyed what, in a preface to the posthumous *The Acceptable Sacrifice* (1689), his ministerial colleague George Cockayne, called *'Extraordinary Circumstances'* (MW, XII:7). This the printing trade had quickly realised: though put out by publishers other than Ponder, the title pages of *Mr Badman* and of *The Holy War*, and of other texts (MW, X:106; XI:97), capitalised on his success by identifying Bunyan no longer as 'the servant of Jesus Christ' but as the 'Author of the *Pilgrim's Progress*'. Bunyan was now a bestseller, his name a marketing tool. It was the beginning of an even more remarkable posthumous literary career as Bunyan's name entered the English literary canon.[36]

NOTES

1. In fact, Bunyan rather overstated the case: see Greaves, *Glimpses*, pp. 3–4.
2. For statistical data, see John Barnard, D. F. McKenzie and Maureen Bell, *The Cambridge History of the Book in Britain*, vol. IV, *1557–1695* (Cambridge University Press, 2002), chapters 1, 2 and 26 (especially pp. 557–67), and appendix 1, from which these figures are taken; also Ian Green, *Print and Protestantism in Early Modern England* (Oxford University Press, 2000), pp. 13–14 and appendix 1.
3. On Thomason and the 'explosion of print' see Joad Raymond, *Pamphlets and Pamphleteering in Early Modern Britain* (Cambridge University Press, 2003), esp. pp. 161–201, and 'The Literature of Controversy', in Thomas N. Corns (ed.), *A Companion to Milton* (Oxford: Blackwell, 2001), pp. 191–210; Sharon Achinstein, 'Texts in Conflict: The Press and the Civil War', in N. H. Keeble (ed.), *The Cambridge Companion to Writing of the English Revolution* (Cambridge University Press, 2001), pp. 50–68.
4. Greaves, *Glimpses*, p. 11.
5. Richard Baxter, *Aphorismes of Justification* (1649), sigs. a1r–a1v.
6. The phrase provides the title of Christopher Hill, *The World Turned Upside Down: Radical Ideas during the English Revolution* (London: Temple Smith, 1972).
7. Greaves, *Glimpses*, pp. 54, 61–7.
8. Nigel Smith, *Literature and Revolution in England, 1640–1680* (New Haven and London: Yale University Press, 1994), p. 24.
9. Green, *Print and Protestantism*, p. 26; David Cressy, *Literacy and the Social Order: Reading and Writing in Tudor and Stuart England* (Cambridge University Press, 1980), esp. pp. 72–5.
10. John Spurr, *English Puritanism, 1603–1689* (London: Macmillan, 1998), p. 151.
11. Richard Baxter, *A Christian Directory* (1673), Book 2, p. 348.
12. See Tessa Watt, *Cheap Print and Popular Piety, 1550–1640* (Cambridge University Press, 1991); Margaret Spufford, *Small Books and Pleasant Histories* (London: Methuen, 1981); Green, *Print and Protestantism*, pp. 445–502.
13. See further Sharon Achinstein, *Milton and the Revolutionary Reader* (Princeton University Press, 1994).
14. See further Frederick Siebert, *Freedom of the Press in England, 1476–1776* (Urbana: University of Illinois Press, 1952); Christopher Hill, 'Censorship and English Literature', in his *Writing and Revolution in Seventeenth Century England* (Brighton: Harvester Press, 1985), pp. 32–71; Raymond, *Pamphlets*, pp. 66–71, 196–201; N. H. Keeble, *The Literary Culture of Nonconformity in Later Seventeenth-Century England* (Leicester University Press, 1987), pp. 93–126.
15. *The Complete Prose Works of John Milton*, gen. ed. Don Wolfe, 8 vols. (New Haven: Yale University Press, 1953–82), II:554.
16. On this legislation and its effect see G. R. Cragg, *Puritanism in the Period of the Great Persecution, 1660–1688* (Cambridge University Press, 1957); Keeble, *Literary Culture*, pp. 25–92; for Bunyan's imprisonment, see Greaves, *Glimpses*, pp. 127–72.
17. Greaves, *Glimpses*, pp. 211, 216–18, 226.
18. See further below, p. 18.
19. See further below, pp. 18, 23.
20. For further readings of Bunyan in this way, see Hill, *Turbulent*, pp. 125–30, 212–21, 243–50.

21. In an extraordinarily helpful appendix in his *Glimpses*, pp. 637–41, Greaves lists editions of Bunyan's titles put out in his lifetime, with their dates of publication, licensing and advertisement, identification of their publishers and conjectural dates of composition.
22. Richard L. Greaves, *Deliver Us from Evil* (New York: Oxford University Press, 1986), pp. 207–25 and *Enemies under His Feet* (Stanford University Press, 1990), pp. 167–90; Keeble, *Literary Culture*, pp. 120–6.
23. Frank Mott Harrison, 'Nathaniel Ponder: the Publisher of *The Pilgrim's Progress*', *The Library*, 4th ser., 15 (1934), 257–94; Elizabeth Lane Furdell, ' "At the King's Arms in the Poultrey": The Bookshop Emporium of Dorman Newman, 1670–1694', *London Journal*, 23.1 (1998), 1–20; H. R. Plomer, *Dictionaries of the Printers and Booksellers who were at work ... 1557–1775* (London: Bibliographical Society, 1977), s.vv; Greaves, *Glimpses*, p. 347.
24. For Doe's edition, see below, p. 23 and chapter 10.
25. These details derive from Greaves, *Glimpses*, pp. 637–41 and throughout, and *MW*, vols. XII and XIII. Doe's list of sixty works included 'A Christian Dialogue' and 'A Pocket Concordance', both as '*Manuscripts*, yet unprinted' and not otherwise known (but on the concordance see Greaves, *Glimpses*, pp. 269–71).
26. For an acute discussion of the significance of the published forms of Bunyan's name and authorial presentation throughout his career, see Tamsin Spargo, *The Writing of John Bunyan* (Aldershot: Ashgate, 1997), pp. 6–42, and 'Bunyan's Abounding', in N. H. Keeble (ed.), *John Bunyan: Reading Dissenting Writing* (Bern: Peter Lang, 2002), pp. 79–101.
27. Greaves, *Glimpses*, pp. 4–6.
28. Gordon Campbell, ' "Fishing in Other Men's Waters": Bunyan and the Theologians', in Keeble (ed.), *Conventicle*, pp. 137–51; Greaves, *Glimpses*, pp. 603–7.
29. Doe does not identify Smith; for the episode in 1659, see Greaves, *Glimpses*, pp. 121–3.
30. Roger Sharrock, ' "When at the first I took my Pen in hand": Bunyan and the Book', in Keeble (ed.), *Conventicle*, pp. 71–90 (p. 75).
31. As noted by Spargo, *Writing of John Bunyan*, p. 21.
32. Baxter, *Christian Directory*, Book 1, p. 60. See on this Keeble, *Literary Culture*, pp. 78–92.
33. 1 Timothy 1:14–15: 'the grace of our Lord was exceeding abundant ... Christ Jesus came into the world to save sinners; of whom I am the chief'; Hebrews 11:13: 'These all died in faith ... and confessed that they were strangers and pilgrims on the earth.'
34. See, on this theme, John R. Knott, *Discourses of Martyrdom in English Literature, 1563–1694* (Cambridge University Press, 1993); Keeble, *Literary Culture*, pp. 187–214; Greaves, *Glimpses*, pp. 493–8.
35. As argued in W. R. Owens, 'Reading the Bibliographical Codes: Bunyan's Publication in Folio', in Keeble (ed.), *John Bunyan*, pp. 59–77; see further *MW*, XII:xvii–xxiii.
36. See further N. H. Keeble, ' "Of him thousands daily sing and talk": Bunyan and his Reputation', in Keeble (ed.), *Conventicle*, pp. 241–63; Greaves, *Glimpses*, pp. 619–34; Isabel Hofmeyr, *The Portable Bunyan: A Transcultural History of 'The Pilgrim's Progress'* (Princeton University Press, 2004).

2

NIGEL SMITH

John Bunyan and Restoration literature

Most of the works John Bunyan published in print, and indeed most of what he wrote, was compiled during the Restoration. This was a period with clear boundaries in English history, witnessing the return of the monarchy in the shape of the two sons of Charles I, first Charles II between 1660 and 1685 and then James II between 1685 and 1688. The shape of these regimes was particularly relevant to Bunyan since as a dissenter he suffered from the policies of religious discrimination that the government of each monarch adopted towards Protestant nonconformists, although James II favoured toleration of dissenters in order to gain the same for Roman Catholics. The pathetic end of James's reign in the Glorious Revolution, in the year of Bunyan's death, ensured greater freedom for dissenters and the end of the 'great persecution', but even before Charles's ascent to the throne in 1660 the twenty years of the 'Puritan Revolution' had seen advocates of the Baptist Calvinism for which Bunyan stood grow from a tiny and persecuted minority to become a flourishing community.

The fortunes of the literary history of the Restoration fluctuate. Eighty years ago drama, much of it libertine in character, was the subject of much fascination.[1] Three or four decades ago, a flourishing industry was devoted to reconstructing and restoring the texts, reputation and activities of John Dryden.[2] Between the 1960s and the 1980s, however, the Restoration was largely eclipsed by the dazzle of the 1640s and 1650s, and study of major Restoration themes and authors dwindled significantly, with the possible exception of the study of Puritan literature. Now there is renewed interest in the decades of the Restoration, with publications and conferences holding out the promise of more sustained attention to the crucial period of transition when Bunyan grew to fame as a minister and an author.[3] It was once the case that conventional literary period division made the Restoration the beginning of a 'long eighteenth century' that lasted until the French Revolution in 1789. Now it might equally be claimed that the Restoration is viewed as the denouement of the Civil War and Commonwealth period.

The Restoration is not short on literary masterpieces by any measure. There is John Milton's *Paradise Lost* (1667), John Bunyan's *The Pilgrim's Progress* (1678), John Dryden's *Absalom and Achitophel* (1681), George Etherege's *The Man of Mode* (1676), Aphra Behn's *Oroonoko* (1688), and it is bustling with original intellectual energy. There was the attempt to build a proper tradition of English letters: to make a calculated recovery from what was regarded as the cultural desecration of the Civil Wars by improving upon the achievements of the heyday of drama and poetry in the late sixteenth and early seventeenth centuries. At the centre of this activity was John Dryden, determined also to establish himself as laureate and pre-eminent literary authority, and scoring brilliant goals in the fields of drama, poetry and the critical essay.[4] The drama had been revived at the return of the King and flourished, in new conditions of official approval, as a facet of both the court and the city.[5] Female actors now trod the boards of the public theatres and once the anxiety of regicide had been expelled in the tragedies of the 1660s, a distinctive drama was developed in the following decade. It gave the dramatic canon several classics, such as Etherege's *The Man of Mode* (1676), Wycherley's *The Country Wife* (produced 1672–3) and Dryden's *The Conquest of Granada* (1671–2). We might add the Duke of Buckingham's *The Rehearsal* (written *c*.1667; first performed 1671), a hard text to appreciate today, but the most frequently performed comedy for the next century. Classicism was one impulse behind the infamous rewriting of older plays, especially those of Shakespeare, and the influence of the French theatre was also felt with Molière and Corneille in particular inducing imitations as royalists returned from exile in Paris and brought new tastes with them.[6]

The world of the theatre was the world of London, whose West End was being laid out at this time and with greater rapidity after the Great Fire in 1666. It was, or was reputed to be, a salacious world. Actresses had open and extra-marital relationships with people as important as the King, or with aristocratic poets like John Wilmot, Earl of Rochester. The sexually generous habits of the King were continuous with a libertine culture that prized sexual bravado but cringed at the thought of its retributions in more reflective and philosophical moments.[7] Rochester's audacious poetry, designed to outrage, was the work of a young victim of venereal disease. This poetry, and Rochester's small body of drama, was part of a much larger network of sexually frank expression; its literary materials were almost wholly circulated in manuscript within the court, and more widely in the city, at the time of their composition, but many of them gained a foothold later in anthologies of printed verse. This world was the seedbed of the great satire that would follow in the early eighteenth century, but it also had its own rich harvest: in addition to Rochester, an unlikely contributor was the former Cromwellian secretary turned Restoration MP Andrew Marvell, with his many Puritan credentials, who was responsible for 'The Last Instructions to a Painter', possibly the greatest and funniest of the Restoration anti-court satirical poems, and for the innovative treatise *The Rehearsal Transpros'd*, Parts I and II (1672–3).[8] John Oldham was another fine and discriminating poetic satirist.[9] Bunyan would have looked with horror at these men and their world.

He might have looked with a different kind of disapproval at the second main area of literary activity during the Restoration. This was the writing of the new scientists given official sanction by the creation of the Royal Society in 1660. Robert Boyle, Robert Hooke and Isaac Newton were merely the most famous of an astonishing generation of discoverers, by whose measurements of the physical world we still live.[10] They were famous in their lifetimes as writers as well as intrepid researchers. The graininess of their writing bears some comparison, as has been suggested, to Bunyan's very differently directed project.[11] There were also aspects of their collective thought that Bunyan would have regarded as a road to destruction. Despite their seeming conformity with the teachings of the church as well as the state, they were often philosophically or theologically of very heterodox views. The teaching of the ancient Greek Epicureans with its atomistic description of the universe, helpfully (or unhelpfully) transmitted through Lucretius's *De rerum natura*, maintained its hold upon the imagination of many, and was widely seen as a version of atheism.[12] Nonetheless, and despite any feelings the Puritans harboured against natural philosophers and those who deployed human 'invention' – which is to say the imagination – some measure of Puritanism remained close to the centre of early scientific endeavour. While the group that preceded the Royal Society as the pre-eminent gathering of natural philosophers, namely the circle of correspondents gathered around Samuel Hartlib, certainly entertained connections with the Commonwealth regimes and had hopes for greater patronage therein, some individuals came from backgrounds that imbued them with elements of Puritan piety.[13] Robert Boyle, for example, the youngest son of the Earl of Cork, emerged as one of the most important early scientists and his spirituality was undoubtedly founded upon Puritan piety, although he remained a member of the Church of England. His *Occasional Meditations* of 1665 insisted upon finding spiritual significance in its examination of the natural world.

Since Bunyan was a persecuted Puritan, we might have expected him to pay more attention to the literature of protest that accompanied the years of the Restoration with growing anger. Yet while his writing reflects the experience of persecution, as instanced in the martyrdom of Faithful in *The Pilgrim's Progress*, Part I (1678), or James II's interference with the government of local corporations in *The Holy War* (1682), and while some material from the *Mirabilis Annus* tracts of 1661–2 functioned as a source for *The Life and Death of Mr Badman* (1680), Bunyan was a true separatist who really did turn his back on the world. The literature of Whig protest that grew with the Exclusion Crisis from late 1678 onwards, and the oppositional writing that preceded it, exerted no influence upon his work. There is none of the boisterous agit-prop of Ralph Wallis's pamphleteering, none of the engaged millenarianism of the *Mirabilis Annus* tracts and none of the profane sexual satire of the republican Henry Neville in *The Isle of Pines* (1668) with its mischievous parody of the Book of Genesis, and its Machiavellian account of a society destined for division, and with the further evidence of Neville's considerable Italianate learning and his friendship with the Duke of Tuscany.[14] Many of the godly and some former Levellers, godly or not, remained engaged with the political and religious disputes of the Restoration, especially after the fall from power of Edward Hyde, Earl of Clarendon, in 1667, and their writings, when they did write, reflected this. A good example of a Baptist with a complex involvement in politics would be the printer George Larkin, coincidentally the printer of some of Bunyan's works.[15] But Bunyan has none of this.

Nonetheless, Bunyan's writing belongs with the large body of nonconformist writing produced and disseminated during the Restoration years. This very large body of work, which has been well mapped in the last two decades, ranges from considerable, learned works of theology and ecclesiology to much less sophisticated pastoral treatises, from the sermons and commentaries of Presbyterians to the visionary and messianic prophecy of the Quakers.[16] It includes several works that have come to have a major place in the literary canon, not least the major poetry of John Milton, and Bunyan's autobiographical and allegorical writings. Milton's *Paradise Lost* and Milton's reputation would quickly come to enjoy a far more celebrated and enduring place in the canon than Bunyan's.

Bunyan's career as an author probably began when he joined the Bedford congregation of Baptists under the pastorship of John Gifford in the 1650s. Since this was an 'open' Baptist church, with believers either undergoing adult baptism or making a confession of faith and experience in order to be church members, it is likely that Bunyan's great autobiographical classic *Grace Abounding* began life as a confession of experience or a conversion narrative. In this way, many other people of humble origins became authors as members of such congregations. No doubt the text was revised (and was certainly augmented) after its initial publication in 1666 as Bunyan's retrospective view of his early days changed with continuing experience. The immediacy of this text is very striking, much of its vividness being imparted by the personification of abstract entities, especially likely to arise from particular texts in the Bible, which become urgent, nagging or alarming persons. There are also the medicinal metaphors, with the Bible becoming a leech that bleeds Bunyan, the would-be believer, for his own good. We might say that these qualities of 'literal figure', where the metaphor becomes more literal than the signified, betoken someone with a lively imagination but little education or training.[17] It was perhaps Bunyan's greatest literary asset.

After conversion and confession came a life of preaching, turning into the preached word the 'language of Canaan', the godly speech that he had first heard spoken by the group of women 'sitting at a door in the Sun' in Bedford (GA, p. 14).[18] The body of Bunyan's literary output, most of it lost to us now, was comprised of sermons. We have no sermon books to show how he composed them or where he stood on the complicated issue of the use of sermons in worship or for other pious purposes. We cannot tell where he was located on the spectrum of sermon style from high to low church. He preached his first sermon in 1655 in the midst of the Cromwellian Protectorate, when the position of the Baptists was more fortunate than at any other point in his lifetime. These early sermons were barely competent, to judge by what was published in 1658 as A Few Sighs from Hell, although certainly with significant power and signs of what was to come. The continued repetition and composition of the sermons was the quickest way by which Bunyan was able to establish himself not merely as a preacher but also as an author. In this respect, he was a typical product of Puritan culture.

The first text that he wrote and saw printed was his attack on the Quakers, Some Gospel-truths Opened (MW, 1: 1656), a work that elicited responses from Edward Burrough and George Fox, both major figures in the nascent charismatic movement that had swept England in the early 1650s.[19] It was typical of these years that a printed dispute about doctrine should have been thought necessary and important. Indeed, throughout the country Baptist congregations found themselves threatened with loss of members to the rising Quaker movement that so resourcefully exploited the opportunities of print culture to proselytise.[20] Like many people from a similar background, Bunyan in his writing struggled with the demands of controversy. Sentences mount up under the weight of the author's conviction that the position of the opponent is dangerously erroneous:

> And for this cause God hath sent them strong delusions, that they should believe a lye: That they all might be damned, who believed not the truth, but had pleasure in unrighteousness, as it is written, 2 Thes. 2. 11, 12. And indeed if you marke it, you shall see, that they be such kinde of people, who at this day are so carried away with the Quakers delusions; namely, a Company of loose Ranters, and light Notionists, with here and there a Legalist, which were shaking in their principles from time to time, sometimes on this Religion, sometimes on that: and thus these Unstable Souls are deluded and beguiled at last, 2 Pet. 2. 14.

So that these who before (as one would have thought) had something of God in
them, are now turned such enemies to the glorious truths of the Gospel that there
is none so obstinately erroneous as they. And indeed it is just with God, to give
them over to believe a lye, 2 Thes. 2. 11. *who before were so idle that they wou'd*
not receive the Truth of God into their hearts, in the love of it: And to be
bewitched by the Divell to obey his temptations, and be damned, who would
not obey the truth, *Gal.* 5.1. *that they might be saved.* (MW, 1:15–16)

The Quakers were not fit company, despite the fact that Quaker speech-habits
of address ('thou' to one but 'you' to many, which is historically correct) have
been detected in *The Pilgrim's Progress*.[21]

Two quite different features explain how Bunyan progressed from this kind
of published discourse to the masterful and distinctive expression that char-
acterises his great works of literature. First of all, he put his hand to the many
different kinds of pastoral literature that typified Puritan writing both before
and after 1660. *The Holy City* (1665) is an allegorical treatise, much like a
sermon in character, but extending an explanation of the figure of the Holy
City or 'New Jerusalem'. It began, so Bunyan claims in his prefatory epistle, as
a Sunday ministering to those with whom he was imprisoned. He claimed to
feel 'empty, spiritless, and barren', and therefore incapable of delivering any
substantial words of 'Truth, with Life and Evidence' (*MW*, III:69), but after a
while he saw something in Revelation 21:11 and in the following verses. The
allegorical explanation of the meaning of the holy city follows this scriptural
text with great narrative energy, connecting different parts of the Bible, nearly
all of which have very vivid imagery. The effect is utterly memorable and the
reader is helped along by marginal references to Biblical texts and pointers to
key themes. This is textbook Puritan writing: clarifying, edifying and purify-
ing. So were Bunyan's forays into other genres such as *A Book for Boys and*
Girls: Or, Country Rhimes for Children (1686), which has connections not
merely with educational writing but also with catechism (since Bunyan offers
precepts of faith in a series of delightful, homely emblematic poems to which
engravings were added in the eighteenth century), the means by which all, but
especially the young, were brought to understand theological doctrine.[22]
The Life and Death of Mr Badman (1680) is a dialogue.

Also striking are the instances of Bunyan's ability with extremely vivid
figures drawn from everyday activity. The liveliness of lived experience is
underscored, even if the signified lies far in the realm of the transcendental.
Sometimes skeins of imagery are run in a loosely connected way through quite
large textual distance. 'We did all eat, and were well refreshed' (*MW*, III:70),
he says of his growing Holy City address, but the food has to become something more substantial: 'while I was in the distributing of it, it so increased in
my hand, that of the Fragments that we left, after we had well dined,

I gathered up this Basket-full' (MW, III:70), alluding to the parable of the loaves and the fishes. By the next paragraph, the food has become drink: 'that much more then I do here crush out, is yet left in the Cluster: Alas! I shall onely say thus, I have crush'd out a little Juyce to sweeten their Lips withal' (MW, III:70). Then we return to solid food to explain that while some readers may wish to discard the text as 'an empty Bone', 'others may pick both good and wholsom Bits; yea, and also out of that suck much nourishing Marrow. You find by experience that that very bit that will not down with One, may yet not onely down, but be healthful and nourishing to another' (MW, III:70). This is eminently practical, and sounds like a dietary manual.

Few were as skilled as Bunyan, or so happily unconstrained by a formal education, in the art of writing so feelingly. Bunyan reproved those divines who offered the learning of ancient philosophy in their sermons because he wanted the simplicity of the gospel to shine forth. These embedded quotidian metaphors are so effortlessly and naturally placed that we literally pass them by unless we pay careful attention. There is a sense too with Bunyan that the pious book, such as the copies of Arthur Dent's *The Plaine Mans Path-way to Heaven* (1601) and Lewis Bayly's *The Practise of Pietie* (1612?), with which he began his marriage (GA, p. 8), is of the same order with other helpful books, such as cookbooks or medical manuals, all useful guides for the godly and attentive people in this life. Thus, aspects of the great allegories have been connected to the local medical treatises that circulated in Bunyan's community.[23] When these ways of expressing a physical sense of being in the world arise in states of acknowledged stress, as in *Grace Abounding*, the effect is of the most impressive kind of conversion narrative:

> By this Temptation also, I was greatly beaten off my former foolish practice, of putting by the Word of Promise when it came into my mind: for now, though I could not suck that sweetness and comfort from the Promise, as I had done at other times, yet, like to a man asinking, I should catch at all I saw: formerly I thought I might not meddle with the Promise, unless I felt its comfort; but now 'twas no time thus to do, the Avenger of blood too hardly did pursue me.   (GA, p. 77)

The second major feature in Bunyan's mature writing is the remnant in his imagination of the very condition of worldliness from which he hastened to escape. Indeed, in both *The Heavenly Foot-man* (comp. c.1667–8, pub. 1698) and in *The Pilgrim's Progress*, this is likened to a sprinting away from one's pre-converted state into a godly state as fast as one's legs could run. Bunyan is happy to confess that he was a kind of seventeenth-century hooligan: frequently drunk, delinquent, lazy, a prodigious swearer and generally a very unpleasant young man: 'from a childe, that I had but few Equals, (especially considering my years, which were tender, being few) both for cursing, swearing, lying and blaspheming the holy Name of God' (*GA*, p. 6). His engagement with the world of seventeenth-century popular culture must have been as sensually intense as his expression of it. When he finally came to construct the narrative of *The Pilgrim's Progress* he did the work with a decisive return of what he had banished; the narrative has an astonishing and famous vividness by virtue of the sensory boldness of that early, profane and supposedly repudiated imagination. That Bunyan says he often felt guilty as a young man, so that he felt the Lord tortured him with terrifying dream visions or apprehensions of devils on account of his sinfulness, is a measure of how, even as a child and long before his conversion, he felt that his sensory perceptions were dangerous to him (*GA*, p. 6).

By contrast Benjamin Keach, another Baptist author whose works sold very well, for all his knowledge of rhetoric cannot sustain as convincing an allegory because he will insist on reminding his readers that they are reading allegory, and because, while we are in a domestic seventeenth-century narrative world, the episodes are extraordinary rather than believable:

> *Riches*, Sir I am troubled I have not minded you all this while, for I have a great reverence and respect for *Godliness*, God forbid I should keep you out any longer.
>
> Upon this, the whole House was in an uproar, for he had (as I told you before) divers loose, ill-bred, or rather Hell-bred Servants, all bitter Enemies to *True Godliness*, their Names were *Presumption, Pride, Unbelief, Ignorance, Malice, Vain-hope,* and *Covetousness*, &c. These and several other base companions of like quality (whom he had brought up, and a long time cherished in his House) seemed mightily concerned that the least heed or attention should be given to *True Godliness*; they also enquired who was the cause of it; at last they understood it was Mr. *Fearful*, they then presently joyned together to fall upon *Fearful*, and turn him out of the House. *Presumption* struck the first blow, and spake also to this purpose.
>
> *Presump.* Are not you a base Fellow, thus to disturb my Master, as to cause him in the least to doubt of the strength of his strong and impregnable fortification [Note '*' in margin: *Riches Bags of Gold and Silver.*], wherein he hath placed his long confidence, and now to force him to incline to open unto *True Godliness*, who is our utter Enemy? Is he not an honest man? what can you charge him with? What cause or ground is there for this disturbance? Hath he not done much good in the Parish where he lives, and given many a piece of Bread at his Door? I warrant you it will go well with him, *Fearful*, what do you say?[24]

The difference is subtle but finally the gap between the two writers is considerable.

The unity of *The Pilgrim's Progress* is probably a result of early immersion in the stories of popular heroism that featured in the national chapbook market, offering the cheapest kinds of available books: *Guy of Warwick, Bevis of Hampton* and *The Seven Champions of Christendom*.[25] It is within this structure, with its sparse sense of direct narrative drive, that the other compelling elements on the level of the signifier operate: the sense of class abjection that underpins the relationship between Christian and his persecutors.[26] Behind this there is probably a story of the decline of the Bunyans, for if Bunyan's father was a tinker his grandfather had been a yeoman farmer. There were plenty of dissenting writers with humble backgrounds, but few could equal Bunyan in articulating class abjection so acutely. While other divines and lay nonconformists focused on public issues, such as arguments for religious toleration, Bunyan is striking in his disinterestedness, despite suffering at the hands of conformist legislation. A text intended to have the broadest possible reach, *The Life and Death of Mr Badman*, is notable for the stories it tells of the terrible fates of gross sinners (in addition to its eponymous anti-hero) like Dorothy Mately, who was swallowed by the ground for denying that she had stolen coins from a child (*LDB*, pp. 32–3). The incidental detail that makes all the difference is that she was washing ore on a hillside at the time – perhaps searching for precious metal. The fall into the ground was presumably the consequence of collapsed mining works. In this way, many characters that Bunyan was able to remember from his former days, especially religious radicals from the 1650s, are projected forwards into this world of clear and absolute allegory. Bunyan's allegorical characters exist as exemplary counterparts to the biographies of godly ministers that constituted a large part of nonconformist publishing. The Presbyterian minister Samuel Clarke was notable in this respect with his *The Lives of Sundry Eminent Persons* (1683).[27] But while Bunyan was typical in stressing the values of godly community in his writing, as seen especially well in *The Pilgrim's Progress*, Part II (1684), his portrayal of the lonely road to salvation stands apart from the measured and capacious godliness, with its full sense of history and politics, that we find in Richard Baxter's works, and Baxter might stand here as the example of the educated, broad-minded Puritan.

Much has been written about plain style during the course of the seventeenth century and in the Restoration in particular, belonging in different versions to Puritans, Anglican rationalists and new scientists.[28] In his way, Bunyan is without doubt one fine example of this manifestation, although one quite contrary to the civility and sociability that marks the pages of the Anglican Latitudinarians, figured in *The Pilgrim's Progress* as the offensive Mr Worldly Wiseman.[29] But when he writes about setting down what 'he smartingly did feel' (*GA*, p. 85) he is opening the door to another quality that is not customarily addressed in standard literary histories. Puritan writing was open to trauma, to the recording of trauma, because conversion was either preceded by, or embodied, that experience.[30] However sharp-sighted the nonconformist minister is, when the trauma is situated so centrally inside the writing it necessarily acquires an entirely different and notable quality. It is so complete that we can say Bunyan buried his trauma entirely inside his calling as a minister. Into predestination theology was sewn the sense of always feeling guilt, and in the splendid envisionings of crossing into heaven came release. It is Bunyan's particular narrative gift to make us feel that trouble, and as Bunyan might have put it, the softening of the heart that comes with it, in lived reality and mental reflection on it that is immediately recognisable and so very believable. It is worth quoting at length from the original edition of *The Pilgrim's Progress*:

But thinking again of what he heard from the men, he felt in his bosom for his Roll, that he might read therein and be comforted; but he felt and [Note 'k' in margin: Christian *missed his Roll, wherein he used to take comfort.*] found it not. Then was *Christian* in great distress, and knew not what to do, for he wanted that which used to relieve him, and that which should have been his Pass into the Celestial City. Here therefore he began to be much perplexed, and knew not what to do; at last he bethought himself that he had slept in the Arbour that is on the side of the Hill: and falling down upon his knees, he asked God forgiveness for that his foolish Fact; and then went back to look for his Roll. But all the way he went back, who can sufficiently set forth the sorrow of *Christians* heart? somtimes he sighed, somtimes he wept, and often times he chid himself, for being so foolish to fall asleep in that place which was erected only for a little refreshment from his weariness. Thus therefore he went back; carefully looking on this side, and on that, all the way as he went, if happily he might find his Roll, that had been his comfort so many times in his Journey. He went thus till he came again within sight of the *Arbour*, where he sat and slept; but that sight renewed [Note 'l' in margin: Christian *bewailes his foolish sleeping.* Rev. 2. 2.] his sorrow the more, by bringing again, even a fresh, his evil of sleeping unto his mind. Thus therefore he now went on bewailing his sinful sleep, saying, *O wretched Man that I am*, that I should sleep in the daytime! that I should sleep in the midst of difficulty! that I should so indulge the flesh, as to use that rest for ease to my flesh, which the Lord of the Hill hath erected only for the relief of the spirits of Pilgrims! How many steps have I took in vain! (Thus it happened to *Israel* for their sin, they were sent back again by the way of the Red-Sea) and I am made to tread those steps with sorrow, which I might have trod with delight, had it not been for this sinful sleep. How far might I have been on my way by this time! I am made to tread those steps thrice over, which I needed not to have trod but once: Yea now also I am like to be benighted, for the day is almost spent. O that I had not slept! Now by this time he was come to the

Arbour again, where for a while he sat down and wept, but at last (as *Christian* would have it) looking sorrowfully down under the Settle, there he espied his Roll; the which he with trembling and haste catch't up, and put it into his bosom; but who can tell how joyful this Man was, when he had gotten his Roll again![31]

It was these qualities that impressed the early readers and convinced publishers to keep the book in print. It was also these qualities that alarmed the authors and literary critics of the early eighteenth century, Alexander Pope, John Dennis and Joseph Addison among them, who saw literary virtue as a more elevated matter.[32] In their eyes, the great work of English literary imagination was Milton's *Paradise Lost*, the one work by a Puritan that was regarded as incontestably great in this period. Bunyan's reputation relied upon his appeal to the evangelical revival in the mid eighteenth century; extensive confirmation of his literary genius would have to wait for the Romantics.[33] Bunyan was indubitably of the Puritan milieu, and the Restoration one at that; and yet his writings, *The Pilgrim's Progress* in particular, have been globalised and have played a significant role in globalising enterprise.[34] Bunyan's distinctness among his contemporaries was and is very evident. Not merely is his pastoral approach singular, but he displays none of 'Howe's own inelegancy, Bate's fluency, Penn's poised and often aphoristically pointed lucidity, Baxter's unpretentious and direct urgency, Owen's ponderous comprehensiveness, Fox's visionary fervour and admonitory trenchancy'.[35] He may indeed have offered 'shifting registers ... colloquial, biblical, theological, personal, narrative',[36] but all of it was indubitably 'grounded', as he would have put it, and it 'smarted' even to the gates of heaven.

NOTES

1. See Leslie Hotson, *The Commonwealth and Restoration Stage* (Cambridge, Mass.: Harvard University Press, 1928; New York: Russell and Russell, 1962).
2. See for instance, John Dryden, *The Works of John Dryden*, ed. Edward Niles Hooker and H.T. Swedenberg, Jr., 20 vols. (Berkeley: University of California Press, 1956–96); Alan Roper, *Dryden's Poetic Kingdoms* (London: Routledge and Kegan Paul, 1965); Earl Miner, *Dryden's Poetry* (Bloomington: Indiana University Press, 1967).
3. See for instance, John Dryden, *Poems*, ed. Paul Hammond, 5 vols. (London and New York: Longman, 1994–2000); Paul Hammond, *The Making of Restoration Poetry* (Cambridge: D. S. Brewer, 2006); *The Prose Works of Andrew Marvell*, ed. Annabel Patterson *et al.*, 2 vols. (New Haven and London: Yale University Press, 2003); James Turner, *Schooling Sex: Libertine Literature and Erotic Education in Italy, France, and England 1534–1685* (Oxford University Press, 2003); Derek Hughes, *English Drama, 1660–1700* (Oxford: Clarendon Press, 1996).

The biennial interdisciplinary Restoration conference at the University of North Wales, Bangor, since 2005, has been a major focus of revival. Literary scholars have benefited from the significant work of historians, including Justin Champion, Mark Goldie, Tim Harris, John Marshall, Steven Pincus and John Spurr.

4. See James A. Winn, *John Dryden and his World* (New Haven: Yale University Press, 1987).

5. See Robert D. Hume, *The Development of English Drama in the Late Seventeenth Century* (Oxford: Clarendon Press, 1976); Nancy Klein Maguire, *Regicide and Restoration: English Tragicomedy, 1660–1671* (Cambridge University Press, 1992).

6. See Derek Hughes, *English Drama, 1660–1700* (Oxford: Clarendon Press, 1996); Cynthia Wall, *The Literary and Cultural Spaces of Restoration London* (Cambridge University Press, 1998).

7. See James Turner, *Libertines and Radicals in Early Modern London: Sexuality, Politics, and Literary Culture, 1630–1685* (Cambridge University Press, 2002); Warren Chernaik, *Sexual Freedom in Restoration Literature* (Cambridge University Press, 1995).

8. See Andrew Marvell, *Poems*, ed. Nigel Smith (2003; Harlow: Longman, 2007); Andrew Marvell, *Prose Works*, ed. Annabel Patterson *et al.*

9. For examples and more authors, see Paul Hammond (ed.), *Restoration Literature: An Anthology* (Oxford University Press, 2002); for discussion, see Margaret Doody, *The Daring Muse: Augustan Poetry Reconsidered* (Cambridge University Press, 1985).

10. Of many accounts, see for instance Michael Hunter, *Science and Society in Restoration England* (Cambridge University Press, 1981) and his *Science and the Shape of Orthodoxy: Intellectual Change in Late Seventeenth-Century Britain* (Woodbridge: Boydell, 1995).

11. See Cynthia Wall's note on Boyle in John Bunyan, *The Pilgrim's Progress*, ed. Cynthia Wall, Norton Critical Editions (New York and London: Norton, 2009), p. 310.

12. See Reid Barbour, *English Epicures and Stoics: Ancient Legacies in Early Stuart Culture* (Amherst: University of Massachusetts Press, 1998); Catherine Wilson, *Epicureanism at the Origins of Modernity* (Oxford University Press, 2008).

13. See Mark Greengrass, Michael Leslie and Timothy Raylor (eds.), *Samuel Hartlib and Universal Reformation: Studies in Intellectual Communication* (Cambridge University Press, 1994).

14. See Stephen K. Roberts, 'Wallis, Ralph' and Nicholas von Maltzahn, 'Neville, Henry', *Oxford DNB*.

15. See Martin Dzelzainis, 'George Larkin and the London Literary Underground, 1666–1690', delivered at 'Radicalism and the Book' Conference, Center for the Study of Books and Media, Princeton University, March 2006: www.princeton.edu/cbs/conferences/march_2006/papers/dzelzainis.pdf. For another, ex-Leveller conspirator, John Wildman, and his association with the Duke of Buckingham and William III, see Richard L. Greaves, 'Wildman, John', *Oxford DNB*.

16. For more details, see N. H. Keeble, *The Literary Culture of Nonconformity in Later Seventeenth-Century England* (Leicester University Press, 1987).

17. See Thomas Luxon, *Literal Figures: Puritan Allegory and the Reformation Crisis in Representation* (University of Chicago Press, 1995).

18. See chapter 4 below.

19. See Edward Burrough, *The True Faith of the Gospel of Peace Contended For* (1656) and his answer to Bunyan's *A Vindication ... of Some Gospel-Truths* (1657), *Truth (the Strongest of All) Witnessed Forth* (1657); George Fox, *The Great Mistery of the Great Whore Unfolded* (1659).

20. Ann Hughes, 'The Pulpit Guarded: Confrontations between Orthodox and Radicals in Revolutionary England', in Anne Laurence, W. R. Owens and Stuart Sim (eds.), *John Bunyan and His England, 1628–1688* (London and Ronceverte, W.Va.: Hambledon Press, 1990), pp. 31–50; Kate Peters, *Print Culture and the Early Quakerism* (Cambridge University Press, 2005).

21. Paul Davis, 'John Bunyan and Heavenly Conversation', *Essays in Criticism*, 50 (2000), 215–41 (p. 222).

22. Ian Green, *The Christian's ABC: Catechism and Catechizing in England, c. 1530–1740* (Oxford: Clarendon Press, 1996). For *A Book for Boys and Girls*, see below, chapter 9.

23. Jacqueline Phillips, 'Transformation by Allegory in John Bunyan's Writing', unpublished D.Phil. thesis, University of Oxford, 1998.

24. Benjamin Keach, *The Travels of True Godliness* (1684), 17–18.

25. See further, Margaret Spufford, *Small Books and Pleasant Histories: Popular Fiction and its Readership in Seventeenth-Century England* (Athens: University of Georgia Press, 1982).

26. James Turner, 'Bunyan's Sense of Place', in Vincent Newey (ed.), *'The Pilgrim's Progress': Critical and Historical Views* (Liverpool University Press, 1980), pp. 91–110.

27. Peter Lake, 'Reading Clarke's *Lives* in Political and Polemical Context', in Kevin Sharpe and Steven N. Zwicker (eds.), *Writing Lives: Biography and Textuality, Identity and Representation in Early Modern England* (Oxford University Press, 2008), pp. 293–318.

28. Roger Pooley, 'Language and Loyalty: Plain Style at the Restoration', *Literature and History*, 6.1 (Spring 1980), 2–18.

29. As discussed in Isabel Rivers, 'Grace, Holiness, and the Pursuit of Happiness: Bunyan and Restoration Latitudinarianism', in Keeble (ed.), *Conventicle*, pp. 63–7.

30. See Vera J. Camden (ed.), *Trauma and Transformation: The Political Progress of John Bunyan* (Stanford University Press, 2008).

31. John Bunyan, *The Pilgrim's Progress* (1678), 45–7.

32. For eighteenth- and nineteenth-century views on *The Pilgrim's Progress*, see Roger Sharrock (ed.), *'The Pilgrim's Progress': A Casebook* (London and Basingstoke: Macmillan, 1976).

33. See N. H. Keeble, ' "Of him thousands daily Sing and talk": Bunyan and his Reputation', in Keeble (ed.), *Conventicle*, pp. 246–53.

34. Isabel Hofmeyr, *The Portable Bunyan: A Transnational History of 'The Pilgrim's Progress'* (Princeton University Press, 2004).

35. Keeble, *Literary Culture*, p. 246.

36. *Ibid.*

3

W. R. OWENS

John Bunyan and the Bible

In the opening scene of *The Pilgrim's Progress* we are presented with the spectacle of a burdened man, wearing ragged clothing, and reading a book: 'I dreamed, and behold *I saw a Man cloathed with Raggs, standing in a certain place, with his face from his own House, a Book in his hand, and a great burden upon his Back.* I looked, and saw him open the Book, and Read therein; and as he read, he wept and trembled' (*P'sP*, p. 8). His family and friends cannot understand what is troubling the poor man, and he for his part withdraws from them, still anxiously reading his book. Then one day, we are told, 'when he was walking in the Fields ... reading in his Book, and greatly distressed in his mind ... he burst out ... crying, *What shall I do to be saved?*' (*P'sP*, p. 9). The book that prompts this outburst is the Bible, to which a series of references is given in the margin, and indeed the very words are those of the trembling jailer to the Apostle Paul as recounted in Acts 16:30. This memorable scene establishes at the outset that Bible-reading will be a central theme in Bunyan's allegory, and, as we shall see, the pilgrim's developing ability to read and understand the Bible parallels in many ways the account Bunyan gives of his own experience in his spiritual autobiography, *Grace Abounding to the Chief of Sinners* (1666).

For Bunyan, the Bible was the only book that really mattered. 'Thou must give more credit to one syllable of the written Word of the Gospel', he says on one occasion, 'than thou must give to all the Saints and Angels in Heaven and Earth' (*MW*, II:191). 'All Scripture is given by inspiration of God', he says elsewhere (citing II Timothy 3:16), and is 'able to give a man perfect instruction into any of the things of God necessary to faith and godliness' (*MW*, 1:324). He would sometimes claim that the Bible and a concordance were the only books he used in his writing (*MW*, VII:9). Such reverence for the Bible was far from unique in England in the seventeenth century. At that time the Bible was not only regarded as the central authority in religious matters, it was also considered absolutely central to artistic, scientific, political and economic thought (as we would now term them).[1] Bible reading dominated

English culture in the early-modern period to an extent that is difficult for us now to comprehend. It was linked to the acquisition of literacy itself: the main point of learning to read was to be able to read the Bible, and it was the first book a child read once the ABC and primer had been mastered. Bunyan himself, in a book of poems for children that he published in 1686, included an alphabet, and an explanation of how words are divided into syllables, as 'An help to Children to learn to read English', explaining that the purpose was to prepare them for reading 'Psalter, or Bible' (*B&G*, pp. 194, 196). Once basic literacy had been attained, it was expected that the Bible would be read daily, and that portions of it would be committed to memory. Much of this reading would take place communally, in the home as well as in the church. In his book, *Print and Protestantism in Early Modern England*, Ian Green shows how completely Bible reading penetrated everyday life:

> The act of reading [the Bible] varied according to time and place – study, bedchamber, field – and milieu – school, church, study group – and normal habit, which sometimes included methods such as reading aloud in pairs or groups ... Heads of households might read the Bible ... out loud to servants who were illiterate; children in elementary schools were urged to read the Bible to their parents, especially if the latter themselves could not read; neighbours might read to each other, in an alehouse or at home; and in church the text of the Bible, and the official liturgy, catechism and psalms were regularly declaimed from a printed copy.[2]

This unprecedented access to and knowledge of the printed Word of God was a relatively recent phenomenon. William Tyndale's translation of the New Testament into English had been published in 1526, just over a hundred years before Bunyan was born, and the first complete Bible in English, edited by Miles Coverdale, had appeared in 1535. Another complete Bible, the so-called Matthew Bible, edited by John Rogers, a friend of Tyndale, was published in 1537. In 1539 Coverdale published a revision of the Matthew Bible, known as the Great Bible because of its size and lavish adornment, and a copy of this was ordered by Henry VIII to be placed in every parish church. Then, in 1560, early in the reign of Elizabeth I, a new translation was produced by a group of English Protestant scholars working in Geneva, published in a handy octavo format, in roman type, and with the verses numbered. Although the Geneva Bible, as it was known, became enormously popular, the marginal annotations it included were greatly disliked by Church of England bishops and it was never given any form of official approval. In 1568 a revision of the Great Bible prepared by a panel of bishops was published, but the Bishops' Bible, as it was known, failed to supplant the Geneva Bible, over eighty editions of which were published between 1568 and

1611. James I shared the bishops' dislike of the Geneva Bible, regarding its annotations as 'very partial, untrue, seditious, and savouring too much of dangerous, and traitorous conceits'.[3] Upon coming to the throne in 1603 he authorised the establishment of a body of some fifty Biblical scholars whose task was to prepare a new translation to replace both the Geneva and the Bishops' Bible. This new Bible was ordered by James to be '*set out and printed, without any marginal notes, and only to be used in all churches of England in time of divine service*'.[4] The resulting Bible, first published in 1611, has become known as the 'Authorised Version' or the 'King James Bible'. Green estimates that about 140 separate editions of the Authorised Version were produced between 1611 and 1640, with editions of the Geneva Bible also continuing to appear until 1644. By the middle of the seventeenth century, however, the Authorised Version had ousted all its rivals, and had established itself as the most popular version in English, a position it would hold for about three centuries.

Although Bunyan generally quotes the Authorised Version, it is clear that he knew the Geneva Bible well, and he also refers to the work of Tyndale.[5] The circulation of such enormous numbers of bibles led to concerns about whether it was safe for such an important book to be in the hands of ordinary readers. The Bible was a complicated book, whose meaning was open to widely differing interpretation, and early-modern translators and publishers went to some lengths to direct people how to read it effectively and with proper understanding. The Geneva Bible owed its popularity not only to its smaller format, and therefore cheaper price, but also to its provision of an elaborate apparatus of aids for readers. These included summaries of books and chapters, subject headers at the top of its pages, maps, genealogies, historical tables and translations of Hebrew names. There was also a flow diagram setting out general advice on 'How to take Profite in Reading of the Holy Scriptures'. Most important of all was the provision of extensive marginal notes, explicating the text, and encouraging readers to apply the Biblical stories to their own situations. It would be difficult to overstate the importance of the Geneva Bible in giving generations of English readers the equipment and the confidence with which to read the Bible.

Perhaps in response to the lack of assistance in the Authorised Version, other publications began to appear, offering help of this kind to readers. Indeed, it is an indication of the continuing demand for such assistance that several editions of the Authorised Version were produced with the Geneva apparatus of marginal notes inserted. Among the numerous works designed to assist readers were doctrinal commentaries, paraphrases and abridgements, but of particular interest are the manuals or guidebooks which gave advice on how the Bible should be read. One of the two books Bunyan's first wife brought with her as her dowry was Lewis Bayly's immensely popular devotional work, *The Practise of Pietie*, first published in about 1612. A chapter in this was entitled 'Brief directions how to read the Holy Scriptures, once every yeare over, with ease, profit, and reverence'. In order to accomplish this Bayly recommends reading three chapters a day, in the morning, at midday and at night. Each reading should be followed by a period of reflection: 'meditate a while with thy selfe, how many *excellent things* thou canst remember'. Then, 'apply these thinges to thine owne heart, and read not these Chapters, as matters of *Historicall* discourse; but as if they were so many *Letters* or *Epistles* sent downe from God out of *Heaven* unto thee'.[6]

This stress on what we might call active reading strategies was taken up by other authors. Edmund Calamy, for example, especially recommended the practice of writing out lists of the 'promises' of salvation in the Bible. In *The Godly Mans Ark*, first published in 1657, he notes that many excellent books of promises have been published, which may be of help to readers. And yet, says Calamy, 'let mee advise you not to rest satisfied with the Collections of others; but when you read the Bible, and meet with a suitable promise ... take the pains to write it down, and one such promise of your own writing, will work more powerfully upon your souls, than many others of anothers gathering'.[7] In a later work, *The Art of Divine Meditation* (1680), Calamy emphasises that the Bible should be read 'in a different way than you read any other Book whatsoever'. In particular, he says, the Bible should be used as an aid to religious meditation:

> [W]ould you meditate of Christ? go and take the *Bible*, and *read* the History of his Passion; and when thou readest any thing remarkable, *lay thy book aside*, and meditate seriously of that passage. As for example, when thou comest to *read of Christ sweating drops of blood*; that Christ in a cold Winter night upon the cold ground for thy sake should shed drops of blood: *lay thy book aside, and meditate of these drops of blood.*[8]

The emphasis Calamy places here on imaginative engagement with the Biblical text as part of the reading experience brings us back to Bunyan, whose spiritual autobiography, *Grace Abounding*, gives a vivid account of his own development as a reader of the Bible. As a young man, he tells us, he took 'great pleasure' in reading 'the historical part' of the Bible, though disliking the epistles of St Paul and other doctrinal scriptures of that kind. His reading at this time, we might say, was reading for mere enjoyment – in Bunyan's eyes a mark of his unregenerate state. Later, however, a turning point came when he met 'three or four poor women sitting at a door in the Sun, and talking about the things of God'. Bunyan was 'greatly affected' by what they said: 'they spake with such pleasantness of Scripture language, and with such appearance of grace in all they said, that they were to me as if they had found a new world' (*GA*, pp. 14–15). Inspired by their example, he 'began to look into the Bible with new eyes, and read as I never did before; and especially the Epistles of the Apostle *S. Paul* were sweet and pleasant to me: and indeed, I was then never out of the Bible, either by reading or meditation, still crying out to *God*, that I might know the truth, and way to Heaven and Glory' (*GA*, p. 17).

Bunyan's reading, as this passage suggests, was becoming more frequent, repeated and purposeful. We notice, too, the reference to reading 'with new eyes', and to reading 'as I never did before': Bunyan is learning to read in new ways, but at this stage he has not yet discovered how to read with what he would regard as true spiritual understanding, and in the remainder of *Grace Abounding* he describes how he became a more competent reader. His conversion experience is marked by obsessive, neurotic wrestling with texts of scripture, as he finds one that seems to promise hope of salvation only to be plunged into despair by another one that threatens him with damnation. He uses powerfully graphic physical terms to convey the impact with which Biblical verses would take hold of his mind: 'these words were to my Soul like Fetters of Brass to my Legs'; 'suddenly this sentence bolted in upon me'; 'that piece of a sentence darted in upon me'; 'these words did with great power suddainly break in upon me' (*GA*, pp. 44, 64–5). He describes violent mood swings, and how sometimes he had 'sudden thoughts to question all I read' (*GA*, p. 34). He could not bring himself to believe that the promises of salvation in the Bible could apply to him: 'as for me, I had cut my self off by my transgressions, and left myself neither foot-hold, nor hand-hold amongst all the stayes and props in the precious Word of Life' (*GA*, p. 62). On other occasions he would catch himself nursing absurd resentments or reproaches against the Bible. After all, he would complain, there were only three or four texts against him: 'cannot God miss them, and save me for all of them?' (*GA*, p. 66). In an extraordinary passage he tells how one day, after weeks of feeling 'oppressed and cast down . . . as I was now quite giving up the Ghost of all my hopes of ever attaining life, that sentence fell with weight upon my spirit, *Look at the generations of old, and see, did ever any trust in God and were confounded?*' (*GA*, p. 21). The problem was that he could not recollect where in the Bible he had seen this verse, and so for over a year he read his way through the entire Bible, searching for it, before, finally, finding it in Ecclesiasticus, one of the books of the Apocrypha.[9]

Elsewhere in *Grace Abounding* we find Bunyan visualising the Biblical text and imagining himself into the situations he is reading about in very much the ways recommended by Calamy. Of the account of Christ in the Gospels, he writes, me thought I was as if I had seen him born, as if I had seen him grow up, as if I had seen him walk thorow this world, from the Cradle to his Cross; to which, also, when he came, I saw how gently he gave himself to be hanged and nailed on it for my sins and wicked doings ... When I have considered also the truth of his resurrection, and have remembred that word, *Touch me not Mary*, &c., I have seen, as if he leaped at the Graves mouth for joy that he was risen again.   (*GA*, p. 38)

Eventually Bunyan overcame his neurosis, gradually learning how to interpret and understand the Bible so that he was no longer at the mercy of apparently conflicting texts. Now, he says, he was enabled 'with careful heart and watchful eye, with great seriousness to turn over every leaf, and with much diligence mixed with trembling, to consider every sentence, together with its natural force and latitude' (*GA*, p. 77). Those last few words, and especially 'latitude', are the crucial ones here. Bunyan had described elsewhere how at one time he had felt as if the apostles Peter, Paul and John 'did look with scorn upon me, and hold me in derision; and as if they said unto me, All our words are truth, one of as much force as another; it is not we that have cut you off, but you have cast away yourself' (*GA*, p. 66). The hermeneutic principle he has now discovered is that none of the various books or texts of scripture is in itself decisive. The Bible needs to be read as a whole, and it is its own best interpreter.[10] Once Bunyan had persuaded himself of the truth of this principle, he was able to see that apparent contradictions could be resolved, with one text being interpreted in the light of other texts. When, in prison, he was challenged by the Clerk of the Peace to say who was to judge between competing interpretations of scripture, Bunyan answered that the scripture itself would be the judge, 'and that by comparing one Scripture with another; for that will open itself, if it be rightly compared' (*GA*, p. 123).

Behind the idea that the Bible, for all its diversity, was a unity was the long-standing belief that the Old Testament pointed forward to the New Testament. It needs to be remembered that the Christian Bible incorporated within it the Hebrew Bible. To what Christians called the 'Old Testament' was added by them a 'New Testament', a collection of twenty-seven Christian writings, including the Gospels, gathered together in their final form in the fourth century CE. The word 'testament' means 'covenant', and in speaking of 'Old' and 'New' testaments Christians were implying that the special covenant (or compact) that God had with Israel, by which he would protect them as his special people, and which was confirmed by the giving of the Torah (law) to Moses on Mount Sinai (Exodus 19–20), had been superseded by a new covenant between God (in the person of Christ) with the Christian church. So, for example, the author of the letter to the Hebrews speaks of Christ as 'the mediator of the new covenant' (12:24).

According to the earliest Christian writers, persons, events and things in the Old Testament were to be understood as not only historical, but also as symbolic 'types' or prefigurations of persons, events and things in the New Testament. So, for example, in the Gospel of John the brass serpent which cured the Israelites of snake-bites in the wilderness is described as a foreshadowing of the crucifixion of Christ: 'as Moses lifted up the serpent in the wilderness, even so must the Son of man be lifted up [i.e. on the cross]' (John 3:14–15). Similarly, St Paul interpreted the passing of the Israelites through the Red Sea at the time of the exodus from Egypt to the Promised Land as a type of the baptism of Christ in the Jordan, and of Christian baptism in general (1 Corinthians 10:1–4). Again, in his letter to the Romans, Paul refers to Adam as 'the figure [type] of him [Christ] that was to come' (5:14), meaning by this that the obedience of the 'Second Adam' would undo the mortal harm done by the disobedience of the 'First Adam'.

This typological method of interpreting the Bible was subsequently incorporated within a more elaborate exegetical system by which scripture was interpreted as having four senses: the literal, the allegorical (including typology), the tropological (or moral, especially in application to the individual Christian life) and the anagogical (pointing towards the ultimate goal of the Christian life). Although in the Protestant Reformation of the sixteenth century the 'fourfold' method of interpretation was rejected as departing too far from the literal sense, typology itself was not rejected, and indeed it was developed and extended throughout the seventeenth century.[11] It offered not only a way of understanding the sacred text, and how the Old and New Testaments related to each other, but a way of applying the Biblical stories to the lives and experiences of individual readers. In reading the Bible typologically, the Puritan Thomas Taylor said, a believer will be 'able to parallel his Estate in some of the Saints, he shall see his own case in some of them, and so shall obtain instruction, direction, and consolation by them'.[12] In the revolutionary upheavals of the mid seventeenth century, there were many who saw in the Bible prophetic types of events which were currently being fulfilled in England. As Arise Evans put it, 'afore I looked upon the Scripture as a History of things that passed in other Countreys ... but now I looked upon it as a mysterie to be opened at this time belonging also to us'.[13] In a sermon preached before Parliament in 1644, Herbert Palmer told Members that the Bible contained '*not onely* Stories *of things done in that Age, but* Prophesies *also of future events in succeeding Generations*'.[14] This typological approach to the Bible was widespread, and by no means restricted to Puritans. Thomas Carles, preaching in 1661, gave thanks to God for having restored Charles II to the throne as 'a *Moses* to conduct us ... a second *Joshua* too, to give possession of our *Canaan* to the redeemed ones'.[15]

In *Grace Abounding* Bunyan describes how he learned to interpret the Bible typologically, taking as his example a chapter in Deuteronomy setting out Jewish dietary laws by which some animals are to be regarded as 'clean', and may be eaten, and others as 'unclean' and not to be eaten.

> I was also made about this time to see something concerning the Beasts that *Moses* counted clean, and unclean. I thought those Beasts were types of men; the *clean* types of them that were the People of God; but the *unclean* types of such as were the children of the wicked One. Now I read, that the clean beasts chewed the Cud; that is, thought I, they shew us we must feed upon the Word of God: They also parted the hoof, I thought that signified, we must part, if we would be saved, with the ways of ungodly men. (*GA*, p. 23)

It was his developing skill in this method of interpretation that enabled him to overcome his terror of a terrible passage from Hebrews 12:17, about how Esau, having sold his birthright and been denied a blessing, could find 'no place of repentance, though he sought it carefully with tears'. For months these words had haunted Bunyan, until after a mighty struggle they were overcome by another text, 'My grace is sufficient for thee' (II Corinthians 12:9). Bunyan came to see that, regarded in 'a New-Testament stile and sence', 'the *Birth-right* signified *Regeneration*, and the *Blessing* the *Eternal Inheritance*', and that the story was meant as a warning to believers not to cast off God's blessings, 'lest they become as *Esau*' (*GA*, p. 71). He had become a more confident reader and interpreter of the Bible, able to find 'concurrance and agreement in the Scriptures' (*GA*, p. 61), and, as he put it in a later work, to 'reconcile the seeming contradictions that are in ... Texts' (*MW*, XIII:224).

What these accounts of his struggles with scripture reveal is the extent to which for Bunyan, and readers like him, Bible reading was heavily exegetical and homiletic. Every word or passage was understood to hold a deeper spiritual meaning to be discovered or puzzled out by careful thought and analysis, and given a personal or contemporary application. The Old Testament descriptions of the ceremonies of the law were worthy of particular study, Bunyan thought, 'for though they be out of use now, as to *practice*, yet the signification of them is rich, and that from which many Gospellers have got much' (*MW*, XIII:331). In an extended treatment of the first ten chapters of Genesis, he interprets Noah's Ark as a type both of Christ, 'in whom the Church is preserved from the Wrath of God', and of 'the Works of Faith of the Godly ... by which the Followers of Christ are preserved from the rage and tyranny of the World' (*MW*, XII:201). Examples of this kind of typological interpretation may be found in nearly everything Bunyan wrote, and indeed they became particularly prevalent in works written or published towards the end of his life.[16]

asked why it was said, *That the Savior is said to come out of a dry ground, and also that he had no Form nor Comliness in him?*

Greath. Then said Mr *Great-heart*, To the first I answer, Because, the Church of the Jews, of which Christ came, had then lost almost all the Sap and Spirit of Religion. To the Second I say, The Words are spoken in the Person of the Unbelievers, who because they want *that* Eye that can see into our Princes Heart, therefore they judg of him by the meanness of his Outside.   (*P'sP*, pp. 265–6)

Towards the end of the Second Part there is a whole series of allegorical representations of the Bible. It is presented as a looking glass – a very special looking glass, because as well as showing a man what he looks like himself, it also, if turned another way, shows 'the very Face and Similitude of the Prince of Pilgrims himself' (*P'sP*, p. 287). Later on it is a map, which shows all the ways leading to the Celestial City, and which it is essential for a pilgrim to have in his pocket at all times (*P'sP*, 297). Finally, it is a lantern, by the help of which the pilgrims could see to continue their journey for the rest of the way, 'tho the Darkness was very great' (*P'sP*, p. 299).

Intensive reading of the Bible of the kind represented by Bunyan can perhaps hardly be described as mere reading, but represents instead a quite extraordinary immersion and absorption in a text regarded as the very Word of God. For a reader as sensitive and as intensely engaged as Bunyan, the outcome was to have his mind saturated with scriptural texts. It is clear from all his writings – and not least from *The Pilgrim's Progress* – that he had absorbed the language of the Bible so thoroughly that his own prose was infused in the most natural way with Biblical references, phrases and idioms. In Christian's encounter with the fiend Apollyon, to take one brief example, the materials of folk tale and popular romance are clothed in Biblical language: 'Now the Monster was hidious to behold, he was cloathed with scales like a Fish (and they are his pride) he had Wings like a Dragon, feet like a Bear, and out of his belly came Fire and Smoak, and his mouth was as the mouth of a Lion' (*P'sP*, p. 56). No actual Biblical texts are cited here, but the whole passage is a tissue of intertextual allusion. The name Apollyon is taken from Revelation 9:11, where it is given to 'the angel of the bottomless pit'. In describing his appearance, Bunyan adapts details from Job 41:15, 20–1 (Leviathan's 'scales are his pride … out of his nostrils goeth smoke … his breath kindleth coals, and a flame goeth out of his mouth') and from Revelation 13:2 ('the beast … was like unto a leopard, and his feet were as the feet of a bear, and his mouth as the mouth of a lion').

Finally, of course – and nothing could be more triumphantly apt – Christian defeats Apollyon not by his own strength but by wielding verses from the Old and New Testaments. The words of Micah 7:8, '*Rejoyce not against me, O mine Enemy! when I fall, I shall arise*', and of Romans 8:37,

'*Nay, in all these things we are more than Conquerours, through him that loved us*' are '*the two-edg'd Sword*' (see Hebrews 4:12) that give Apollyon his deadly wound and cause him to speed away, so that '*Christian* saw him no more' (*P'sP*, p. 60).

NOTES

1. See Christopher Hill, *The English Bible and the Seventeenth-Century Revolution* (1993; London: Penguin, 1994), pp. 20–31 and throughout.
2. Ian Green, *Print and Protestantism in Early Modern England* (Oxford University Press, 2000), p. 25.
3. Cited in David Daniell, *The Bible in English* (New Haven and London: Yale University Press, 2003), p. 434.
4. Cited in Alister McGrath, *In the Beginning: The Story of the King James Bible* (London: Hodder & Stoughton, 2001), pp. 163–4.
5. See *MW*, VII:150, where Bunyan remarks that 'in some of your old Bibles, that which in one place is called a *Target*, in another is called, a *Shield*'. In 2 Chronicles 14:8, the Geneva Bible has 'shields' where the Authorised Version has 'targets'. For the reference to Tyndale, see *MW*, XII:27, 426n.
6. Lewis Bayly, *The Practice of Piety*, 1612? (1624), pp. 244–51.
7. Edmund Calamy, *The Godly Mans Ark*, 1657; 2nd edn (1658), pp. 113–14.
8. Edmund Calamy, *The Art of Divine Meditation* (1680), pp. 140, 118–19.
9. The Apocrypha was included in the Geneva Bible and in the Authorised Version in the seventeenth century, and indeed right up until the 1820s, when the British and Foreign Bible Society decided to exclude it from all the editions it distributed, and it came to be omitted more generally.
10. See Patrick Collinson, 'The Coherence of the Text: How it Hangeth Together: The Bible in Reformation England', in W. P. Stephens (ed.), *The Bible, the Reformation and the Church* (Sheffield Academic Press, 1995), pp. 84–108 (esp. pp. 100–3).
11. See Barbara Kiefer Lewalski, *Protestant Poetics and the Seventeenth-Century Religious Lyric* (Princeton University Press, 1979), pp. 111–44.
12. Thomas Taylor, *David's Learning, or The Way to True Happinesse* (1659), p. 93.
13. Arise Evans, *An Eccho to the Voice from Heaven* (1652), p. 17.
14. Herbert Palmer, *The Glasse of Gods Providence Towards His Faithfull Ones* (1644), sig. A2r, 'The Epistle Dedicatorie'.
15. Thomas Carles, *A Sermon Preached at the Cathedral Church in Gloucester* (1661), p. 12.
16. For discussions of Bunyan's use of typology, see Introductions by Richard L. Greaves, Graham Midgley and W. R. Owens respectively to *MW*, VII:xv–xliii, VIII:xliii–l and XII:xxxviii–xlvi.

4

VERA J. CAMDEN

John Bunyan and the goodwives of Bedford: a psychoanalytic approach

> For where two or three are gathered together in my name, there am I in the midst of them.
>
> (Matthew 18:20)

In his youth, John Bunyan knew what it was to feel keenly the reproach of a woman. In *Grace Abounding to the Chief of Sinners* (1666), he describes how he was once shamed by an encounter with a local shopkeeper's wife:

> But one day, as I was standing at a Neighbours Shop-window, and there cursing and swearing, and playing the Mad-man, after my wonted manner, there sate within the woman of the house, and heard me; who, though she was a very loose and ungodly Wretch, yet protested that I swore and cursed at that most fearful rate, that she was made to tremble to hear me; And told me further, *That I was the ungodliest Fellow for swearing that she ever heard in all her life . . .*
>
> At this reproof I was silenced, and put to secret shame; and that too, as I thought, before the God of Heaven: wherefore, while I stood there, and hanging down my head, I wished with all my heart that I might be a little childe again, that my Father might learn me to speak without this wicked way of swearing . . . (GA, p. 11–12).

The effect of this blunt admonition awakens feelings in Bunyan that will be stirred again in his famous encounter with a few goodwives in the town of Bedford:

> But upon a day, the good providence of God did cast me to *Bedford*, to work on my calling; and in one of the streets of that town, I came where there were three or four poor women sitting at a door in the Sun, and talking about the things of God; and being now willing to hear them discourse, I drew near to hear what they said . . . but now I may say, *I heard, but I understood not*; for they were far above out of my reach, for their talk was about a new birth, the work of God on their hearts, also how they were convinced of their miserable state by nature . . . moreover, they reasoned of the suggestions and temptations of Satan in particular . . . and how they were borne up under his assaults: they also discoursed of their own wretchedness of heart, of their unbelief, and did contemn, slight, and abhor their own righteousness, as filthy and insufficient to do them any good.

> And me thought they spake as if joy did make them speak: they spake with
> such pleasantness of Scripture language, and with such appearance of grace in
> all they said, that they were to me as if they had found a new world, as if they
> were people that dwelt alone, and were not to be reckoned among their
> Neighbours, Num. 23.9.   (GA, pp. 14–15)

This providential arrival at the Bedford doorway 'upon a day', when the sun
was shining, is one of the most evocative scenes in all of conversion literature in
English. It opened a self-proclaimed profligate to a discourse of joy and
tenderness: to a way of hearing and understanding the gospel he had never
experienced before. His meeting with the 'poor women of Bedford' represents a
turning point in his conversion narrative. In the presence of these women, he
hears talk of a new birth that awakens in him an awareness of his own distance
from grace and his longing to be part of the world inhabited by these women
with their message of love and redemption. Even though he feels that they are
'far above' him at first, and out of his reach, he comes to recognise the offering
of God's grace in the gentle talk of these Bedford wives.[1]

Bunyan's meeting with these women, his later interpretations of its meaning for his spiritual rebirth and his eventual adoption into the family of the
Bedford church, mobilise and yet also monumentalise the place of the feminine in his life and work. The women touched Bunyan spiritually by the
affective authority of their testimony. This formative moment laid the foundation for his ultimate and inexorable flourishing as man and minister in his
inner and outer world. Speaking together in a doorway, the women open
Bunyan to a domestic interior that inspires an accompanying exploration of
his own interiority. Further, they inhabit a geographical place as 'goodwives'
of Bedford, leading young Bunyan to their church, and to its minister John
Gifford, a man who will do much for what Bunyan calls his 'stability' (GA,
p. 37). Finally, their gathering rather contradictorily foreshadows Bunyan's
eventual mandates against women assembling for prayer. For in Bunyan's
church, as opposed to that of the Quakers, women could neither speak in the
public congregation nor congregate (although they could deliver their conversion narratives in public, show repentance for their sins and testify in
disciplinary cases). 'They are not builded to manage such Worship, *they are
not the Image and Glory of God*, as the Men are, 1 *Cor.* 11. 7. They are placed
beneath and are *called the Glory of the Man*' (MW, IV:306).

The trend in Bunyan studies over the last twenty years has demonstrated
how often Bunyan's women were imagined as the 'Other', excluded from full
humanity. Most recently we hear from Thomas Luxon that 'The equations
are painfully familiar . . . Woman=Flesh=World. All are always already types,
signifying what a "fair and comely man" is not. Such figures are never
permitted a being of their own apart from signifying something else.'[2]

Bunyan inherited the belief, partly derived from scripture, that women's 'place' in the natural and social order allows for no true mind or soul.[3] Critics and biographers of Bunyan, very much like Bunyan himself, have accordingly minimised the place of women in his life and work, largely because they have accepted the severe limitations he placed upon their position in church society, without looking further. In a recent historical reading of Bunyan's women, however, Margaret Ezell questions the view that Bunyan 'did not deal well with or avoided the company of women, even godly ones, and, by extension, also excluded or did not deal well with them as a writer'.[4] She suggests that we should look more closely at what really happened to Bunyan in the company of women and give less emphasis to his rulings. Accordingly, I shall explore what Bunyan's own record of his transformational and repeated encounters with the women of the town can reveal about his spiritual life and work. I conclude my discussion of Bunyan's relationship to these Bedford wives by recognising in *A Case of Conscience Resolved* (1683) traces of his sustained early attachment to their devout discourse.

Feeling and rebirth

Psychoanalyst Marion Milner has written that in order to experience the 'subtle tenderness' that allows the artistic imagination to absorb and to create, one must surely find 'some way of coming to terms with nature inside; or rather, with those parts of nature inside that one had repudiated as too unpleasant to be recognised as part of oneself'.[5] The manner in which the Bedford women spoke about their sinfulness clearly gave Bunyan a way to accommodate his own intolerable sense of condemnation for sin. The women claimed an experience of God that alleviated guilt by acknowledging it and then moving from condemnation to reconciliation, from reconciliation to a relationship with God, and finally from relationship to redemption. Listening to them, Bunyan finds his hardness of heart dissolving, and his mind opening, as his emotions are stirred. Only when his heart is softened does his mind 'bend' to a 'continual meditating' on their use of scripture. Bunyan's relationship to these women – his 'tarrying' with them in his heart – is what makes his assent to their doctrine of redemption possible:

> Thus therefore, when I had heard and considered what they said, I left them, and went about my employment again: but their talk and discourse went with me, also my heart would tarry with them, for I was greatly affected with their words ...
> Therefore I should often make it my business to be going again and again into the company of these poor people; for I could not stay away; and the more I

went amongst them, the more I did question my condition; and as still I do remember, presently I found two things within me, at which I did sometimes marvel, (especially considering what a blind, ignorant, sordid, and ungodly Wretch but just before I was) the one was, a very great softness and tenderness of heart, which caused me to fall under the conviction of what by Scripture they asserted; and the other was, a great bending in my mind to a continual meditating on them, and on all other good things which at any time I heard or read of. (GA, p. 15)

Michael Davies has argued that Bunyan's encounter with the Bedford women moves him one step away from the rigid mandates of church legalism to the embrace of grace. Davies notes the irony that the comforting language of these poor women arises from the strictures of Calvinist theology. 'What is remarkable about this episode is the profound sense of estrangement and disorientation that Bunyan, with great subtlety, manages to convey here.'[6] The 'unparalleled homeliness, tranquility, and happiness' of their words, Davies continues, 'are revealed suddenly as built not upon the easy moralism familiar to the ignorant young Bunyan but on a harsh and oxymoronic vocabulary of Calvinist self-abhorrence'.[7] How, in other words, can an admission of guilt that had earlier made Bunyan hang his head in the presence of the shopkeeper woman succeed now in inspiring joy? I would suggest that the profundity of the scene in the Bedford doorway is not fully captured by emphasising, with Davies, Bunyan's acceptance of a theology of grace that makes him 'teachable'. Instead, the power of the scene is affective. Bunyan is highly susceptible to these women because of the power that they exert over his psychology at this moment.

Like Johannes Vermeer, whose portrayals of domestic interiors also evoke the divine through rooms, doorways and other places that he almost exclusively shows occupied by women, Bunyan's doorway in Bedford is luminescent. Bunyan's women, like Vermeer's, are sunlit or 'Son'-lit with an illumination that brightens the divine and the domestic alike. Vermeer's depictions of windows and doors do not draw the viewer to the exterior world but illuminate instead the enclosed interior, suggesting a metaphor for the woman's inner life: her soul within. Lawrence Gowing, in his classic study of Vermeer's painting, proposes that the dominant theme of the artist's work is 'the attention man pays to woman'.[8] Lisa Vergara notes that the motif most intimately Vermeer's own is one that shows a woman in whom a sense of life's meaning, its 'affirmative core', is made manifest. She embodies a 'broad range of positive ideals from piety to fertility and judiciousness'.[9] Rodney Nevitt reverses the relationship by observing that 'Vermeer's women seem almost to be called into being by the light'. Even when Vermeer paints male figures he brings them into a 'quiet, domestic space' to illuminate their being.[10] It is just such a moment of illumination, I suggest, that is offered to Bunyan when he approaches the sunlit doorway of the Bedford women and hears them speak.

When Bunyan leaves the women's presence, the very thought of them leads him to a vision of his own rebirth:

> About this time, the state and happiness of these poor people at *Bedford* was thus, in a kind of Vision, presented to me: I saw as if they were set on the Sunny side of some high Mountain, there refreshing themselves with the pleasant beams of the Sun, while I was shivering and shrinking in the cold, afflicted with frost, snow, and dark clouds; methought also betwixt me and them I saw a wall that did compass about this Mountain; now, thorow this wall my Soul did greatly desire to pass, concluding that if I could, I would goe even into the very midst of them, and there also comfort myself with the heat of their Sun.
>
> About this wall I thought myself, to goe again and again, still prying as I went, to see if I could find some way or passage, by which I might enter therein, but none could I find for some time: at the last I saw as it were, a narrow gap, like a little door-way in the wall, thorow which I attempted to pass: but the passage being very straight, and narrow, I made many offers to get in, but all in vain, even untill I was well nigh quite beat out by striving to get in: at last, with great striving, me thought I at first did get in my head, and after that, by side-ling striving, my shoulders, and my whole body; then was I exceeding glad, and went and sat down in the midst of them, and so was comforted with the light and heat of their Sun. (*GA*, pp. 19–20)

Bunyan here accepts an allegorical but homely doctrine of rebirth. In the Gospel of John, Nicodemus had asked Jesus 'How can a man be born when he is old? Can he enter the second time into his mother's womb, and be born?' (John 3:4). For Bunyan, the question has ceased to be rhetorical and has a positive answer. At first, he searches fruitlessly for a passageway until he finally discovers a narrow gap, 'like a little door-way in the wall'. The simile immediately recalls his meeting with the Bedford women, which took place in a doorway, just as it prefigures the 'straight, and narrow' wicket gate of *The Pilgrim's Progress*. The most remarkable aspect of this passage, however, is the extent to which Bunyan evokes the travails of a literal birth to describe how difficult it is to be metaphorically reborn into the Kingdom, pushing his head and shoulders through the narrow way. It seems that this rebirth is harder for the one who is called than the first, biological birth.

Some critics have described this vision as 'hallucinatory', but that is an unfortunate term here for it invokes the underlying anxiety about Bunyan's mental illness that has always characterised Bunyan criticism.[11] This scene does not describe a hallucination but a mystical experience, one of the peak and formative moments in Bunyan's psychological as well as his spiritual development.[12] This early dream vision, not unlike the dream that will inspire the narrative of his great allegory to come, is made possible by his renewed capacity for feeling and his deep attachment to a presence in the Bedford women that is maternal. It is almost as though they are united to become the composite mother that allows for the young Bunyan's rebirth into a new life and language: a new way of being in the world.

Beyond the Bedford wives

The Bedford women introduce Bunyan to their pastor John Gifford, who does much for his 'stability'. Bunyan's heart is 'prepared' to receive the language of love offered by this man, who was once part of the rakish world Bunyan had known from the military life, and from his own shenanigans, but who was now the devoted pastor of the Bedford flock. The enveloping return to the mother in Bunyan's dream vision, quoted above, is followed directly by Bunyan's attachment to Gifford, the figure who directs him to God with, as it were, the blessings of the maternal goodness embodied in the women of Bedford who commend Gifford to Bunyan. One sermon in particular rouses Bunyan: 'when comforting time was come, I heard one preach a sermon upon those words in the *Song* (*Song* 4.1), *Behold thou art fair, my Love; behold, thou art fair*; but at that time he made these two words, *My Love*, his chief and subject matter' (*GA*, p. 29). Notably, Bunyan admits that he 'got nothing' from the actual content of the sermon in its various applications of this verse to the work of Christ, though he does summarise those meanings as the almost bland background to the real drama of the Word's impact on him:

> So as I was a going home, these words came again into my thoughts, and I well remember as they came in, I said thus in my heart, What shall I get by thinking on these two words? this thought had no sooner passed thorow my heart, but the words began thus to kindle in my Spirit, *Thou art my Love, thou art my Love*, twenty times together; and still as they ran thus in my minde, they waxed stronger and warmer, and began to make me look up . . .   (*GA*, p. 29)

Following this sermon Bunyan 'began to give place to the Word' (*GA*, p. 29), an expression that suggests an opening of an interior place, now given over to the Word in a gradual submission.

The sermon with its text of love nurtures the tenderness of heart begun at Bedford. Within this maternal matrix, Bunyan first received the message of love that is here continued by the sermon, probably delivered by Gifford and therefore by his spiritual father: one in authority and inspired by grace. Erik Erikson, whose seminal work on Martin Luther I have called upon elsewhere to illuminate the dynamics of 'Young Man Bunyan', emphasises the cardinal importance of a revival of 'basic trust' in any religious conversion.[13] Erikson compares Luther's struggle to cross the bridge from isolation to a relationship with his spiritual guide, Staupitz, to the psychoanalyst's struggle to revive the love in his patient: 'This is the therapeutic leverage: the therapist knows how to say that right particular thing which, given favorable circumstances, and the condition of the patient's needy openness, strikes a deep note – in Martin's case, undoubtedly the long lost note of infant trust which preceded the emergence of his morbid conscience.'[14] The sermon Bunyan heard, I would argue, also provided this 'retroactive sanction to the efficacy of maternal trust, and trusts the good which has been there from the beginning'.[15] The sermon is drawn from an erotic passage of scripture and allows for a revival of erotic energy in Bunyan that is attached to something good within him: his celebration of this moment, however fleeting, foreshadows the distinctly homely lyricism that will flavour so much of his best writing. '[Y]ea, I was now so taken with the love and mercy of God, that I remember I could not tell how to contain till I got home; I thought I would have spoken of his Love, and of his mercy to me, even to the very Crows that sat upon the plow'd lands' (GA, p. 30). He does not affirm fine points of doctrine in this scene. His assent is emotional. In his late allegory, The Holy War (1682), he describes the ways in which people can be penetrated by a sermon in language that is plainly and wittily the language of love: 'The people when Sermon was done, were scarce able to go to their homes, or to betake themselves to their imploys the week after; they were so Sermon-smitten, and also so Sermon-sick by being smitten, that they knew not what to do' (HW, pp. 157–8). The discourse of the Bedford women has led him into a place of feeling within himself that virtually smites him with love.

In an important study of religious conversion and asceticism, R. W. Medlicott has questioned Freud's hypothesis that the father figure is the primary image of the divine being. He notes that it is usually the parent of the opposite sex, or the preferred parent, that is associated with the divine, the latter clearly showing that it is a projection of the love object.[16] The God image nonetheless has elements of both parents and reveals the bisexual conflicts that prevail in human development. Most discussions of religious imagination in literary criticism miss these points and remain unaccountably wedded to Freud's denigration of religion and to his insistence upon the primacy of the paternal.[17] We should recognise that the place of the maternal has been overlooked in many modern studies of Puritan religious experience; the presence of the maternal has certainly been excluded from considerations of Bunyan's conversion experience, theology and art.

Recent attempts in psychoanalytic theory to explain the failure of classical and even much postmodern psychoanalysis premised on classical notions of the phallus provide a context for understanding the place of Bunyan's encounters with the feminine, and with the maternal, in his psychic development. In the speech of the Bedford women, Bunyan gains access to part of his own history, opening up new ways of speaking and (as argued above) of being. Christopher Bollas has described the maternal order of speech as a historically neglected terrain in psychoanalysis. Recent clinical work, however, has sought to establish ways of illuminating the landscape. Bollas writes that the voice of the mother is 'a complex of associations made up of the greatest variety of visual, acoustic, tactile, kinesthetic and other presentations. If language is a third object derived from the paternal order, one that divides selves from imaginary unity, then maternal speech is an acoustic signifier, a body-ego action.' The maternal order is composed of 'unthought known' forms of knowledge that are foundational to the evolution of ratiocination, speech, imagination and affect.[18] For Bollas, any repudiation of the maternal realm must necessarily restrict and inhibit development, both cultural and psychological. Far from being something that can safely be disavowed, the maternal order that is so tied to free association, and to ways of knowing offered by unconscious knowledge, needs to be recovered, recognised and revisited if we are to understand our being and the meaning of human creativity and culture. Jessica Benjamin has sustained her critique of the 'insufficiently theorised' maternal dyad that has produced, both in 'theory and in life', an inability to represent identification with the mother as a desiring subject whose containing functions the boy as well as the girl can accommodate and appropriate. Very suggestively for our discussion of Bunyan, Benjamin writes of a culturally constructed pathology whereby 'the boy repudiates the identification with the mother, thus losing access to an important means of remaining in relation to her ... all the more so because he cannot identify with her as container of his own feelings'.[19] Bunyan breaks with the pathology of his youthful profanity when he can embrace the offer of grace embodied in the women of Bedford.

Erikson seeks to reclaim the place of the mother. As a clinician, he speculates that Luther received from his mother a pleasurable and 'more sensual' attitude towards nature and God:

> nobody could speak and sing as Luther later did if his mother's voice had not sung to him of some heaven; that nobody could be as torn between his masculine and his feminine sides, nor have such a range of both who did not at one time feel that he was like his mother; but also, that nobody would discuss women and marriage in the way he often did who had not been deeply disappointed by his mother – and had become loath to succumb the way she did to the father, to fate. And if the soul is man's most bisexual part, then we will be prepared to find in Luther both some horror of mystic succumbing and some spiritual search for it, and to recognize in this alternative some emotional and spiritual derivatives of little Martin's 'pre-historic' relation to his mother.[20]

It is tempting to consider Bunyan's experience of the Bedford women in a similar light, since they may well revive for him feelings and memories of his own mother's death while he was an adolescent. In the Bedford doorway, he crosses the threshold into a new world; following this luminous moment he envisions the mountain he must traverse in a manner evoking a birth-archetype, as argued above. It seems that he has been reborn through the womb of the Bedford doorway. But if this is his rebirth, then the rest of *Grace Abounding* charts the difficult burden of growing into the promises of the Bedford women's new discourse, the language of love. This is not so much a foreign as a forgotten tongue for Bunyan. His narrative chronicles the struggle he must undergo to become fluent in this promise of joy, but the encounter, glowing as it is, provokes a great longing, uncertainty and despair. It dislodges him from the false comforts of his libertine pleasures. Hitherto, they had concealed the anxiety that now surfaces in the multiplicity of his imminent battles with scripture, with the Lord, with the Devil and with the myriad 'interpellated' characters – what Louis Althusser calls the 'competing sociolinguistic identities' – that he will now encounter along his way.[21] Aileen Ross revealingly but incorrectly refers to the Bedford women as 'old'. Bunyan does not say they are old, only that they are 'poor', and it is misguided to think that they are any less erotically charged for him than the shopkeeper's wife.[22] The difference lies in the way their tenderness allows him to experience love in a manner that helps him integrate maternal eroticism and paternal law: the journey towards creativity and maturity that Erikson famously called 'identity' in his work on Luther.

Bunyan associates his deepening attachment to scripture with his experience among the Bedford women; their language arrests his attention and keeps his mind fixed on their presence. Under their influence, he gives way to the Word of God and relinquishes the profane eloquence that had so transfixed his rowdy peers. The oaths and curses that had previously given him authority are now replaced by the scripture verses that wrestle for mastery of his soul. As I have argued elsewhere, the replacement is direct and almost concrete.[23] Erikson explored the maternal meaning of the Bible to Martin Luther many years ago; his work on the maternal qualities of scripture in Christian experience emphasises that the origins of human speech and human relationships lie in the early maternal bonds that provide the foundations for later flourishing. He associates Luther's acceptance of the 'matrix' of scripture with his earliest modes of relating to the 'mater', and he shows that the great reformer's pose as 'suckling mother' to his followers derived from that acceptance of his own bodily memory and desire.[24] Bunyan will later speak of himself as a travailing mother to his congregation, 'I have really been in pain, and have as it were travelled to bring forth Children to God' (*GA*, p. 89).

However, the most important point to emphasise about Bunyan's encounter with the Bedford wives is that scripture becomes part of his inner dialogue from that moment on. It is also the case, of course, that the terrifying penetration of the Word will also come to torment him; after his 'taking in' of the discourse of the Bedford congregation, Bunyan's anguish was unrelenting. Yet the awakening to such feeling – to the range of emotions that his youthful profligacy had been numbing and repudiating – is what he will eventually work through in the full course of his rocky conversion experience. The saving moment for Bunyan arrives when he starts to feel – when he allows for tenderness of heart – and the rest of his journey flows from that. The attachment to the scriptures as a maternal object links Bunyan to Luther in a manner that is consistent with his sense that Luther's *Commentary on the Galatians* had been written out of his own heart. The maternity of the Word highlights the heartfelt connection (*GA*, p. 40).[25]

> Intrinsic to the kind of passivity we speak of is not only the memory of having been given, but also the identification with the maternal giver: 'the glory of a good thing is that it flows out to others.' In the Bible Luther at last found a mother whom he could acknowledge; he could attribute to Scripture a generosity to which he could open himself, and which he could pass onto others, at last a mother's son.[26]

This insight into the bisexual origins of religious objects has not, to my knowledge, been pursued further, either for historical or contemporary subjects. The postmodern imagination has been too concerned with the phallic significance of language for that. A case like Bunyan's, once again, calls this absolutism into question. The Word is awakened in Bunyan's heart when the tenderness of the Bedford women's discourse stirs his capacity to feel God's love. It is the 'maternity' of God that bridges him to eternity in these early years of his search.

A Case of Conscience Resolved (1683)

One of the ironies of Bunyan's career is that a man transformed by his encounter with a small gathering of holy women chose, when he became pastor of the Bedford church, to forbid women's separate prayer meetings in *A Case of Conscience Resolved* (1683). Underlying all of Bunyan's arguments, certainly, is his 'belief in the fundamental weakness and inferiority of women' (*MW*, IV:xliii). Yet despite the voice that *A Case of Conscience Resolved* gives to patriarchy, the treatise is also interesting for what it suggests about his construction of the feminine in his church, in his writings and even in himself. '[F]or,' he writes, 'I have not in anything sought to degrade them, or to take from them what either Nature or Grace, or Appointment of God hath invested them with; But have laboured to keep them in their place' (*MW*, IV:329). What is the 'place' of the women of Bunyan's church? Does it bear any relation to his celebration, even veneration, of the small gathering of women so movingly described in *Grace Abounding*? I will conclude this chapter on the 'place' of Bunyan's women by reflecting upon the ways that, despite his stern judgements, he allows for the special calling of holy women.

Bunyan acknowledges a special function for women's prayer that resonates with the ways the Bedford women brought him to God and to himself. *A Case of Conscience Resolved* emphatically resists all female power in the church; for Bunyan, women bear most heavily the burden of original sin because of Eve's first disobedience. Women who are holy are thoroughly convinced of their 'miserable state by nature' (*GA*, p. 14) and duly shamed by it. The Bedford women's frank, joyful acceptance of their inheritance speaks to the young Bunyan, who is so devastated by 'the inward wretchedness of [his] wicked heart' (*GA*, p. 25). As pastor, Bunyan insists that the burden of original sin is specially 'shouldered' by women, but he hastens to add that the painful legacy of Eve is not applicable to the 'Mystical Body' of the Church but only to its 'Body *Politick*'. This distinction allows him to be strict in his rulings about congregations while allowing for a different, mystical side of female spirituality. 'And I will add, that as *they*, and *we*, are united to Christ, and made members of his mystical body, the fulness of him that fills all in all: So there is no superiority, as I know of, but we are all one in Christ' (*MW*, IV:322). Bunyan tenderly concedes that this political hierarchy will pass away: 'Wherefore my beloved Sisters, this inferiority of yours will last but a little while: When the day of Gods Salvation is come ... these distinctions of Sexes shall be laid a side, and every pot shall be filled to the Brim' (*MW*, IV:323). Almost as a consolation for his insistence on the restricted role of women in his congregation, Bunyan refers to the feminine function of intercessory prayer in language that echoes the role of the Holy Spirit according to St Paul. 'Likewise the Spirit also helpeth our infirmities: for we know not what we should pray for as we ought: but the Spirit itself maketh intercession for us with groanings which cannot be uttered' (Rom. 8:26). Bunyan describes women's public role in prayer in similar terms of utterances beyond language: 'They should also not be the mouth of the Assembly, but in the heart, desires, grones, and Tears, they should go along with the Men. In their Closets they are at Liberty to *speak* unto their God, who can bear with, and pitty them with us; and pardon all our weakness for the sake of Jesus Christ' (*MW*, IV:324). Their silence is filled with unspeakable desire and wordless supplication. He reiterates, regarding the 'Body Politick' of the church, 'Let the Men in Prayer be the mouth to God, and the VVomen [*sic*] lift after with groans and desires ... When Women keep their places, and Men manage their Worshipping God as they should, we shall have better days for the Church of God' (*MW*, IV:329).

The woman is not in the place of the 'mouth' of the congregation but in the place of silent intercession; even her discourse is most stirring in its unspeakable resonance. Young Bunyan dropped both his blasphemy and his 'brisk-talking' when he felt the presence of the divine; perhaps he is alluding to his Bedford encounter when he concludes:

> Nor are Women, by what I have said, debarred from any Work, or imploy, unto which they are enjoyned by the Word. they [*sic*] have often been called forth to be Gods witnesses, and have Born famous Testimony for him ... I remember many of them with comfort: Even of these Eminent Daughters of *Sarah*, whose Daughters *you also are* ...   (*MW*, IV:324)

Women's discourse has a special place; it is tender, intercessory and often too deep for words. Bunyan's blasphemous speech as a young man was terrifying to himself, and to others, in its sheer power. When he contains that affective power in the matrix of the scriptures, he finds the core of his true self. It is important to acknowledge the ways that such foundation – such a place – in the scripture derived from his saturation in women's ways and women's words. It is certainly not the place that we would assign the myriad female voices that echo over the centuries, and it may not be even the place progressively assigned to the female prophet, preacher or poet by more enlightened figures of Bunyan's day. But it is a place that remains pivotal in Bunyan's inner development, without which he simply could not have progressed as preacher or writer.

NOTES

1. My title invokes the 1970s dystopian, feminist novel *The Stepford Wives*, in which housewives in the idyllic town of Stepford, Connecticut, become robots in perfect servitude to their husbands. In popular American usage, the term 'Stepford wife' has come to stand for women who lose their humanity in order to be put in their place within the patriarchy. In this ironic allusion, there is a chilling recognition that the mandates against women's worship in Bunyan's late treatise, *A Case of Conscience Resolved*, may seem to resemble the rules of the fictional town of Stepford as much as they reflect the rules of the Bedford church. By the time the mature Bunyan resolved in his 'conscience' to forbid the women of his congregation to gather for prayer, the Bedford women idealised in his autobiography may well seem to have devolved into dutiful and silenced Stepford wives. On Bunyan's 'reach', see also *GA*, p. 26.
2. Thomas H. Luxon, 'One Soul Versus One Flesh: Friendship, Marriage, and the Puritan Self', in Vera J. Camden (ed.), *Trauma and Transformation: The Political Progress of John Bunyan* (Stanford University Press, 2008), pp. 81–99 (p. 98).

3. On Bunyan's misogyny, see Michael Mullett, *John Bunyan in Context* (Keele University Press, 1996), pp. 246–8.
4. Margaret J. M. Ezell, 'Bunyan's Women, Women's Bunyan', in Camden (ed.), *Trauma and Transformation*, pp. 63–80 (p. 65).
5. Joanna Field, pseudonym for Marion Milner, *On Not Being Able to Paint* (1957; Los Angeles: J. P. Tarcher, 1983), Foreword by Anna Freud, p. 44.
6. Michael Davies, *Graceful Reading: Theology and Narrative in the Works of John Bunyan* (Oxford University Press, 2002), p. 124.
7. *Ibid.*
8. Lawrence Gowing, *Vermeer* (1952; 2nd edn, London: Faber and Faber, 1970), p. 52.
9. Lisa Vergara, 'Perspectives on Women in the Art of Vermeer', in Wayne E. Franits (ed.), *The Cambridge Companion to Vermeer* (Cambridge University Press, 2001), pp. 52–72 (p. 61).
10. H. Rodney Nevitt, Jr., 'Vermeer on the Question of Love', in Franits (ed.), *Cambridge Companion to Vermeer*, pp. 89–110 (p. 108).
11. Roger Sharrock, 'Spiritual Autobiography: Bunyan's *Grace Abounding*', in Anne Laurence, W. R. Owens and Stuart Sim (eds.), *John Bunyan and His England, 1628–1688* (London and Ronceverte, W.Va.: Hambledon Press, 1990), pp. 97–104 (pp. 100–4).
12. See my discussion of Richard Greaves's definitive 'diagnosis' of Bunyan, 'Young Man Bunyan', in Camden (ed.), *Trauma and Transformation*, pp. 41–62.
13. *Ibid.*
14. Erik H. Erikson, *Young Man Luther: A Study in Psychoanalysis and History* (New York: Norton, 1962), pp. 167, 168.
15. *Ibid*, p. 168.
16. R. W. Medlicott, 'St Anthony Abbot and the Hazards of Asceticism: An Analysis of the Artist's Interpretation of the Temptations', *The British Journal of Medical Psychology*, 42 (1969), 133–40.
17. For the individual, the power of the image of God lies in its libidinal charge. He ... harks back to the mnemic image of the father whom in his childhood he so greatly overvalued. He exalts the image into a deity and makes it into something contemporary and real. The effective strength of this mnemic image and the persistence of his need for protection jointly sustain his belief in God.

    Sigmund Freud, 'The Psychology of Women', in *New Introductory Lectures on Psychoanalysis*, trans. James Strachey (New York: W. W. Norton, 1965), p. 202
18. Christopher Bollas, *The Freudian Moment* (New York: Karnac Press, 2007), p. 6.
19. Jessica Benjamin, 'The Primal Leap of Psychoanalysis from Body to Speech: Freud, Feminism, and the Vicissitudes of the Transference', in Muriel Dimen and Adrienne Harris (eds.), *Storms in Her Head: Freud and the Construction of Hysteria* (New York: Other Press, 2001), p. 57.
20. Erikson, *Young Man Luther*, p. 73.
21. 'I shall then suggest that ideology "acts" or "functions" in such a way that it "recruits" subjects among the individuals ... by that very precise operation which I have called *interpellation* or hailing, and which can be imagined along the lines of the most commonplace everyday police (or other) hailing: "Hey, you there!" '

This hailing is most dramatically witnessed in *The Pilgrim's Progress* when Christian must preserve his identity by resisting the lure of the sideline 'hail-fellow well-met' of Talkative, Mr Worldly Wiseman and other seducers whose predecessors are such characters as 'Harry' in Bunyan's personal pilgrimage (*GA*, p. 16); Louis Althusser, 'Ideology and Ideological State Apparatuses', in *Lenin and Philosophy and Other Essays*, trans. Ben Brewster (New York: Monthly Review Press, 1972), cited in Tony Tanner, *Adultery and the Novel: Contract and Transgression* (Baltimore, Md.: Johns Hopkins University Press, 1979), 241n.

22. Aileen Ross, ' "Baffled, and Befooled": Misogyny in the Work of John Bunyan', in David Gay, James G. Randall and Arlette Zinck (eds.), *Awakening Words: John Bunyan and the Language of Community* (Newark: University of Delaware Press; London: Associated University Presses, 2000), pp. 153–68 (p. 167).
23. Vera J. Camden, 'Blasphemy and the Problem of the Self in *Grace Abounding*', *BS*, 1.2 (Spring 1989), 5–21.
24. Erikson, *Young Man Luther*, p. 208.
25. For an extended meditation on the maternity of the word and rebirth, see Bunyan's *Last Sermon*, *MW*, XII: 83–94.
26. Erikson, *Young Man Luther*, p. 208.

PART II
John Bunyan's major works

5

MICHAEL DAVIES

Grace Abounding to the Chief of Sinners: John Bunyan and spiritual autobiography

> One day I was very sad, I think sader [*sic*] then at any one time in my life; and this
> sadness was through a fresh sight of the greatness and vileness of my sins: And as I was
> then looking for nothing but *Hell*, and the everlasting damnation of my Soul,
> suddenly, as I thought, I saw the Lord Jesus look down from Heaven upon me,
> and saying, *Believe on the Lord Jesus Christ, and thou shalt be saved.*
> But I replyed, Lord, I am a great, a very great sinner; and he answered, *My grace
> is sufficient for thee.*
> (*P'sP*, pp. 142–3)

This passage from Bunyan's most famous allegory commands our attention
for two obvious reasons: first, because it gives us Hopeful's spiritual autobiography – a vivid account of his awakening into what Bunyan considers
saving faith – and, secondly, because of its closeness to Bunyan's own conversion narrative, published twelve years before *The Pilgrim's Progress*
appeared, *Grace Abounding to the Chief of Sinners* (1666). The same, yet
not the same, Hopeful's story might seem little more than '*Grace Abounding*
in miniature'.[1] It is useful to begin with Hopeful's conversion not only to spot
connections between *Grace Abounding* and *The Pilgrim's Progress*, exemplary works of Bunyan's religious experience and imagination, but also
because it illustrates 'in miniature' some key features of seventeenth-century
spiritual autobiography: a form which, focusing on an individual's religious
conversion, often excludes details of a straightforwardly biographical kind,
concentrating more on the convert's 'inner world' than upon 'the ordinary
historical course of a life'.[2] What we notice about Hopeful's account, then,
even from the short extract quoted above, is just how *inward* it is: the word 'I'
dominates this narrative, and it is an 'I' contemplating its own sadness as 'a
great, a very great sinner', before undergoing a remarkably direct communication with 'the Lord Jesus'. This style marks something important about
the kind of account that *Grace Abounding* likewise exemplifies, albeit even
more intensely: the trials of a first-person 'subject' profoundly sensitive to its
own fragility and to the ongoing struggles of the soul.

Yet, there is much more to Hopeful's narrative than just an introspective
obsession with the self. An eloquent expression of '*Saints Fellowship*' (as

'*The Dreamers note*' prefacing this episode describes it, *P'sP*, p. 137),
Hopeful's spiritual autobiography serves a distinct purpose in *The Pilgrim's
Progress*: a purpose both personal and pastoral, sociable and salvatory.
'*Good discourse prevents drowsiness*', a marginal note tells us, and so these
pilgrims do the right thing in order to stay awake while crossing the deadly
'*Inchanted Ground*': '*They begin at the beginning of their conversion*' (*P'sP*,
p. 137). Narrated in order to keep the two travellers awake and alive, no less,
Hopeful's story of conversion is not just edifying and instructive, but life-
saving, and this in itself can offer a salutary reminder to readers embarking
upon *Grace Abounding*. Bunyan's spiritual autobiography, as interior and
inward-looking, and as strange and as strained as it may sometimes seem,
is geared nevertheless to awakening a sharp sense of religious community as
well as of individuality in its readers. As '*a Relation of the work of God upon
my own Soul*' (*GA*, pp. 1–2), its '*good discourse*' about conversion is, like
Hopeful's, intent upon offering fellowship, not just soliloquy.

The purpose of this chapter is to address *Grace Abounding to the Chief of
Sinners* in these terms: as a stylistically fascinating first-person 'relation' of
religious experience, and as a work written in communal conversation with
others. In order to do so, it will be helpful to consider *Grace Abounding* in
relation to some other seventeenth-century conversion narratives, as well as
to the period during which Bunyan wrote and published *Grace Abounding*,
well over a decade after his conversion had originally taken place, and while
separated from his church and community – from '*Saints Fellowship*' – as an
imprisoned nonconformist preacher. On this basis, the graceful compression
of *Grace Abounding* into Hopeful's version in *The Pilgrim's Progress* barely
does justice to Bunyan's own unique and sustained account, because it elides
so much of what makes *Grace Abounding* a major literary achievement: one
of the greatest spiritual autobiographies in the English language. In order to
gain its proper measure as such, it is as well for us to follow Hopeful's
example and to '*begin at the beginning*'.

Into a maze

But the same day, as I was in the midst of a game at Cat, and having struck it one
blow from the hole; just as I was about to strike it the second time, a voice did
suddenly dart from Heaven into my Soul, which said, *Wilt thou leave thy sins,
and go to Heaven? or have thy sins, and go to Hell?* At this I was put to an
exceeding maze; wherefore, leaving my Cat upon the ground, I looked up to
Heaven, and was as if I had with the eyes of my understanding, seen the Lord
Jesus looking down upon me, as being very hotly displeased with me, and as if
he did severely threaten me with some grievous punishment for these, and other
my ungodly practices. (*GA*, p. 10)

This famous passage from *Grace Abounding* recalls the first encounter of a young, unregenerate John Bunyan with the rather bewildering world of spiritual experience. Occurring one Sunday while he is playing at 'Cat' (or 'tipcat', the 'cat' in question being a piece of wood hit by the players), this extraordinary incident marks a turning point in Bunyan's story, for it is from this moment in *Grace Abounding* that his journey towards salvation could be said really to begin. As such, it seems to give us just what we might expect from a spiritual autobiography: a point of conversion. The sense of this being a life-changing event is reinforced by the affinities it bears with that other, more famous spiritual transformation, the scriptural text of which remains legible beneath Bunyan's own: Paul's conversion on the road to Damascus (Acts 9: 1–8). Like Paul, young man Bunyan (though no persecuting Saul, of course) similarly finds himself stunned by a voice (unbidden, and seemingly from heaven) which speaks to him suddenly and directly about his sinful condition (his 'ungodly practices'), and in terms that command an unequivocal change. Bunyan's first 'experience' is thus both strikingly dramatic and very familiar. Bunyan, at this stage, appears to be another Paul, that classic archetype of the Christian convert with whom Bunyan has already signalled a number of connections. The title of Bunyan's conversion account – *Grace Abounding to the Chief of Sinners* – is drawn from Paul's first letter to Timothy (1 Tim. 1:14–15), and the prefatory epistle of *Grace Abounding* seems distinctly Pauline too, addressing the '*Children*' of his church '*now from the* Lions Den' (*GA*, pp. 1–4). Such associations prepare us well for the game of cat as a point at which, as for Paul, grace too seems to be abounding for Bunyan.[3]

However, far from seeing this moment as an offer of spiritual reprieve, a sign to leave sin and repent, the inexperienced Bunyan misunderstands it. He takes it not as an offer of salvation but, we soon discover, as confirmation of his sinfulness and of his reprobation, and so immediately concludes, with a logic that is perfectly rational but also perverse, that if 'I can but be damned' then 'I had as good be damned for many sins, as be damned for few' (*GA*, pp. 10–11). The outcome of this experience is no sudden or definitive conversion in the style of Paul, then, but quite the opposite. On hearing the voice speak to him of choosing between Heaven and Hell, Bunyan does not convert at all. Instead, Faustus-like, he 'returned desperately to my sport again', he tells us, and 'found within me' not great 'grace', but rather 'a great desire to take my fill of sin' (*GA*, p. 11). Far from receiving Pauline clarity, the young Bunyan is in fact put into 'an exceeding maze' by all of this. Yet, conjuring this image of an 'exceeding maze' is also one of the reasons why this episode is one of the most important within *Grace Abounding*. After all, this is an 'amazing' encounter, not just for the unconverted Bunyan but also for the reader.

We have to wonder, for example, what really is going on here? Is this a conversion moment or not? If it is (and the affinities with Paul's conversion might encourage us to think so, at least initially), then what kind of conversion leads to further sin and despair? Equally, are we to accept that something supernatural is occurring? Is Bunyan (like Paul, and like Hopeful too, as well as some other seventeenth-century converts) actually 'hearing' a 'voice' from heaven, and 'seeing' Christ looking down on him? Or is all of this metaphorical? After all, Bunyan uses an interesting phrase when describing what happened to him: it 'was as if'. So, it was only 'as if' he heard a voice darting into his 'soul', then, while the vision he 'sees' is likewise only 'as if', and in any case through the scriptural 'eyes of my understanding' (Ephes. 1:18). Is this an inward, or an outward 'experience'? Is it literal, or figurative? Real, or imagined? Our response to Bunyan's first extraordinary description of a supercharged spiritual life might well be as amazed as his own.

It can be helpful to dwell on the game-of-cat episode and how it puts the gamesome Bunyan, as well as Bunyan's readers, into 'an exceeding maze' because it seems exemplary of the text as a whole. Indeed, the game-of-cat passage establishes an overall pattern or shape for *Grace Abounding*, which subsequently is full of mistakes and misunderstandings, doctrinal wrong turns and providential lucky escapes from them. No sooner does the converting Bunyan describe feeling 'all on a flame to be converted', for instance, than just as suddenly he confesses how 'my desires also for heaven and life began to fail', leaving him 'farther from conversion than ever I was before' (*GA*, pp. 24–6). It is because Bunyan's relation of such things is always 'twining and twisting' (*GA*, p. 49) that Bunyan's spiritual autobiography can perplex readers. Unlike Paul's instantaneous conversion, *Grace Abounding* can appear confusing, diffuse and labyrinthine. When, for example, might Bunyan's conversion be said to have occurred? Is it during Bunyan's game of cat, or is it later when, having reformed himself as 'a brisk talker ... in the matters of Religion', he encounters the 'poor women' of Bedford 'sitting at a door in the Sun' talking of the 'new birth', a conversation which amazes him once again, as if a door had just been opened to 'a new world' (*GA*, pp. 14–15)? Or is it actually much later, when, having received the guidance of 'holy Mr *Gifford*', the Bedford congregation's pastor, Bunyan's 'Soul' is 'led from truth to truth by God!', until he 'had an evidence, as I thought, of my salvation from Heaven, with many golden Seals thereon, all hanging in my sight' (*GA*, pp. 37–40)? If so, what do we then make of the despair that follows hard upon this last 'evidence', when Bunyan is 'most fiercely assaulted with this temptation, to *sell and part with Christ*' (*GA*, p. 43)? At the end of the book, as a successful preacher, Bunyan confesses to being 'violently assaulted' still 'with thoughts of blasphemy, and strongly tempted to speak them with my mouth before the

Congregation' (*GA*, p. 90). To the undiscerning reader, one might begin to wonder exactly how and where grace has abounded for Bunyan. But even for the most discerning reader, *Grace Abounding* remains an amazing account: our experience of reading it can indeed be likened to 'travelling in a mighty maze whose plan is far from clear, and where at every turn we meet some new and puzzling psychodrama'.[4]

Poor Bunyan's troubles

For Bunyan, then, conversion is neither as swift nor as final as Paul's falling off his horse. A long and painful business, the 'concept of conversion' as an instantaneous 'alteration in chemical state, an alchemy of person' does not readily apply to Bunyan, or perhaps anyone other than Paul, whose conversion might be seen 'as much anti-type as archetype' in providing an example that few other converts, including Bunyan, could hope to replicate.[5] Nevertheless, Bunyan's mode of conversion has a powerful impact upon the style of *Grace Abounding*. The slowly converting Bunyan is often depicted not just as caught in 'an exceeding maze' but at a loss, more often than not, which way to turn. Being 'at a very great stand' (*GA*, p. 24) is how Bunyan describes himself at key points in his spiritual progress. As a result, the most characteristic experience that Bunyan recalls is one of hesitation. He is continually 'ready to sink' or indeed 'always sinking, whatever I did think or do', at times into 'a miry bog' and at others in 'a very great storm', or he is 'racked upon the wheel', or even like a child fallen into a 'mill-pit', who could 'scrable and scraul', able to 'find neither hold for hand nor foot' (*GA*, pp. 21, 26–7, 31, 33, 46, 62). '[T]ossed to and fro', Bunyan's 'Soul' becomes 'like a broken Vessel, driven, as with the Winds, and tossed sometimes head-long into dispair' (*GA*, pp. 48, 58).

It is this accumulation of images (of shipwreck, of sinking and drowning, of amazement) that makes *Grace Abounding* such a profoundly moving spiritual autobiography, but also one that remains dramatic, tense and full of suspense, even as it seems so often to stall in its progress towards any conclusive state of conversion. When Bunyan writes how he felt that '*now* was I both a burthen and a terror to myself, nor did I ever so know, as *now*, what it was to be weary of my life, and yet afraid to die. Oh, how gladly now would I have been anybody but myself!' (*GA*, p. 45), we are struck not only by the force of his desperate yearning to disown his own 'self' and to inhabit instead 'anybody' else, but also by the sheer immediacy – the *now*ness – of this outcry. Suspended between weariness of 'life' yet still 'afraid to die', becoming both 'a burthern and a terror to myself', Bunyan's prose performs a high-wire balancing act here: the 'I' teeters on a tightrope of taut existence, its fearful footsteps marked by the

breathtaking '*now ... now ...* now'. So extreme are such experiences at times
that commentators have often taken them as signs of mental illness rather than
of religious conversion, treating *Grace Abounding* more as a psychiatric casebook than a seventeenth-century spiritual autobiography. As William James
noted in his famous work, *The Varieties of Religious Experience* (1902), 'Poor
Bunyan's troubles' bear all the hallmarks (according to James, at least) of 'a
typical case of the psychopathic temperament, sensitive of conscience to
a diseased degree, beset by doubts, fears and insistent ideas, and a victim of
verbal automatisms, both motor and sensory'.[6] Similar diagnoses have followed, often interpreting the game-of-cat passage, or when a bell-tower seems
about to fall upon Bunyan (*GA*, pp. 13–14), or when Bunyan describes reading
the Bible 'as if it talked with me' (*GA*, p. 21), among other apparently 'auditory'
encounters in *Grace Abounding*, as indicative of mental disorder, depression or
obsessive-compulsive behaviour.[7]

We might be less inclined to diagnose Bunyan as psychologically ill, however, if we consider other seventeenth-century spiritual autobiographies, and
the conventions that they adopt when relating experiences of conversion.
Although rarely as detailed or simply as well written as *Grace Abounding*,
nevertheless most seventeenth-century conversion accounts – especially of the
Puritan or nonconformist brand – display the same patterns of experience,
and share the vocabulary and narrative shape characterised by Bunyan's
'*castings down, and raisings up*' (*GA*, p. 2). Anthologies such as *Spiritual
Experiences of Sundry Beleevers* (1653) and Charles Doe's *Collection of
Experience of the Work of Grace* (1700) include narrative after narrative of
the same kind of '*castings down, and raisings up*' experienced by numerous
'chiefs of sinners'. In her *Legacy For Saints* (1654), Anna Trapnel likewise
explains how 'my spirit had thus been upon the rack for a season, and tossed
up and down with the waves of a continual accusing troubled conscience',
and she too describes how 'sometimes as I have been going along the streets,
I have looked behind me, thinking I had heard some locall voice, a voice
without me, but sure it was because I was unacquainted with the voice of the
Spirit speaking in, or to the soul'.[8] While Bunyan's *Grace Abounding* could
hardly be said to be simply par for the course – it remains still the most
engaging and affective of all Puritan spiritual autobiographies, even without
any of the sensational prophecies and dreams that can be found in some –
nevertheless, its structure of falling and fighting amid spiritual storms, which
we might find bewildering now, would not have seemed so to early-modern
readers sensitive to the ways in which 'flouds of temptation' can 'over-whelme
the poore distressed, doubting, despairing and drowning soule'.[9]

Reading *Grace Abounding* alongside other conversion narratives, from
Augustine's *Confessions* to the spiritual autobiographies of much later

converts, helps to illustrate how deeply Bunyan's account is rooted in literary convention rather than in psychic derangement. When Bunyan describes himself as no more than 'a very Cast-away indeed' (*GA*, p. 18), foundering like a distressed ship amid dreadful tempests, he is adopting an imagery of spiritual seafaring which, within an English literary tradition, takes us back to Wyatt, Spenser and Milton, and which is continued too in the eighteenth-century writings of John Newton and William Cowper. We should not, in other words, assume that the way in which *Grace Abounding* has been written grants us access in any straightforward sense to Bunyan's allegedly disturbed mind. What we must negotiate when reading *Grace Abounding* is not Bunyan's hysteria but his style, and it is a style particular, at times, to seventeenth-century nonconformists (involving a gospel- or scripture-language, heavily allusive to the Bible and its allegorical and 'spiritual' meanings) and, at others, traditional to the ways in which religious writing has always struggled with 'the unfathomable grammar of grace' which, especially when it comes to recounting conversion, 'defies the ordinary usages of language to express it'.[10] Far from anything crude or rustic, Bunyan's *'plain and simple'* style of relating the *'experience of the grace of* God' upon his *'Soul'* (*GA*, p. 3) exemplifies in remarkably subtle ways how 'Grace is an enigma, a grammar unto itself'.[11] There is very little that is *'plain and simple'* about it.[12]

Grace Abounding and the shape of conversion

Like many seventeenth-century spiritual autobiographies, *Grace Abounding* also follows the ups-and-downs of what has been termed a 'morphology of conversion': a Calvinist *ordo salutis* or order of salvation, the sequence of which begins (as for Christian at the start of *The Pilgrim's Progress*) with a powerful conviction of sin and moves through a series of stages towards faith in salvation by grace alone.[13] Such a pattern provides a narrative structure that can be discerned quite clearly in *Grace Abounding*, as Bunyan describes moving from an outward conformity to formal religion early on in his religious life (believing that 'I pleased God as well as any man in *England*' (*GA*, p. 12)) into more profound convictions of sin and of faith that develop following his momentous encounter with the women of Bedford (*GA*, pp. 14–15). Recognising the shape of Bunyan's *ordo salutis* – of moving from law to grace, from the pain of a legalistic conscience and from guilt over sin to a justification by faith, which is followed, in turn, by sanctification and a perseverance in that faith – can certainly make sense of *Grace Abounding* as an account that follows a clear theological scheme.[14] Far from being a random sequence of unconnected experiences, impossible to fathom or to follow by convert and reader alike, *Grace Abounding* can be read according to a lucid process of salvation, charting the sinning believer's journey from a guilt-ridden state of enslavement under the covenant of law and works (according to the terms of Bunyan's covenant theology) to the liberty offered by a covenant of grace, faith in which brings blessed release for Bunyan from incarcerating fears and doubts.

Moreover, because faith in grace for Bunyan is not something simply to be accepted but to be worked for continually, through faithful perseverance, then the ups-and-downs of conversion are, in a sense, never-ending for Bunyan. As he illustrates in later works such as *Saved by Grace* (1676) and *Come, and Welcome, to Jesus Christ* (1678), for Bunyan great sin begets great grace, for which reason none should despair. Bunyan's concept of saving faith thus involves not only a full understanding of how sinners are saved by grace, but also an acceptance of those slips and backslidings that can, and will, befall even the most devout of believers or 'saints', but which grace can always encompass. The condition of the believer under grace is undoubtedly one of striving for sanctification or holiness in life amid a continual battle against temptations, but when faults and falls do occur, they can be accommodated nonetheless and in a way exemplified by Bunyan's own experience in *Grace Abounding*. 'Here is Grace!', Bunyan can exclaim: 'So many times as the soul backslides, so many times God brings him again ... he renews his pardons and multiplies them.' Because of the 'Heart-wandrings', 'daily Miscarriages' and 'common Infirmities that are incident to the best of saints, and attend them in their best Performances', abundant grace provides simply 'Millions of pardons from God for these' (*MW*, VIII:208). No wonder that the most triumphant moment in *Grace Abounding* comes with Bunyan's hard-won conviction, after a long and painful backsliding into despair, that God's '*grace is sufficient for thee*' (*GA*, pp. 64–5).

With this theological frame of redemption by grace in mind, we can begin to see how and why it is so important for *Grace Abounding* to *remain* labyrinthine and seemingly repetitive as an account of conversion. On the one hand, faith in grace is something to be maintained continually for Bunyan through perseverance, with all its ups-and-downs. On the other, what *Grace Abounding* depicts are the stages through which the convert may have to pass to realise true faith, a process which naturally encompasses movements both forwards and backwards, through faith and despair and back again: all those '*castings down, and raisings up*'. Bunyan's *Grace Abounding* is not so much a maze for us to fathom after all, then, but a type of map by which its readers may be guided through the difficult labyrinths of conversion. So detailed and precise is Bunyan's spiritual autobiography as a doctrinal acting-out of the Calvinist *ordo salutis* that, not surprisingly, it can be compared directly to Bunyan's other, more famous guidebooks for coming believers, from his early treatise *The Doctrine of The Law and Grace Unfolded* (1659) to his most famous work about salvation-by-stages, *The Pilgrim's Progress*, as well as that perhaps less well-known chart, *A Mapp Shewing the Order and Causes of Salvation and Damnation* (MW, XII:415–23).

Sola scriptura and 'Saints Fellowship'

What makes *Grace Abounding* unique among early-modern conversion accounts is that it elaborates this recognisable pattern of experience – this 'morphology of conversion' – with a doctrinal and pastoral finesse absent from most other spiritual autobiographies. As such, we are reminded of just how deeply Bunyan's 'spiritual life is invested in theological language' in *Grace Abounding*: as a conversion account, it overturns any 'presiding assumption that theology is an activity separate from the personal and psychological sphere of religious experience', or that doctrine somehow offers 'a language subsequent, and supplementary, to the spiritual life which it (merely) "describes" '.[15] To borrow Brian Cummings's formulation, 'without theology' any attempt to understand *Grace Abounding* as 'psychological history is meaningless'.[16] Equally, we should also be clear about what kind of 'theology' we are dealing with, given that there is more to *Grace Abounding* as an account of a converting soul than an obsession with Calvinist predestination and its forbidding power (as has often been assumed, at least) to distress the uninitiated. *Grace Abounding* is a narrative of much more than just an anxiety over whether Bunyan is predestined to damnation or not.[17] But this, in itself, should not surprise us. For the story that *Grace Abounding* tells is not simply an emotional or a psychological one, marked by the 'hearing' of voices and the suffering of despair for years at a time, but profoundly an intellectual one. *Grace Abounding* is a narrative of a convert's growth in understanding. It involves a strenuous, almost physical striving to interpret scripture, faith and salvation not as they appear through the kaleidoscope of a fractured mind, nor through the frame of a persecutory theological imagination, but as they look through 'the eyes of my understanding'.

For this reason, *Grace Abounding* remains a tremendously vigorous account of Bunyan's early struggles to make sense of scripture as a reader. His is a conversion achieved as much through dedication to interpretation and the decipherment of texts – through reading, that is – as is Augustine's *Confessions*, and it is centred as firmly as Luther's conversion in the Reformation tradition of receiving salvation *sola scriptura*: through scripture alone. Bunyan's often astonishing encounters with the Bible in *Grace Abounding* – how its 'words broke in upon my mind' (*GA*, pp. 22–3), how its sentences 'fell in upon me' (*GA*, p. 29) and how it would at times seem like a

voice 'sounding and ratling in mine ears' (*GA*, p. 31) – mark a relationship with
scripture that is remarkably intense, but nevertheless hermeneutic rather than
unhinged. When Bunyan's conversion reaches its climax, it is marked by an
unmistakable progress in reading and understanding the Word: he feels his
'Soul' suddenly 'led from truth to truth' through every aspect of scripture,
'even from the birth and cradle of the Son of God, to his ascension and second
coming', so that there remains 'not one part of the Gospel of the Lord Jesus, but I
was orderly led into it' (*GA*, p. 37). Like Luther before him, Bunyan 'presents a
history of reading' in *Grace Abounding* 'which demands of the reader a corre-
sponding energy and patience in interpretation', Bunyan aiming thereby 'to
replicate in his readers the reformatory powers he attributes to his own experience of reading'. As of Luther, then, so too we might say of Bunyan in *Grace
Abounding*: 'By reading he was converted, and by reading he hopes to convert
his readers.'[18]

Yet, for as much as the Reformed doctrine of salvation *sola scriptura* might
give us the impression that Bunyan is left to wrestle with the Word all alone,
Grace Abounding represents more than the lonesome drama of a lonely soul
incarcerated in the prison-house of the 'self'. Bunyan's conversion may work
firmly and authentically towards a sense of salvation *sola scriptura*, *sola
gratia* and *sola fide* (that is, by scripture, grace and faith 'alone'), but he
does not come to understand such things solo. A community peoples the
pages of *Grace Abounding*, facilitating Bunyan's conversion providentially
from the outset: from his nameless first wife, whose dowry of devotional
works ('*The Plain Mans Path-way to Heaven*, and *The Practice of Piety*')
encourages Bunyan the newlywed to take up 'somewhat pleasing' thoughts of
religion (*GA*, p. 8), to the women of Bedford whose talk of 'new birth'
introduces him with more lasting efficacy to an entirely 'new world' of
religious belief (*GA*, pp. 14–15). While books other than scripture likewise
play a key role in Bunyan's progress in *Grace Abounding* (Luther's 'comment
on the *Galathians*' and 'that dreadful story of that miserable mortal, *Francis
Spira*' falling into his hands at crucial moments: *GA*, pp. 40–1, 49–50), it is
the Independent congregation at Bedford and, its pastor John Gifford in
particular, who perform a vital though almost secret service for Bunyan,
whose conversion occurs precisely as a result of sitting 'under the Ministry
of holy Mr *Gifford*'. Gifford's 'Doctrine, by Gods grace, was much for my
stability', Bunyan recalls, and this pastor's ability 'to deliver the People of
God from all those false and unsound rests that by Nature we are prone to
take and make to our Souls' results directly in Bunyan's spiritual transformation: his 'Soul thorow Grace' became 'very apt to drink in this Doctrine',
which led him in turn to understand 'how God did set me down in all the
things in Christ' (*GA*, pp. 37–40). Bunyan's seemingly ecstatic experience in

becoming 'inflamed' at this point 'with the sight, and joy, and communion of him, whose Head was crowned with Thorns' (*GA*, p. 40) thus comes through a much less spectacular but no less significant 'communion' with the Bedford congregation, 'those poor people' to whom Bunyan turns early on in his ordeals in order to 'break my mind' and 'tell them of my condition', and with whom he could witness John Gifford 'confer with others about the dealings of God with the Soul' (*GA*, p. 25).

We can see how the remarkable 'kind of Vision' that Bunyan recounts in *Grace Abounding* – in which he saw 'these poor people at *Bedford . . .* as if they were set on the Sunny side of some high Mountain' while he, 'shivering and shrinking in the cold', strove to join them by squeezing himself through 'a little door-way' in a 'wall' – is a poignant expression of the desire to be 'born again', as the spiritual language of 'new birth' dictates.[19] Yet it also fulfils a wish to be reborn specifically into this community: to be a part of rather than apart from it, and to be 'comforted with the light and heat of their Sun' (*GA*, pp. 19–20). Such passages serve as powerful reminders of how conversion in *Grace Abounding* is never far from convergence with others. For Bunyan, as for Christian and Hopeful in *The Pilgrim's Progress*, to convert is also to converse. The story *Grace Abounding* tells is, after all, perhaps no more than a detailed elaboration of the kind of account or 'confession of faith' that members of the Bedford congregation gave upon joining the church, and which Bunyan himself must have made in the early 1650s (see *MW*, XIII:453). Offering a spiritual autobiography – an oral, rather than a written account of conversion, detailing how one became convinced of saving faith – was a basic requirement of church membership in order for others 'to be satisfyed of the truth of the worke of grace in their heartes'.[20] The business of having to '*begin at the beginning of their conversion*', in other words, stood at the very basis on which '*Saints Fellowship*' was founded for Bunyan and his church.

Yet there are other reasons why *Grace Abounding* is especially motivated by '*Saints Fellowship*'. The book's 'Preface' makes it clear that Bunyan is offering his '*Relation of the work of God upon my own Soul*' to his '*Children*' so that '*if God will, others may be put in remembrance of what he hath done for their Souls, by reading his work upon me*' (*GA*, p. 2). Turning his most painful and personal experiences into a text upon which God's grace has become legible performs a key pastoral service: it ensures the congregation's '*further edifying and building up in Faith and Holiness*' while Bunyan is '*taken from you in presence, and so tied-up*' in prison, unable to '*perform that duty that from* God *doth lie upon me*'. In this sense, Bunyan's account of the converting self has been '*published*' for selfless reasons: '*if you are down in despair, if you think* God *fights against you, or if heaven is hid from your eyes*', Bunyan writes, even while incarcerated himself in a Restoration gaol, '*remember 'twas thus with your father*, but out of them all the Lord delivered me' (*GA*, pp. 2–3). As echoed in Hopeful's similar words of support for the despairing Christian in the dreadful dungeons of 'Doubting Castle', Bunyan's sustaining exhortation to *'remembrance'* resonates throughout the 'Preface' of *Grace Abounding*: '*Remember . . . the Word that first laid hold upon you; remember your terrours of conscience*' and '*remember also your tears and prayers to God*', and '*the Word, the Word . . . upon which the Lord hath caused you to hope*' (*GA*, p. 3).

Why Bunyan calls for such powerful acts of memory from his '*Children*' can be explained, to an extent, by the Puritan habit of recalling experiences of grace, as part of both church and indeed everyday life. But it can also be explained by political circumstance. Published in 1666, *Grace Abounding* appeared at a high point in the ongoing persecution of nonconformists during the first decade of the Restoration. Bunyan had already been in prison over five years when *Grace Abounding* appeared, the penal legislation against nonconformists – the 'Clarendon Code' – having come into full effect with the passing of the First Conventicle Act in 1664. With fellow church leaders being imprisoned, and with many members 'having in these troublous times withdrawne themselves from close walking with the Church', it must have seemed that the Bedford congregation was falling apart by the mid-1660s owing to the 'sore persecutions now come upon them'.[21] This context indicates why a Biblical typology of exile and of endurance resurfaces throughout the 'Preface' to *Grace Abounding*, with the Bedford congregation being likened to the Israelites during '*their forty years travel in the wilderness*' (*GA*, p. 2), and why too Bunyan concludes his conversion narrative with further accounts of his call to the ministry and of his experience of imprisonment. Yet this context also underscores why Bunyan published his spiritual autobiography right in the midst of these 'troublous times' of 'sore persecution': to comfort and to bind his church, presumably, against further disintegration and collapse through '*remembrance*' of grace. For ''*twas thus with your father*', as Bunyan puts it, 'but out of them all the Lord delivered me' (*GA*, p. 3). Far from being simply the confessions of a solitary, private 'I', then, *Grace Abounding* bespeaks a powerful spirit of solidarity – of '*Saints Fellowship*' – both for and with a community very much in the 'Wilderness' (*GA*, p. 4): for and with those, like Christian and Hopeful in *The Pilgrim's Progress*, very much on dangerous ground.

NOTES

1. U. Milo Kaufmann, '*The Pilgrim's Progress' and Traditions in Puritan Meditation* (New Haven and London: Yale University Press, 1966), p. 228. For an earlier version of Bunyan's conversion, see *MW*, II:156–9.

2. Roger Sharrock, 'Spiritual Autobiography: Bunyan's *Grace Abounding*', in Anne Laurence, W. R. Owens and Stuart Sim (eds.), *John Bunyan and his England, 1628–1688* (London and Ronceverte, W.Va.: Hambledon Press, 1990), pp. 97–104 (p. 99). See also Owen C. Watkins, *The Puritan Experience* (London: Routledge and Kegan Paul, 1972) and D. Bruce Hindmarsh, *The Evangelical Conversion Narrative: Spiritual Autobiography in Early Modern England* (Oxford University Press, 2005).

3. On Bunyan and Paul, see Rebecca S. Beal, '*Grace Abounding to the Chief of Sinners*: John Bunyan's Pauline Epistle', *SEL*, 21 (1981), 147–60.

4. Vincent Newey, ' "With the Eyes of My Understanding": Bunyan, Experience, and Acts of Interpretation', in Keeble (ed.), *Conventicle*, pp. 189–216 (p. 192).

5. Brian Cummings, *The Literary Culture of the Reformation: Grammar and Grace* (2002; Oxford University Press, 2007), pp. 370–1.

6. William James, *The Varieties of Religious Experience: A Study in Human Nature* (1902; London: Longmans, 1952), pp. 8–9, 23–5, 154.

7. On medical readings of *Grace Abounding* see Michael Davies, *Graceful Reading: Theology and Narrative in the Works of John Bunyan* (Oxford University Press, 2002), pp. 81–116, and Anne Dunan-Page, *Grace Overwhelming: John Bunyan, 'The Pilgrim's Progress', and the Extremes of the Baptist Mind* (Bern: Peter Lang, 2006), pp. 149–73.

8. Anna Trapnel, *Legacy for Saints* (1654), pp. 7–8.

9. Vavasour Powell, *Spiritual Experiences of Sundry Beleevers* (1653), p. ii, 'Preface'.

10. Cummings, *The Literary Culture of the Reformation*, p. 413.

11. *Ibid.*

12. See Roger Pooley, 'Language and Loyalty: Plain Style at the Restoration', *Literature and History*, 6.1 (1980), 2–18 and 'Plain and Simple: Bunyan and Style', in Keeble (ed.), *Conventicle*, pp. 91–110.

13. See Edmund S. Morgan, *Visible Saints: The History of a Puritan Idea* (New York University Press, 1963) and Patricia Caldwell, *The Puritan Conversion Narrative: The Beginnings of American Expression* (Cambridge University Press, 1983).

14. See further, Davies, *Graceful Reading*, pp. 81–174, and Pieter de Vries, *John Bunyan On the Order of Salvation*, trans. C. van Haaften (New York: Peter Lang, 1994).

15. Cummings, *The Literary Culture of the Reformation*, p. 378.

16. *Ibid.*, p. 388.

17. On Bunyan and predestination, see John Stachniewski, *The Persecutory Imagination: English Puritanism and the Literature of Despair* (Oxford: Clarendon Press, 1991), pp. 127–216. See also Davies, *Graceful Reading*, pp. 17–80.

18. Cummings, *The Literary Culture of the Reformation*, p. 63, and pp. 57–101 for a reading of Luther's conversion. See also Graham Ward, 'To Be a Reader: Bunyan's Struggle with the Language of Scripture in *Grace Abounding to the Chief of Sinners*', *Journal of Literature and Theology*, 4 (1990), 29–49.

19. On this episode, see chapter 4.

20. *The Minutes of the First Independent Church (now Bunyan Meeting) at Bedford, 1656–1766*, ed. H. G. Tibbutt (Bedfordshire Historical Record Society, 1976), p. 24.

21. *Ibid.*, pp. 38–9.

6

ROGER POOLEY

The Pilgrim's Progress and the line of allegory

Look at the title page of the first edition of *The Pilgrim's Progress* (1678), and one word stands out, in the largest typeface: 'DREAM.' The full title, with the fullness characteristic of early-modern books, runs as follows, with line breaks marked: 'THE/Pilgrim's Progress/FROM/THIS WORLD,/TO/That which is to come:/Delivered under the Similitude of a/DREAM/Wherein is Discovered,/The manner of his setting out,/His Dangerous Journey; And safe/Arrival at the Desired Countrey'. Between rules there is a quotation from the Old Testament prophet Hosea, '*I have used Similitudes*'; and then the author's name (*P'sP*, opposite p. xxxvi). So it is not strictly a dream, but the 'similitude' of a dream. The carefulness of the distinction, we might think, relates to Bunyan's need to be frank, even defensive, about the relationship between dreams and reality, not to mention the relationship between truth and fiction. However, when it comes to describing life as a passage 'From This World, To That which is to come', the criteria of truth, or of realism, that Bunyan is employing, need to be examined more closely. That there is a real world beyond this one is a more common view in the late seventeenth century than now, but how one got there, and what counted as reliable information about it, was more hotly disputed.

Dreams, it appears, give us a privileged entry into a world that is hidden to ordinary perception.[1] The way in which they are interpreted and explained has varied throughout history, of course, but the feeling that there is something special about dreams is equally widespread. The need to explain, or interpret them is something they share with allegories. Bunyan recounts a 'a Dream or Vision' of the poor Christian people of Bedford as a crucial episode early in his conversion experience in *Grace Abounding* (1666). Like Joseph interpreting Pharaoh's dreams in Genesis 41, Bunyan interprets his dream allegorically:

> Now, this Mountain and Wall, *&c.*, was thus made out to me; the Mountain signified the Church of the living God; the Sun that shone thereon, the comfortable shining of his mercifull face on them that were therein: the wall I thought was the Word that did make separation between the Christians and the world:

and the gap which was in this wall, I thought was Jesus Christ, who is the way to
God the Father.   (*GA*, p. 20)

There is an interesting mixture of the active and passive voice here. It seems as
though sometimes Bunyan indicates that he is receiving a reliable interpretation from the Holy Spirit ('was thus made out to me'). At others, he is relying
on his own thoughts ('the wall I thought was the Word'). The text betrays
little anxiety at the difference here, though the question of correct interpretation does occur at some points in the narrative.

The First Part of *The Pilgrim's Progress* is, in many ways, indebted to *Grace
Abounding*. It is an oversimplification to say that the First Part is a fictional,
allegorised and universalised version of Bunyan's conversion experience,
because, as we have seen, the visionary aspects of *Grace Abounding* are already
a pretext for allegorising. While the shape of Bunyan's conversion experience, as
he describes it in *Grace Abounding*, is closer to that of Hopeful than Christian's,
the psychological emphases are similar for both. So, for example, the Doubting
Castle episode is the longest time that Christian and his companion are out of the
Way; they are subject to Giant Despair's prison and cudgelling for a symbolic
three days before they remember the key of promise that gets them out. This
corresponds to the lengthier periods when Bunyan despaired of his salvation.
However, although they are cudgelled and fearful, the fictional pilgrims are not
destabilised in the way that Bunyan seems to have been for a time.

What needs stressing here is that the allegory contains both the dream
vision and a running commentary on what it means. The question of correct
interpretation is as important to the continuing impetus of the pilgrims'
journey as their reaction to clear and present danger. This is not unique to
allegorical narrative, but it is a common feature. Dante's pilgrim and
Spenser's questing knights are often tested most in their ability to recognise
what is really going on behind the appearances. Allegories do not just present
the vision and expect the reader to do all the work; rather, the work of
interpretation is shared between readers and characters.

In the introductory 'Author's *Apology*' Bunyan describes the genesis of *The
Pilgrim's Progress* as something that happened while he was writing something else:

> *. . . I writing of the Way*
> *And Race of Saints in this our Gospel-Day,*
> *Fell suddenly into an Allegory*
> *About their Journey, and the way to Glory,*
> *In more than twenty things, which I set down;*
> *This done, I twenty more had in my Crown,*
> *And they again began to multiply.*   (*P'sP*, p. 1)

One should always be sceptical of authors' descriptions of how they came to write books – and the *Apology* is already an uneasy defence of a Puritan fiction in the face of anticipated scepticism – but it is worth thinking why Bunyan should have 'fallen' into an allegory. It could just mean a happy accident, which, within Bunyan's way of looking at the world, could imply the providence of God. But, tucked behind the word, is something potentially more dangerous, a fall that might be connected to The Fall; and so it needs to be examined and tested.

Allegory is distinctive among the symbolic modes as being a mode of reading as much as a mode of composition. The history of allegory is not just that of its literary monuments – Dante's *Divine Comedy*, Orwell's *Animal Farm* (1945), and so on. It is also a history of reading, of finding hidden meanings in texts, and in so doing, bringing recalcitrant or heterodox texts into line. The medieval tradition of the 'Ovide moralisé', where the pagan gods of the *Metamorphoses* are allegorised into examples of Christian virtue and theology, is one example where allegorical reading is an act of theological and moral appropriation.[2] The link is that allegory, whether engaged in as reading or writing, is about making meaning – a meaning which is ideological, ethical or theological.

But what is a Protestant like Bunyan doing with allegory? After all, one of the earliest ways that Protestantism defined itself against Catholicism was in its manner of reading the Bible. In preferring the literal sense against the allegorical, Luther and Tyndale redefined the scriptures as plain texts for plain people without the need for a priestly caste to mediate and explain them for them. They didn't just translate the Bible into the vernacular German, or English; they insisted that the plain sense of the Bible was clear and available to anyone who could read. Bunyan is in a direct line of descent from that first wave of the Reformation – writing for the people in the vernacular, not Latin; presenting himself as an individual in direct contact with God's word; and following an aesthetic of plainness with an ethical, spiritual and even democratic motive. Bunyan had read about Tyndale in Foxe's *Actes and Monuments* (1563), the book that most influenced him after the Bible.[3]

The controversy between Tyndale and More, however, shows that the argument for the simplicity and accessibility of the Bible quickly becomes complex. Tyndale did not want to give the Bible back to the clergy for safe keeping. He accused the Catholic church of removing the literal sense altogether: 'the pope hath take[n] it cleane awaye'.[4] Tyndale is commenting here on the widely held fourfold analysis of the sense of scripture: literal, allegorical (especially where Old Testament events are revealed as a foreshadowing of events in the New), tropological (ethical meanings) and anagogical (the heavenly or eternal meanings). As Dante pointed out in his 1319 letter to his patron Can Grande della Scala, there is a sense in which this is really a twofold structure: 'although these mystical meanings are called by various names, they can in general all be said to be allegorical, since they differ from the literal or historic'.[5] Tyndale had agreed with that, and pointed out that the text actually offers allegorising, as when St Paul borrows 'a similitude, a figure or an allegory of Genesis to expresse the nature of the law and of the Gospell'.[6] He argues, however, that when scripture actually uses allegories, that becomes the literal sense: 'The scripture useth proverbes, similitudes, redels or allegories as all other speaches doo, but that which the proverbe, similitude, redell or allegory signifieth is ever the literall sence which thou must seke out dilgently.'[7] This also gets round the established view, that allegories prove nothing. So when Thomas More argues that 'Luther and Tyndale wolde have all allegoryes and all other senses taken awaye, sauynge the lytterall sense alone', he is oversimplifying their position.[8]

There are some parts of scripture that had attracted allegorical interpretation almost to the exclusion of a literal sense. This is particularly the case with the Song of Songs; as John King argues, 'the literalistic gospellers would have had great difficulty in accommodating the sensual language of the work to their principle of the plain simplicity of biblical truth'.[9] So a fresh version of the mystical reading of its erotic account of the lovers as an allegory of Christ and his church appeared in William Baldwin's verse translation, *Canticles or Balades of Solomon* (1549). Bunyan adapts this emphasis in his multiple references to the Song of Songs in the Second Part of *The Pilgrim's Progress*; there, Bunyan's vision of the pilgrim church adapting itself to women pilgrims adds force to the feminised image of the church as the bride of Christ in the allegorical readings of the book.

So, by the time Bunyan was writing, Protestant Christianity had come to an accommodation with allegory; so much so, that it might have appeared obvious to turn to its resources for composition as well as in reading and expounding the Bible. The line of Protestant allegory runs through high culture and popular culture alike. There is Edmund Spenser, whose *Faerie Queene* (1590–6) with its complex, layered allegory based on the Book of Revelation as much as Arthurian legend Bunyan was once thought to have read.[10] There is Richard Bernard, whose *The Isle of Man* was immensely popular from its first publication in 1626, and has affinities with some of the central allegorical devices of *The Holy War* (1680) as well as the journey motif of *The Pilgrim's Progress*; and there is the Leveller Richard Overton's *The Araignement of Mr Persecution* (1645), whose satiric portrait of a prejudiced jury may have suggested some of the names of the jury in Vanity Fair. Each of these combines the allegorical generality of abstract names standing for personal or spiritual qualities with some quite specific topical commentary.

The late seventeenth-century reader of prose fiction in English would have recognised, even expected, another aspect of allegory which has little relation to the arguments about literal and spiritual. The French term *roman à clef* is perhaps a more precise term. A number of fictions published around the time of *The Pilgrim's Progress* were allegories of recent events. *Theophania*, an anonymous royalist romance published in 1655, features a number of historical figures, according to a manuscript key in one surviving copy: the future Charles II as Alexandro, Prince William of Orange as Demetrius and so on.[11] Aphra Behn's *Love-Letters between a Nobleman and His Sister*, published in three parts 1684–7, is based on the scandalous affair of Ford, Lord Grey and his wife's sister Lady Henrietta Berkeley, which had come to trial in 1682. In Behn's epistolary novel Lord Grey appears as Philander and Lady Henrietta as Sylvia, and several other contemporaries are identifiable. The level of decoding that is involved in reading *Love-Letters* or *Theophania* is of a different sort from that demanded of a reader of Bunyan's or Bernard's allegories, for two reasons. The first is that there is no alternative, spiritual world that is beyond the immediate one – and Behn's fictional world is a very sensuous, this-worldly one. Even the scenes that take place in church have a sensuous quality. Still, there is a moral quality to the naming, and the crucial point is that many prose fictions of the later seventeenth century, not just overtly religious ones, present themselves as puzzles to be decoded.[12]

So would Bunyan's early readers have identified specific individuals, or simply types, behind his allegorical names? Very few of them, I suspect. For members of Bunyan's congregation there may have been some recognisable individuals, but Bunyan does not point to any nationally known figures. It is plausible to think that Evangelist might be a version of John Gifford, the first pastor of Bunyan's congregation, who was instrumental in his conversion, but it adds little to our understanding of the text, or indeed of Gifford. More likely is the parallel between Judge Hategood in Vanity Fair and Sir John Kelynge, the judge who passed sentence on Bunyan in 1661. Bunyan's account of the trial was not published until much later, in the eighteenth century, when his family discovered the manuscript of *A Relation of My Imprisonment* (1765); it is unlikely that a work so openly critical of an identifiable judge would have made it into print at the time. Hategood has some political resonance, as representative of the judiciary who took their revenge on the nonconformists they saw as responsible for the civil war. It is possible that there is more local reference than we can now know. Later in life, Bunyan became much better known in London, and he preached and delivered his manuscripts to his printers there. Of the wider circle that he would have encountered as he became a celebrity preacher, only the Welsh evangelist Vavasour Powell, a likely model for Valiant-for-Truth in the Second Part, is identifiable.

So then: allegorical reading, whether theological or topical, would have come relatively easily to Bunyan's readers in the 1670s and 1680s. It was an established line in Biblical reading, but also in the reading of fiction. With the bestseller success of the first part of *The Pilgrim's Progress*, and the publication three years later of Dryden's great political and Biblical allegory *Absalom and Achitophel* (1681), it becomes one of the dominant literary modes of the late Restoration.

However, allegory as a mode of composition has been the focus of critical and ideological attack more than once since Bunyan's time. First, during the Romantic period, it was regarded as a secondary, imaginatively inferior form of imagery to symbolism; and an inferior form of narrative fiction to realism. But some distinguished apologists in the twentieth century – G. K. Chesterton and Walter Benjamin for example – and then a renewed use of allegorical reading in Paul de Man, new historicism and postcolonialism, have moved it back into a central role, if not quite the dominant and prestigious one it had in Bunyan's time.[13]

However, there is now a renewed scepticism, from informed critics of Bunyan and his contemporaries, notably Thomas Luxon, Gordon Teskey and Brenda Machosky. In their different ways their criticisms stem from an opposition to the metaphysics of Christian allegory. Luxon most directly confronts the problem, as he sees it, 'that reality is a particularly problematic category in Christian discourses', and that 'allegory is a mode peculiarly suited to finessing the issue of the real'.[14] In doing so, he rewrites a popular division in literary discussions of Bunyan that, since Coleridge, has produced differentiated verdicts on Bunyan the product of the conventicle, of late Puritan theology (bad, or at least difficult to swallow for many) and Bunyan the literary artist (good, inspired, transcending his doctrinal narrowness). Readers of *The Pilgrim's Progress*, following this line, should not so much dismiss its allegory as inferior to Romantic symbolism or novelistic realism, but recognise that it is a way of making 'the world to come' more real, because more ultimately important, than 'this world'. There is a class of 'this-worldly' figures – Hold-the-World and Mr Worldly Wiseman most obviously – whose false religion is to hold on to the pleasures and rewards of this world. The implication must be that true reading exposes them and therefore, at least provisionally, the reader will need to share in Bunyan's metaphysics.

Naming, protest and politics

Clever, apposite and witty naming is essential to successful allegory, but it goes beyond that. It links Bunyan with a great English comic tradition. There seems to be nothing remarkable about the names of the true pilgrims – Christian,

Faithful and Hopeful – and their helpers, like Evangelist, Piety, Prudence and so on. However, when Ursula Vaughan Williams wrote the libretto for her husband's opera and cantata based on *The Pilgrim's Progress*, she changed Christian's name to Pilgrim, in a bid to make the work of more universal appeal. It's an interesting mistake.[15] Christian's original name, as we learn later, was Graceless, but as soon as he passes through the Wicket Gate on his way to the Celestial City, he has become Christian. The journey he takes is not that of an Everyman figure, but of an elect Christian. John Knott has pointed out that, while the title of Bunyan's book comes from Hebrews 11 ('strangers and pilgrims'), the real, overarching metaphor that drives the allegory comes from the Old Testament Book of Exodus, the flight from Egypt to the Promised Land.[16] Twice in the First Part this Biblical book surfaces explicitly: first, as Christian is deceived by Worldly Wiseman into taking the route of Law rather than Grace, and is frightened by the lightning coming from Mount Sinai; and again at the very end, when Christian and Faithful cross the river, not as Moses crossed the Red Sea, but as the Israelites crossed the Jordan into the Promised Land.

When it comes to Christian's enemies and false pilgrims, Bunyan's acerbic humour comes to the fore, especially when it is the turn of the hypocrites. There are Giants, and the fearsome devil Apollyon, who confront the pilgrims with the threat of violence and death. They are representative of twin threads in Bunyan's inspiration, Apollyon from the apocalyptic scriptures, the Giants from folk tale or heroic romance. But there are also the subtler threats posed by those who pretend to be pilgrims. Some of these false pilgrims are simply inadequate to the challenges. Pliable, who comes early in the journey to persuade Christian to return to the City of Destruction, is at first attracted by the Way, and even hurries Christian along in order to get to the Celestial City quicker. But he soon runs out of enthusiasm by the Slough of Despond, the first obstacle they meet. He loses his temper with Christian and storms off home (*P'sP*, p. 14). Later, when Christian meets Faithful, we hear more of the fate of Pliable. He has become a laughing-stock, even among those who '*despise the way that he forsook*' (*P'sP*, p. 67). Faithful comments, 'I think God has stired [*sic*] up even his enemies to hiss at him, and make him a Proverb, because he hath forsaken the way' (*P'sP*, p. 68). The marginal notes even tell us what the proverb is – Proverbs 15:10, 'Correction is grievous unto him that forsaketh the way.' Even the City of Destruction, in its hostility to the gospel way, acts out the truth.

Not everyone likes their name. By-ends, from the town of Fair-speech, says that his is a 'Nick-name that is given me by some that cannot abide me' (*P'sP*, p. 100). A by-end, according to the Oxford English Dictionary, is 'an object lying aside form the main one … especially a secret selfish purpose, a covert purpose of private advantage'; and the example it gives chronologically just before Bunyan's usage makes the pejorative nature quite clear: 'Tyranny consists in the arbitrary, immoderate, and by-ended exercise of power.' No wonder By-ends objects. After all, he comes from a very polite town, although it's not the kind of politeness Bunyan can respect: By-ends and his former schoolfellows, Mr Hold-the-World, Mr Money-Love and Mr Save-all, have all been taught 'the art of getting, either by violence, cousenage, flattery, lying or by putting on a guise of Religion' (*P'sP*, p. 101). Bunyan lets them condemn themselves out of their own mouths with their unstable mixture of godliness and self-interest: 'God sends sometimes Rain, and sometimes Sunshine', opines Mr Hold-the-world; 'if they be such fools to go through the first, yet let us be content to take fair weather along with us' (*P'sP*, p. 102). Christian and Faithful can have nothing to do with such fair-weather pilgrims, who are likely to compromise at the first sign of difficulty. Such would-be pilgrims also put reason on the same footing as religion, an aspect of Restoration conformist Christianity that Bunyan regarded as deeply suspect. Back in 1659 he had met Thomas Smith, keeper of the Cambridge University Library and Professor of Arabic, and disputed his claim that human learning, particularly the knowledge of formal logic, was essential for the understanding of scripture. Smith's objection to Bunyan's preaching was not just that he was unlearned; he was unlicensed, and 'the meanest of all the vulgar in the country'.[17]

There is an element of class hostility involved, too; although Bunyan became well connected in the City of London later (the Bunyan Meeting Museum has a fancy walking stick given to him by Sir John Shorter, a Lord Mayor), it was the local Bedfordshire gentry who had locked him up. James Turner has pointed out how many of the Giants that threaten Christian do so as the defenders of private property against trespassers.[18] On the other hand, Christ, in his incognito as Lord of the Hill, is a generous and protective landlord; and, as the pilgrims get closer to the Heavenly City, they experience his generosity more directly, in Beulah, for example. The name Beulah comes from the Old Testament prophet Isaiah, where he proclaims God's promise to Israel as follows: 'Thou shalt no more be termed Forsaken; neither shall thy land any more be called Desolate: but thou shalt be called Hephzibah, and thy land Beulah: for the Lord delighteth in thee, and thy land shall be married' (62:4). This is an interesting example of allegory within the Biblical text, where a change of name is a sign of transformation. As Christian leaves the Palace Beautiful, he is shown the delectable mountains in the distance, and is told 'it was *Immanuels Land*: and it is common, said they, as this *Hill* is to [*sic*], and for all the Pilgrims' (*P'sP*, p. 55). This takes the argument into political territory: God's land is common land, in opposition to the rapid growth of enclosure by private landlords in the sixteenth and seventeenth centuries. So, it would seem that many of Bunyan's Giants – Grim and Despair in particular – are representative of an oppressive and unchristian legal and property system. They do not simply represent 'spiritual', other-worldly realities.

The element of protest comes out most clearly in the Vanity Fair episode, which brings together Bunyan's protests at the extremes of the market economy, the persecution of nonconformist Christians and the social snobbery which informed it. Pickthank, the witness, whose name means currying favour, accuses Faithful in these terms: 'he hath railed on our noble Prince *Beelzebub*, and hath spoke contemptibly of his honourable Friends, whose names are the Lord *Old Man*, the Lord *Carnal delight*, the Lord *Luxurious*, the Lord *Desire of Vain-glory*, my old Lord *Lechery*, Sir *Having Greedy*, with all the rest of our Nobility' (*P'sP*, p. 94). As Bunyan's marginal note comments, '*Sins are all Lords and Great ones.*' Now of course there is a spiritual meaning to that; but Bunyan is echoing the warning against the rich and prestigious that he found in the Gospels. In that way the book becomes inescapably political.

Again, what hope of justice is there from this jury: 'Mr *Blind-man*, Mr *No-good*, Mr *Malice*, Mr *Love-lust*, Mr *Live-loose*, Mr *Heady*, Mr *High-mind*, Mr *Enmity*, Mr *Lyar*, Mr *Cruelty*, Mr *Hate-light*, and Mr *Implacable*' (*P'sP*, p. 96)? The effect of this cumulative name-calling energy would be humorous if they were not so resolved on the cruellest form of punishment for their victim – one that echoes Biblical accounts of persecution (Hebrews 11:35–7) as well as those in Foxe. Bunyan's revenge on his persecutors is to call them by their right names.

As a pastor, Bunyan is also compelled to call error by its right name as well, and this may not come over quite as sympathetically to modern readers. There is one particularly troubling case, of Ignorance, here. The hypocrites and the misleaders, from Pliable to Talkative, are easily dismissed. But what is Ignorance ignorant of, and why is he so culpable? Beth Lynch argues that the text shows signs of 'intense strain' at this juncture as Ignorance refuses the arguments of Christian and Hopeful while remaining convinced that he will receive God's mercy. Interestingly, he is less problematic for most explicitly Christian commentators: Barrie Horner sees the episode simply as 'a question as to whether justification is by an objective and complete work of Christ crucified ... or a subjective work taking place within the heart of man'.[19]

Structure

Part of the secret of the book's success is Bunyan's ability to exploit the potential of the journey structure. At one level it is quite rigid and unsubtle.

Everyone that Christian meets is there for the purpose of either hindering or forwarding his journey. No one is there simply for entertainment, or to add a reality effect. So the focus is on Christian's ability to judge who is friend and who is foe, sometimes aided by wise counsellors like Evangelist, sometimes misled by foolish or malicious figures like Worldly Wiseman. But within that rigidity of classification, there is a variety of function. I use the concept of 'function' rather than character here; partly because the notion of 'character' is not quite right for this kind of allegory, but also to signal my indebtedness to Vladimir Propp's groundbreaking formalist account of *The Morphology of the Folk-Tale* (1928). Propp pointed out that, in the Russian folk tale, it is more accurate to put character and action together, and call the resulting compound 'function', because character in the novelistic sense is of little or no interest, whereas certain key moves in the plot are. This takes some translating into the more expansive approach of *The Pilgrim's Progress*, but it fits an important subset of the allegorical figures, who are simply there to perform a function of opposition, or delay or testing. We do find that *The Pilgrim's Progress* follows much of the folk tale at a structural level, as well containing the kind of figures – Giants, the dragon-like Apollyon, or houses of refuge which contain mysterious messages, for example – that are common in what are loosely classified as fairy stories.[20]

The journey motif structures the narrative, then, but so do the moments of interruption. In the First Part these are of two sorts. The Interpreter's House and House Beautiful both function as places for rest and instruction. They provide something of the settled Christian community that Christian has been unable to find at home. In the Second Part, these resting places, such as the house of Gaius, extend the themes of community and hospitality that have become more central to the pilgrimage as Bunyan re-imagines it.

The sequel

The Life and Death of Mr Badman, published just two years later, is the first sequel to *The Pilgrim's Progress*. It depicts the passage from ordinary wrong-doing to shameless damnation, pretty much the opposite of Christian's journey, in a dialogue form that has allegorical elements. It didn't do as well; and there were a series of would-be sequels to the first part, cashing in on its bestseller status, but recognisably not by Bunyan. The best known was by the Baptist Thomas Sherman in 1682. Sherman makes no pretence to be Bunyan, and indeed writes in an ostensibly more polite and educated style. Bunyan does seem to have been protective of his authorship; a poem appended to *The Holy War* begins 'Some say the *Pilgrim's Progress* is not mine', and he proceeds to defend himself against accusations that he did not write it, or didn't write all of it (*HW*, p. 251). Eventually, eight years and several substantial books later, Bunyan brought out the Second Part, 'Wherein is set forth The manner of the setting out of *Christian's* Wife and Children, their Dangerous JOURNEY, AND Safe Arrival at the Desired Country'. In it Bunyan returns to the question asked by Charity in the House Beautiful in the first part, why Christian did not bring his wife and family with him on his journey (*P'sP*, pp. 50–1). No blame attaches to Christian. Christiana, however, begins her journey in repentance for not going with her husband, and as a result is not represented with an external burden.

In what ways does Christiana simply repeat her husband's journey? Does the sequel represent a development in Bunyan's work? And in what ways does it develop a distinctively feminine manner of pilgrimage? The marginal notes in the Second Part continually remind us, even more than the text itself, that Christiana and Mercy are retracing Christian's steps, but that the journey is different as a result of his having taken it. To begin with, they encounter a danger that Christian did not, from the Ill-favoured ones, whose disturbing designs on them are an indication that they cannot travel safely on their own. So Great-heart is appointed as their guide and guard. Whereas Evangelist in the First Part makes important but only occasional interventions to guide Christian, Great-heart is a pretty constant companion, a pastor rather than an evangelist. As they gather a travelling church around them, the emphasis shifts from the confrontation of enemies to the building up of a spiritual community – not that community, or rather companionship, is absent from the First Part, but the balance is quite different.

To what extent is this a feminine fiction?[21] The leadership of the group remains masculine, whether it is Christian's example, or Great-heart's and Valiant-for-Truth's battling. If the phrase 'played the man' is the constant refrain of Bunyan's description of Christian's battles, there seems no equivalent of 'playing the woman' on the spiritual battlefield of the Second Part. Bunyan may have been a radical in many ways, but not in gender politics. Still, the radicalism of the uneducated lay teacher of scripture, which Bunyan's own life and writings embody, does mean that there is a role for women in teaching their children and sharing their thoughts with fellow believers. When Prudence asks Christiana if she can catechise the children, the results are theologically very sophisticated (*P'sP*, pp. 222–6). She concludes by advising them, 'You must still harken to your Mother, for she can learn you more' (*P'sP*, p. 226). When it comes to edifying talk to children or adults, Bunyan's heroines have an intellectual structure for the beliefs and an unquestioned right to speak.

There is another aspect of the pilgrims in the Second Part which one might be tempted to call 'feminine', but one which is a theme of Bunyan's teaching from an early stage; and that is the theme of apparent weakness among believers. In Fearful, Ready-to-Halt and Much-Afraid we have pilgrims whose ability to deal with their own fears is limited but real. This, we might say, is the lighter side of Calvinism's doctrines of grace and election; these pilgrims are weak, and need constant support, but they are part of the elect band, and they cross the River at the end with impressive courage.

Brainerd Stranahan has argued that 'in the friendlier atmosphere of the Second Part, there is much less emphasis on the dreadful prospect of God's wrath'.[22] It is true that, even in the Valley of the Shadow, the pilgrims seem less threatened, and there is no equivalent of the way to Hell from the entrance to Heaven that Ignorance discovers at the end of Part 1. But there is, still, violence; Simple, Sloth and Presumption are hanged, and Giant Despair beheaded and his head set on a pike. The defensive violence of the pilgrims is less heroic, more like policing, in the Second Part.

The poetry

Bunyan began writing poetry in prison. Even his most devoted admirers find *Prison-Meditations* (1663) a little wooden, but by the time he came to write his masterpiece Bunyan had developed a facility in a couple of poetic forms that serve an important role in the way the book works on us. One was heroic couplets, the standard form for poetic argument in the later seventeenth century; and the other was ballad metre, a short stanzaic form that may have been familiar to Bunyan from the metrical psalters. (Bunyan's own gathered church did not sing hymns until after his death, but he visited and preached in churches that did.) Both Parts are prefaced with substantial verse introductions, explaining Bunyan's purpose, anticipating and answering objections. The 'Author's Apology' to the First Part is probably Bunyan's most sustained and successful poem, with its ringing conclusion:

> *Wouldest thou loose thy self, and catch no harm?*
> *And find thy self again without a charm?*
> *Woud'st read thy self, and read thou know'st not what*
> *And yet know whether thou are blest or not,*
> *By reading the same lines? O then come hither,*
> *And lay my Book, thy Head and Heart together.* (P'sP, p. 7)

Bunyan's book may work like other fictions in which readers might lose themselves; but knowing whether their eternal life is or isn't secure is a more unusual feature.

Just as important to the overall effect of the book are the poems (sometimes said to be sung) that pepper the action. They are sometimes a way of commenting on the action, sometimes an expression of emotion. To take a Biblical analogy, they function as some of the Psalms do, as a comment on the historical account of David in 1 Samuel, for example. One of the features of the book is the way it comments on and expounds the lessons to be learned from each encounter, not with an authorial voice, but through the perceptions of one of the main characters. What are the mistakes they have made? What is the true nature of the figure they have just encountered? Poetry releases the emotional tensions of the plot; but it has to be balanced by the unwavering commitment to godly discourse between the pilgrims which keeps them alert and judicious, even if it slows the narrative pace. We have to remember that the first line of the hymn based on the pilgrims' song should not be 'He who would valiant be' as it is in most hymn books, but 'Who would true valour see' (*P'sP*, p. 295);[23] truth and constancy are more important to the pilgrim than out and out bravery.

There is a second layer of poetry, the four lines under each of the illustrations that appeared in the sixth edition of the First Part, and that are there from the beginning in the Second Part. It is not completely clear that they are Bunyan's in the First Part, but there is no plausible alternative in the Second Part; and while they act mostly as captions, they do occasionally have an extra interpretative function.

Bunyan's text continues to be read in Christian as well as academic circles; new children's versions come out almost every year, and there is a steady stream of commentaries aimed, not at the student or academic reader, but at the Christian reader who wants to understand the doctrine, and live out the life. One suspects that Bunyan might have approved of that far more than of academic essays such as this. But he would have appreciated the irony: that the young, unlicensed evangelist who was once berated by a distinguished academic now is admitted on to the humanities syllabus and seen as an important figure in the development of allegory and prose fiction.

NOTES

1. Freud's *Interpretation of Dreams*, first published in 1900, is pivotal for modern understanding; but the practice of interpreting dreams goes back at least to the ancient Egyptians. Freud notes that in classical antiquity there was already a division between theological and psychological interpretations of dreams; *The Interpretation of Dreams*, trans. James Strachey (Harmondsworth: Penguin, 1976), pp. 58–9.

2. See 'Imposed Allegory', chapter 4 of Rosemond Tuve, *Allegorical Imagery* (Princeton University Press, 1966), pp. 215–34.

3. James Simpson, *Burning to Read* (Cambridge, Mass.: Belknap Press, 2007), pp. 108–10; for Bunyan and Foxe, see John R. Knott, *Discourses of Martyrdom in English Literature, 1563–1694* (Cambridge University Press, 1993), pp. 179–215 and Thomas S. Freeman, 'A Library in Three Volumes: Foxe's "Book of Martyrs" in the Writings of John Bunyan', *BS*, 5 (1994), 47–57.

4. William Tyndale, *The Obedie[n]ce of a Christen Man* (1528), sig. R1v.
5. Raman Selden (ed.), *The Theory of Criticism* (Harlow: Longman 1988), p. 292.
6. Tyndale, *The Obedie[n]ce*, sig. R4v.
7. *Ibid.*, sig. R2r.
8. Thomas More, *The Second Parte of the Co[n]futacion of Tyndals Answere* (1533), sig. H2r.
9. John N. King, *English Reformation Literature* (Princeton University Press, 1982), p. 368.
10. Harold Golder, 'Bunyan and Spenser', *PMLA*, 45 (1930), 216–37. Most of the parallels can be ascribed to Bunyan's self-confessed reading in prose chivalric romances.
11. *Theophania* (1655), ed. Renée Pigeon (Ottawa: Dovehouse, 1999). The key is reprinted on p. 66.
12. For a discussion of political allegorical romance in the period, see Paul Salzman, *English Prose Fiction, 1558–1700* (Oxford: Clarendon Press, 1985), chapter 11.
13. Walter Benjamin, *The Origin of German Tragic Drama*, 1963, trans. John Osborne (London: NLB, 1977), pp. 159–235; from the considerable recent literature on allegory, see particularly Angus Fletcher, *Allegory: The Theory of a Symbolic Mode* (Ithaca, N.Y.: Cornell University Press, 1964) and 'Allegory without Ideas', *Boundary* 2, 23.1 (2006), 77–98; Maureen Quilligan, *The Language of Allegory* (Ithaca, N.Y.: Cornell University Press, 1979); Carolynn van Dyke, *The Fiction of Truth* (Ithaca, N.Y.: Cornell University Press, 1985); John S. Pendergast, *Religion, Allegory and Literacy in Early Modern England* (Aldershot: Ashgate, 2006).
14. Thomas H. Luxon, *Literal Figures: Puritan Allegory and the Reformation Crisis in Representation* (University of Chicago Press, 1995), p. 159 and throughout; Gordon Teskey, *Allegory and Violence* (Ithaca, N.Y.: Cornell University Press, 1996); Brenda Machosky, 'Trope and Truth in *The Pilgrim's Progress*', *SEL*, 47.1 (2007), 179–98.
15. For a defence of the Vaughan Williams's approach, see Stan Meares, 'Vaughan Williams' *Pilgrim's Progress*', *Journal of the British Music Society*, 5 (1983), 1–26, itself answering the criticisms of Peter J. Pirie in *The English Musical Renaissance* (London: Victor Gollancz, 1979).
16. See John R. Knott, 'Bunyan's Gospel Day: A Reading of *The Pilgrim's Progress*', *ELH*, 3 (1973), 443–61.
17. See Greaves, *Glimpses*, pp. 121–3, and Thomas Smith, 'A Letter sent to Mr E. of Taft' in *The Quaker Disarm'd* (1659).
18. James Turner, 'Bunyan's Sense of Place', in Vincent Newey (ed.), *The Pilgrim's Progress: Critical and Historical Views* (Liverpool University Press, 1980), pp. 91–110 (esp. pp. 99–101).
19. Beth Lynch, *John Bunyan and the Language of Conviction* (Cambridge: D. S. Brewer, 2004), p. 95; Barrie E. Horner, *John Bunyan's 'Pilgrim's Progress': Themes and Issues* (Darlington: Evangelical Press, 2003), p. 109. For a full discussion and summary of the numerous commentaries on Ignorance, see Anne Dunan-Page, *Grace Overwhelming: John Bunyan, 'The Pilgrim's Progress' and the Extremes of the Baptist Mind* (Bern: Peter Lang, 2006), pp. 255–61.
20. See my 'The Structure of *The Pilgrim's Progress*', *Essays in Poetics*, 4.1 (1979), 59–70, which attempts a full Proppian analysis of Part 1, and Maxine Hancock,

'Folklore and Theology in the Structure and Narrative Strategies of *The Pilgrim's Progress*', BS, 9 (1999–2000), 9–24. For the 'function', see chapter 3 of Vladimir Propp, *Morphology of the Folktale* (1928), trans. Laurence Scott, 1958, 2nd rev. edn (Austin: University of Texas Press, 1990).

21. See Margaret Olofson Thickstun, *Fictions of the Feminine: Puritan Doctrine and the Representation of Women* (Ithaca, N.Y.: Cornell University Press, 1988); and Michael Austin, 'The Figural Logic of the Sequel and the Unity of *The Pilgrim's Progress*', SP, 102.4 (Fall 2005), 484–509.

22. Brainerd Stranahan, 'Bunyan's Satire and Its Biblical Sources', in Robert Collmer (ed.), *Bunyan in Our Time* (Kent, Ohio: Kent State University Press, 1989), pp. 35–60 (p. 57).

23. The words were modified in Percy Dearmer *et al.*, *The English Hymnal* (Oxford University Press, 1906).

7

STUART SIM

Bunyan and the early novel: *The Life and Death of Mr Badman*

The Pilgrim's Progress has played a critical role in the development of the English novel, and one need look no further than Daniel Defoe's *Robinson Crusoe* (1719) to see how it provided both structural and thematic inspiration for the early novelists. Anyone teaching a course on the rise of the novel will make this connection, emphasising the many correspondences that exist between the two works and tracing the line that leads, for example, from Giant Despair in *The Pilgrim's Progress* (1678) to Island Despair in *Robinson Crusoe*. Nonetheless, the point always needs to be made that *The Pilgrim's Progress* is not a novel, and that its allegorical nature aligns it with an earlier tradition of prose fiction than Defoe's. As Ian Watt would say, it lacks 'formal realism': the patina of circumstantial and referential detail that distinguishes Defoe from his immediate literary predecessors, helping to establish what we now generally think of as the 'early novel'.[1] Bunyan's landscape is not Defoe's real world where a protagonist can make his way from York to London, and ultimately to North Africa, Brazil and the Caribbean, rather than from the City of Destruction to the Celestial City by way of the Valley of the Shadow of Death and Vanity Fair (even if Bunyan clearly drew on his knowledge of the Bedfordshire countryside and London to construct that landscape).

To identify a lack of novelistic realism is not to denigrate *The Pilgrim's Progress*, which stands as one of the greatest works of English and indeed of world literature. Far more than a proto-novel, it has provided inspiration for generations of readers through the years in their own struggles against adversity and repressive authority. Yet the sheer success of *The Pilgrim's Progress*, both in literary and social terms, has overshadowed Bunyan's other fiction and narrowed modern appreciation of his range as a literary technician. (His autobiography, *Grace Abounding to the Chief of Sinners* (1666), is the text that tends to attract most interest today, after his allegory.) *The Life and Death of Mr Badman* (1680) is a case in point. Here is a work that invites reappraisal in terms of the novel and deserves to be read as more than a counter-*Pilgrim's Progress*, as the author presents it. The narrative is cast in the form of a dialogue between two devout Christians, Wiseman and Attentive, with the former telling the story of Badman's sinful life from childhood through to death. Badman's questionable morals – his thievery, cheating, sexual infidelity, drunkenness, and so on – are interpreted as those of a character predestined for Hell rather than Heaven.[2] This is the progress of an anti-Christian.

Some commentators have taken the work purely as the author intended, only to find it disappointing. Christopher Hill argues that 'in relating the life of a man predestined to eternal damnation there is no struggle, no conflict, no suspense', and for Monica Furlong Badman 'moves like a tram along the rails of Calvinistic fatalism, and this makes him seem an improbable human being'.[3] I would wish to broaden these readings. *The Life and Death of Mr Badman* represents an extension of the author's technique and is the closest that Bunyan comes to the novel form and the realism that is one of the defining features of its earliest practitioners. Yet it also goes beyond mere realism to demonstrate some of the novel's potential for psychological complexity, narrative tension and social critique, revealing an author concerned to engage with the ideological conflicts of his world in a more direct fashion than his earlier allegorical style would allow.[4] The extent to which we can draw Bunyan more fully into the novel tradition will now be explored.

The Life and Death of Mr Badman and the 'Death of the Author'

The Life and Death of Mr. Badman's novelistic qualities have been recognised before, if not perhaps developed very far. Although Roger Sharrock boldly calls it a novel and 'a cautionary tale of middle-class commercial life in a provincial town', he does not consider it to be a particularly successful example of the genre for 'its merits may have been exaggerated by the enthusiasts of realism'.[5] In their edition, James F. Forrest and Roger Sharrock refer to the work as less of a sequel to *The Pilgrim's Progress* than 'a Puritan rogue novel', a designation that is worth opening out (*LDB*, p. v). As far back as 1880, J. A. Froude praised the work's 'picture of English life in a provincial town', and concluded that '[t]he drawing is so good, the details so minute, the conception so unexaggerated, that we are disposed to believe that we must have a real history before us'.[6] Mr Badman may have an allegory-style name, and the narrators of his career, Wiseman and Attentive, allegorical roles in acting as the judges of his fate, but as Froude's assessment indicates, Badman moves in a convincingly depicted urban world of the seventeenth century, peopled by characters who would not be out of place in a formal realist novel. There are, for example, his ineffective and despairing father, his put-upon first wife and sharp-tongued second wife, as well as his riotous drinking companions. Badman is of his time in a sense that Christian is not (or only with much allegorical interpretation).

Intriguingly enough, and very much against the grain of Bunyan's intentions, Badman turns into a fascinating character who at times is even capable of inspiring sympathy in his audience, his villainy nowithstanding. He cuts a rather sad figure in his relationship with his second wife, even if it is a case of just deserts for his earlier extremely selfish conduct towards his first. Viewed from a twenty-first-century perspective, life for such an energetic and gregarious individual in the hidebound society of mid to late seventeenth-century provincial England must have been difficult. Badman is an uncompromisingly secular figure in a world still largely ruled by religious principles that could lead to an attitude of smugness in the devout (as exhibited memorably by Wiseman, one of his neighbours, and Attentive), and he has no other use for religion than to deploy it to trick his first wife into marriage. Thereafter, as Wiseman's splendidly colloquial phrase so succinctly says, Badman 'hangs his Religion upon the hedge' and resumes his old way of licentious living (*LDB*, p. 69). We can even note the 'Death of the Author' in the work as Badman escapes his creator's control in the manner we have come to expect from fictional characters.[7] Readers today are unlikely to see him in quite the one-dimensional manner of Wiseman and Attentive, and will wish to make up their own minds about his character rather than be forced into summary judgement based on a particularly unforgiving theology.

As Forrest and Sharrock have suggested, Badman is in fact a classic case of the picaro figure that comes to be so prominent in the early novel: a character living by his wits, challenging the social and moral conventions of his time in order to gain wealth and advantage (*LDB*, pp. xxvi–xxx). It is a characteristic of picaros that their behaviour is often reprehensible, and sometimes downright illegal, but still gains the sympathy of their reading audience as they turn into 'lovable rogues' whose adventures are as likely to draw a smile as a reproof. This pattern is repeated over and again in novels from *Crusoe* through *Moll Flanders* (1722) to *Tom Jones* (1749) and so on to many others in later eighteenth-century fiction. Bunyan, knowingly or otherwise, is flirting with the picaresque, although he tries his best to confine it within very tight boundaries. There is certainly no desire on his part for Badman to blossom into a lovable rogue whose escapades the audience will come to applaud. Wiseman and Attentive mark out those boundaries, and it is worth subjecting their roles in the narrative to close scrutiny.

Wiseman and Attentive are discussing Badman's career in retrospect, and they strive from the outset to give it the worst possible interpretation. They repeatedly declare that Badman had all the hallmarks of a damned sinner from birth ('from a Child he was very *bad*: his very beginning was *ominous*, and presaged that no good end, was, in likelyhood, to follow thereupon' (*LDB*, p. 17)), and that his career gives a terrible example of how reprobation becomes manifest and a warning of the horrors awaiting the unrepentant. There is never a sense in Calvinism that good works alone ensure salvation, for that requires unconditional faith from the believer and an unbidden extension of God's grace which no sinner deserves; but a steady stream of bad works offers the opportunity to measure one's own conduct against what is almost undoubtedly collectively a sign of reprobation. Almost undoubtedly, but the small possibility that it may not be so is what moves the narrative away from mere polemic to the world of the novel where such certainties no longer hold sway, and narrators cannot guarantee that their own verdict on the fate of the narrative's characters will satisfy all their readers. In Badman's case, doubts do eventually emerge.

Surprisingly enough, Badman dies an easy death that his narrators struggle to accommodate to their rigidly moralistic scheme wherein one is either unmistakably saved or damned. One's life reveals which of the two states one is destined for: to be a candidate for election or for reprobation, as writers of the period described it. Lives can be 'read' in this respect, and the signs are taken to reveal ultimate spiritual status. Everything about Badman's life seems to point unequivocally towards damnation, except for his death. Wiseman reports that 'Mr *Badman* died like a Lamb, or as they call it, like a *Chrisom* child, quietly and without fear' (*LDB*, pp. 165–6), which forces him into a tortuous round of reasoning to uphold the sentence of reprobation he passed on Badman at the very start of the narrative. He insists that an easy death cannot be interpreted as a sign of God's favour if a sinner dies without recognising the enormity of his sins. That merely constitutes lack of insight, since at such a critical juncture he or she should be racked with guilt and be desperate for God to show mercy. This leaves an interesting loose end in the narrative, and the semiotics seem counter-intuitive; it would make more sense for God to use Badman's death to give a stern warning to others what might be in store for them. Wiseman has to concede that '[h]e that dies quietly, suddenly, or under consternation of spirit, may goe to Heaven, or may goe to Hell; no man can tell whither a man goes, by *any such* manner of death' (*LDB*, p. 157), which seems to leave the matter tantalisingly open. Such an admission positively invites debate as to Badman's fate, which is surely the last thing the author would have wanted. The lack of absolute closure on the issue, for all Wiseman's strident rhetorical efforts, has the effect of making the work seem more modern than the author's other fiction – a point to which we shall return later.

It is the role of Wiseman and Attentive to demonstrate the certainty of Badman's reprobation, and the former in particular is adamant that this is the only conclusion one can reach from the progress of his sin-laden career: 'He died that he might die, he went from Life to Death, and then from Death to Death, from Death Natural to death Eternal' (*LDB*, p. 14). Wiseman makes this point in the very early stages of the dialogue, hoping to preclude any identification with Badman and his ways as the sorry tale of his life unfolds. Wiseman then proceeds to engage in an exhaustive investigation of Badman's actions that his convictions tell him can only be read as signs of eventual damnation.

Badman's world

I have said that Badman inhabits a realistically portrayed seventeenth-century urban milieu. How does this manifest itself? His apprenticeship establishes him in a world that a contemporary reader would have found familiar, and the details of apprentice life ring true. They are such escapades as we would expect from high-spirited young men in such a station of life: drinking, swearing, chasing the opposite sex and generally reacting against the strictures of their subordinate position in society. Badman already has a record of mischievous behaviour behind him in childhood as a thief: 'He took at last great pleasure in robbing of Gardens and Orchards; and as he grew up, to steal Pullen from the Neighbourhood' (*LDB*, p. 21). He rapidly develops into a determined rebel, consorting with villains in taverns and stealing from his master to finance his secret jaunts. There is a strong sense of the period's underworld, with Badman finding this very attractive as an antidote to the servile existence required of him as a bound apprentice. Set up in business by his long-suffering father, Badman soon squanders the money on a debauched lifestyle involving wild nights out in local inns and houses of ill repute with like-minded acquaintances. Throughout his life, Badman will be the enemy of convention, a dissident figure in a strait-laced society: someone who perhaps, as Anne Dunan-Page has suggested, 'fails to mature in both body and spirit', and whose 'extended youth consequently draws Bunyan into a rhetoric of excess'.[8]

Yet if there is a sense of realism in *The Life and Death of Mr Badman*, it has its limitations. There is not the wealth of detail that Watt saw as so characteristic of Defoe and the early novelists (one remembers how carefully Crusoe itemises everything he removes from the wreck of his ship once he is marooned on his island), and there is little physical description of either characters or landscape. Bunyan says that Badman, in wooing his first wife, 'was tall, and fair, and had plain, but very good Cloaths on his back' (*LDB*, p. 66), but that is virtually all we learn about his appearance. His first wife's character as a sincere believer, meek and submissive to her husband in the approved fashion of the time, is well represented, but her appearance remains undefined. As to his second wife, Bunyan mentions her temper, her sexual infidelities and her generally unsavoury character, but her appearance goes unremarked as well. Neither does Bunyan describe the nature of Badman's business, save that it involves weights and measures, thus giving him the opportunity to cheat his customers, a matter of more interest to his author. Badman is a merchant of some kind, but once again the details are scarce in a way they would not be in Defoe and his successors. Crusoe's obsessive listing of his possessions, and Roxana's of her growing wealth, are in sharp contrast to Bunyan's spare rendering of Badman's world, although nowadays we do not expect that degree of detail from every novelist, and have extensive experience of such a minimalist approach, as in the work of Samuel Beckett, for example. What is more, realism is no longer taken to be the defining feature of the novel – not with three centuries of stylistic experiment between the modern reader and the form's early practitioners. *The Life and Death of Mr Badman* need not be compared only with the formal realist school that was so soon to become the norm in prose fiction.

There is, however, a strong sense of psychological realism in the presentation of Badman's character and the way it develops, from the high spirits of youth to the slyness and cunning of the adult always in want of extra money to fund his profligate manner of living.

Character development

Development of character, particularly in the case of the protagonist, has long been expected from the novel. Christian is a more assertive and self-confident character in the latter scenes of *The Pilgrim's Progress* than he is in the work's early stages, when anxiety and fearfulness all but overwhelm him on occasion (as when he is bogged down in the Slough of Despond), but allegory rarely explores its characters' psychology in much detail, except rather obliquely, and Christian's motivation beyond his desire for salvation goes largely unexamined. Badman's motivation, on the other hand, proceeds from attributes that are only too human and universal, such as greed and envy, potentially present in everyone, at least to some degree. Badman is the unacceptable face of the new capitalist order, always looking for ways to short-change his customers or creditors, and untroubled by the immorality of his methods of maintaining a regular cash-flow. He makes it a practice to feign bankruptcy on several occasions, for example, after borrowing heavily, and when his creditors reluctantly accept a reduced settlement of their debts, Badman then becomes 'a better man than when he shut up Shop, by several thousands of pounds' (*LDB*, p. 89). The end manifestly justifies the means for this 'embodiment of *homo economicus*', as he has been dubbed.[9]

Badman's character is sharply observed in terms of the psychology of evil. Most modern readers will probably take a more indulgent view of his youthful conduct than Wiseman and Attentive, but it is easy to see how his increasingly debauched manner of life, with its clear indications of alcoholism and sexual addiction, brings out the very worst in his nature. We may not applaud his actions, but we can understand them. Badman's desperation to uphold his way of life leads him ever more deeply into criminal activity of a depressingly familiar kind. He is not the only one who has found it expedient to run down a company in order to make off with the proceeds for his own use: there are many of his kind still left in our own world where fortunes can be made by asset-stripping and dubious deals on the world's stock markets. The reader may even begin to feel some sympathy for a character so obviously ruled by his addictions, which can only lead him into a downward spiral. Throughout his life, Badman is in the grip of drives which he seems unable to control, and which leave him poised almost permanently on the verge of social disgrace and physical decline.

Badman, spiritual autobiography and the novel

Spiritual autobiography left a strong imprint on the early novel, and Bunyan is one of the key sources for this in the form of *The Pilgrim's Progress* and *Grace Abounding to The Chief of Sinners*, the latter providing the narrative structure for the former. As these two works demonstrate, spiritual autobiography charts an individual's progress to a state of grace, marked in the first instance by his 'conversion', the intense inner realisation that he is after all destined for salvation despite a sinful past that is in some measure universal, since all human beings are stained with the sin of Adam. This is symbolised in *The Pilgrim's Progress* by the burden falling from Christian's back at the sight of Christ on the cross on a hill up ahead, and then by a heavenly messenger's subsequent award of a scroll sanctioning his entry into the Celestial City. But spiritual autobiography has its drawbacks as a scheme for narrative structure, as its first major novelistic proponent, Defoe, was soon to discover. There is something too neat about the 'success story' arc of spiritual autobiography, with its predetermined end, that can rob the narrative of tension, and without tension novels lose much of their interest and may miss their objective to transcend the merely polemical. Defoe uses spiritual autobiography as the basis for most of his narrative structures, but the religious sincerity of characters such as Crusoe or Moll is always surrounded by an uncertainty whether they are as devout as they claim, or whether they are pragmatists appropriating the conventions of the conversion narrative to present themselves in the most sympathetic light to their audience (and perhaps deluding themselves into the bargain?).

The Life and Death of Mr Badman, as Forrest and Sharrock observe, draws heavily on the tradition of judgement narratives (such as Samuel Clarke's

A Mirrour Or Looking-Glass To Both Saints And Sinners (1671), which provides a ready source of examples for Wiseman throughout the dialogue), which leads the book away from the spiritual autobiography to which Bunyan's other fictional works owe allegiance – *The Holy War* no less than both parts of *The Pilgrim's Progress*.[10] Badman is held up for judgement and given few of the redeeming features that might attract sympathy, such as a sense of true repentance when misfortune strikes. When he injures his leg in a fall from a horse (while returning home, very typically, drunk), he appears to turn to God in his distress, but 'when his pain was gone, and he had got hopes of mending, even before he could go abroad, he cast off prayer, and began his old game; to wit, to be as bad as he was before' (*LDB*, p. 132). A later bout of sickness seems to have a more profound effect on his character; fears of imminent damnation give him feelings of remorse about his treatment of his wife, so that upon his recovery 'his wife and her good friends stand gaping to see Mr *Badman* fulfil his promise of becoming new towards God, and loving to his wife' (*LDB*, p. 138). Predictably, this conversion does not last either, and Badman has soon '*returned with the Dog to his Vomit, to his old courses again*' (*LDB*, p. 140). Clearly, this is someone who cannot appreciate the error of his ways, and is incapable of altering his conduct for the better in the long term. In a sense *The Life and Death of Mr Badman* prefigures *Roxana* (1724), traditionally considered Defoe's most problematic narrative, where the author uses the framework of spiritual autobiography without the conversion to signal how the reader should respond to the heroine's actions. Here once again is a character that only experiences remorse in times of adversity and returns to her 'old courses' as soon as trouble passes. Perhaps *Roxana* should be read as a judgement narrative: as Defoe's *Badwoman*?

Today, readers are accustomed to novels in all shapes and sizes; one of the novel's great strengths as a literary practice is this ability to transform itself and discover new methods of constructing a narrative. It is far easier to approach *The Life and Death of Mr Badman* as a novel now than in the days when the form was still being invented. Failure to conform to the conventions of the conversion narrative poses no problem for the present-day reader, who no longer expects novels to have such a set pattern and is more interested in the psychological complexities of the human relationships in the narrative than the spiritual status of fictional characters. There is a 'fascination', as Richard L. Greaves has observed, in following the dealings of a character 'whose life represents the triumph of human nature's darker side'.[11]

Wiseman and Attentive as social critics

It is easy to regard Badman as the centre of the narrative, but the main characters are actually Wiseman and Attentive, whose dialogue constitutes the whole of the text. To what extent can their exchanges be considered novelistic? They share a somewhat Calvinist outlook, bemoaning 'the badness *of the times*' (*LDB*, p. 13) and showing little sympathy for the sinner. Attentive acts as the chorus for Wiseman's weighty judgements, but he is more than a mere foil, and during the narrative interesting differences begin to emerge between the two acquaintances that serve to endow them with distinct identities. (Not everyone is convinced of this; Sharrock complains that 'the differentiation of the two speakers is not pursued very far'.[12]) Wiseman is given to digression and verbosity which Attentive finds irritating, informing his friend at one point that '*it pleases me to hear a great deal in few words*' (*LDB*, p. 100) and complaining at another, '*now I have heard enough of* Mr Badmans *naughtiness, pray now proceed to his Death*' (*LDB*, p. 117). Wiseman, however, is not to be deflected from his purpose, and continues remorselessly to enumerate Badman's many sins: 'Why Sir, the Sun is not so low, we have yet three hours to night' (*LDB*, p. 117). One might also excuse Wiseman's storytelling method on the grounds that, *pace* Hill and Furlong, it creates a sense of expectation with the reader becoming just as eager as Attentive to be given the full details of an event that has immense import, as Wiseman states at the very beginning: 'I was there when he died: But I desire not to see another such man (while I live) die in such sort as he did' (*LDB*, p. 16).[13] Badman's death looms over the whole narrative, although it proves to be a more problematic affair than Wiseman has been insisting.

Wiseman seems to have a limitless supply of cautionary tales, often of a gory and distinctly unpleasant nature that can indeed be 'troubling to a modern reader'.[14] There are assorted suicides by despairing sinners (including one man who disembowels himself with a razor) and persons struck down by God for taking his name in vain or committing adultery. As a result, he appears mean-spirited and more than somewhat pompous, but one should remember that he is a moralist. His faith is deep and sincere. Like the mature Christian, he is truly appalled at the depth of the world's wickedness and feels compelled to broadcast this: ''Tis a folly to look for good dayes, so long as sin is so high, and those that study its nourishment so many' (*LDB*, p. 13). He struggles to accept a world in a process of dramatic change: Restoration England with its dislike of religious enthusiasm and the nonconformist outlook, a society in which the ruling classes are once again pursuing a hedonistic lifestyle that is anathema to Puritans who had tried to banish this from the nation during the days of the Commonwealth. Individuals like Wiseman and Attentive are becoming increasingly beleaguered in such a setting with its more secular orientation, and in truth they communicate a sense of impotence in their railing against a world where, as the Author's Preface puts it: '*Mr* Badman *has left many of his Relations behind him; yea, the very World is overspread with his Kindred. True, some of his Relations, as he, are gone to their place, and long home, but thousands of thousands are left behind; as Brothers, Sisters, Cousens, Nephews, besides innumerable of his Friends and Associates'* (*LDB*, pp. 1–2). Marooned as they are in this unpromising context, Wiseman and Attentive have every reason to bewail the direction in which their world is moving. They represent an older, more spiritual culture where conduct was judged against the loftiest religious principles, and salvation was assumed to be the individual's paramount concern. Badman is an insult to their beliefs and they can only condemn him in the harshest possible terms, particularly since (as they admit) he seems to be the face of the future with 'thousands of thousands' of his 'Relations' and 'Kindred' apparently flourishing around them.

This sense of a society in a transition is one with a powerful appeal to novelists, for it produces a clash of convictions that can be productively explored. The author's claim that *'wickedness like a flood is like to drown our English world'* (*LDB*, p. 7) gives a dramatic edge to what is eventually a tale of incommensurable world orders. While this is rooted in the particularity of the Restoration settlement and the political defeat of the nonconformist cause, it continues to speak to later generations as a situation in which almost anyone can find themselves caught at some point in their lives. Stripped of the allegorical trappings of *The Pilgrim's Progress*, the narrative of *The Life and Death of Mr Badman* becomes all the more eloquent in its outline of a recurrent human dilemma that can leave the individual feeling extremely vulnerable and alienated.

Bunyan and the novel

Bunyan's 'Puritan rogue novel' deserves to be brought out from under the shadow of *The Pilgrim's Progress* and treated on its own considerable merits. In *The Life and Death of Mr Badman*, Bunyan successfully opens out the judgement narrative and makes it responsive to a rapidly changing world order, demonstrating a significant extension of his fictional technique in the process. The book transcends the rigidity of the author's ideological scheme to become a very revealing picture of a society in political and social transition, and it is not unreasonable to discuss it in terms of later developments in the novel tradition since that is a situation numerous novelists have been eager to exploit.

One of the ways that Bunyan most resembles more recent novel writing is in the series of unresolved tensions in the text that leave the reader with much to ponder afterwards. Try as he might, Wiseman never satisfactorily explains Badman's easy death, and the contradictions of his position become plain in consequence. Is Badman quite as bad as he is being painted, one may begin to wonder? Or is his vilification really inspired by his lack of religious enthusiasm: an enthusiasm that appears to be going into sharp decline in his society? Can one really be so sure, with Wiseman, that Badman's death is a clear sign of his reprobation? Most readers today will surely think this question open to many different answers, and might be more inclined to see Wiseman's convoluted reasoning on this count as an indictment of a nonconformist conviction which lacks compassion for human weakness. If Badman's death had been a difficult one instead, that circumstance would surely also have been read by Wiseman as evidence of reprobation, indicating the harshness of the underlying theology. To prove just how uncompromising this theology could be, it seems that even a show of remorse on the deathbed would have availed Badman little; Attentive remarks dismissively that '*Sickbed Repentance is seldom good for any thing*' (*LDB*, p. 139), and this despite Wiseman's insistence that the want of repentance at 'the very last' (*LDB*, p. 162) is the definitive sign of Badman's damnation. From a nonconformist standpoint, Badman simply cannot win. Whatever he does, and however he reacts to situations, he will betray that he is a reprobate.

Given their commitment to a predestinarian scheme on Calvinist lines, it is not surprising that Wiseman and Attentive argue that Badman came into the world 'notoriously infected with Original corruption' and '*Indwelling sin*' (*LDB*, p. 17). The summary judgement will not persuade the vast majority of modern readers, however (although it might still succeed with a confirmed genetic determinist). As presented by his judges, Badman is an unpleasant character, but modern readers are less likely to view this as a sign of damnation and more inclined to see it as open to interpretation, even coming to regard Badman as more to be pitied for his addictive personality than condemned for his vice. We learn more about Wiseman and Attentive from their verdict than about Badman's soteriological position, and their beliefs are explored to deliver a powerful piece of social criticism that exposes the internal divisions in Restoration society. The person of Badman gathers all the traits that the nonconformist community so despised in the new social order: immorality, loose living, lack of religious conviction, a want of probity in business, self-interested behaviour, greed and a general obsession with material wealth and sensual pleasures. While *The Pilgrim's Progress* works as social criticism too, its allegorical framework prevents it from being as forceful and unambiguous as *The Life and Death of Mr Badman*, which prefigures what was soon to become one of the most significant concerns of novelists.

The Life and Death of Mr Badman is a fascinating exploration of evil, and the protagonist a more complex character in this respect than his judges are willing to allow. The psychology of evil has long exerted a fascination for novelists, as the current popularity of crime fiction alone would prove, and Bunyan's work deserves to take its place in that category and to be put in dialogue with more recent contributions. In that sense, too, Bunyan reaches out well beyond the formal realist school to take his place in the wider tradition of the novel.

NOTES

1. Ian Watt, *The Rise of the Novel* (London: Chatto and Windus, 1957).
2. For the role played by the dialogue form in the culture of the period, see Timothy Dykstal, *The Luxury of Skepticism: Politics, Philosophy and Dialogue in the English Public Sphere, 1660–1740* (Charlottesville: University of Virginia Press, 2001).
3. Hill, *Turbulent*, p. 231; Monica Furlong, *Puritan's Progress: A Study of John Bunyan* (London: Hodder and Stoughton, 1975), p. 127. For Michael Davies, however, it is the doctrinal aspect that seems most admirable about Bunyan's work. Thus his reference to the author's 'safeguarding of doctrine over and above narrative interest alone in *Badman*', Michael Davies, *Graceful Reading: Theology and Narrative in the Works of John Bunyan* (Oxford University Press, 2002), p. 303.
4. I discuss those contradictions in more detail in 'Isolating the Reprobate: Paradox as a Strategy for Social Critique in Bunyan's Mr Badman', BS, 1 (1988–9), 30–41.
5. Roger Sharrock, *John Bunyan* (1954; 2nd rev. edn, London: Macmillan, 1968), pp. 108, 117. The narrative's debt to a tradition of such 'cautionary tales' is emphasised in Maurice Hussey, 'John Bunyan and the Books of God's Judgements: A Study of *The Life and Death of Mr. Badman*', *English*, 7 (1948–9), 165–7, and James G. Randall, 'Against the Backdrop of Eternity: Narrative and the Negative Casuistry of John Bunyan's *The Life and Death of Mr Badman*', BQ, 37 (1994), 347–59.
6. J. A. Froude, *Bunyan* (London: Macmillan, 1880), p. 112.
7. Roland Barthes, 'The Death of the Author', in *Image Music Text*, trans. and ed. Stephen Heath (London: Fontana, 1977), pp. 142–8.
8. Anne Dunan-Page, '*The Life and Death of Mr. Badman* as a "Compassionate Counsel To All Young Men": John Bunyan and the Nonconformist Writings on Youth', BS, 9 (1999–2000), 50–68 (p. 52).
9. David Hawkes, 'Master of His Ways? Determinism and the Market in *The Life and Death of Mr Badman*', in N. H. Keeble (ed.), *John Bunyan: Reading Dissenting Writing* (Bern: Peter Lang, 2002), pp. 211–30 (p. 214).
10. For a discussion of Bunyan's use of judgement stories, see Anne Dunan-Page, 'Le châtiment de Dorothy Mately: mise en livre des histoires de jugement', *Bulletin de la Société d'Études Anglo-Américaines des XVIIe et XVIIIe siècles*, 50 (June 2000), 31–50.
11. Greaves, *Glimpses*, p. 377.
12. Sharrock, *John Bunyan*, p. 113.
13. Beth Lynch also finds 'an element of suspense' in the handling of Badman's death throughout the narrative; *John Bunyan and the Language of Conviction* (Cambridge : D. S. Brewer, 2004), p. 107.
14. Roger Pooley, '*The Life and Death of Mr. Badman* and Seventeenth-Century Discourses of Atheism', in Keeble (ed.), *Reading Dissenting Writing*, pp. 199–210 (p. 206).

8

DAVID WALKER

Militant religion and politics in
The Holy War

In the introduction to their seminal edition of *The Holy War* (1682) Roger Sharrock and James Forrest identify a softening of Bunyan's attitude in the 1670s concerning 'the terrors that had haunted his conscience' (*HW*, p. xiv) regarding hell and damnation. They argue that the harsher and more rigidly defined theology of predestination, hitherto predominant in Bunyan's writing, was becoming gentler, being gradually replaced by an inclination towards the 'mercy and relief available to Christians'. An example is provided by the actions of Emanuel in *The Holy War*, a paragon of goodness and mercy, who constantly forgives the ingratitude of Mansoul's citizens for their disobedience, and lack of constancy and discipline (*HW*, pp. xiv, xvi). Yet *The Holy War* is a profoundly violent text where Emanuel's mercy and forgiveness are tempered by his willingness to wage war in a determined and bloody fashion. Violent conflict is everywhere apparent, as a line from the prefatory poem to the text makes clear: 'Mansoul, *it was the very seat of war*' (*HW*, p. 4). When the battle for the town of Mansoul takes place between the forces of good and evil, led by Emanuel and Diabolus respectively, the text informs us that 'many were maimed and wounded, and slain' (*HW*, p. 83). When Emanuel recaptures the town of Mansoul for the first time from the occupying forces of Diabolus, the chief among the ungodly are tried and crucified. In its depiction of armed conflict, and in its characterisation of the warrior for religious truth, Bunyan's narrative closely resembles Milton's in *Paradise Lost* (1667). Neil Keeble has observed that Bunyan, like Milton, was a 'transgressive and subversive author' whose dissent from the established church was lifelong and pronounced. Keeble goes on to argue that both Milton and Bunyan 'fashion textual selves' constructed from bitter experience and 'adverse circumstances', in grave opposition to the contexts in which they were created.[1] This is hardly surprising when one considers Bunyan's career from the 1650s onwards. He constantly engages with the religious controversies of his time: from extensive and violently polemical debate with the Ranters and the Quakers in the 1650s, and on throughout the Restoration period in antagonistic dialogue with the Latitudinarians in the established church.

The Holy War is the fourth volume of Bunyan's allegorical fictions. The text has never attracted the level of critical and popular attention enjoyed by *The Pilgrim's Progress* (1678) or *Grace Abounding* (1666).[2] Perhaps this is because of all Bunyan's fictions, *The Holy War* is most closely engaged with its immediate political and historical context. The intention of what follows is to read *The Holy War* against the politics of religious engagement in the years between the Popish Plot in 1678 and publication in 1682. The text emerged from the maelstrom of anti-Catholicism, exclusion politics and the advent of political parties. The opening chapter of Andrew Marvell's *An Account of the Growth of Popery and Arbitrary Government in England* (1677) captures the intensity of anti-Catholicism and contemporary fears that it was linked to tyranny: 'There has now for divers Years, a design been carried on, to change the Lawful Government of England into an Absolute Tyranny, and to convert the established Protestant Religion into down-right Popery.' For Marvell, 'nothing can be more destructive or contrary to the Interest and Happiness, to the Constitution and Being of the King and Kingdom'.[3] With Marvell's framing of the debate in mind, this chapter is divided into three sections. To assist those readers unfamiliar with the content of *The Holy War* a brief synopsis is provided. In the second section of this chapter the political and historical context of the years immediately preceding publication of the text is discussed, after which an analysis of *The Holy War* follows.

The narrative

In a manner reminiscent of the opening books of *Paradise Lost*, Bunyan introduces us to Diabolus, a figure of magnificent ruin, brought forth by an excess of pride and ambition. Diabolus was once a favoured follower of King Shaddai, 'put by him into most high and mighty place', and the prince 'to the best of his Territories and Dominions' (*HW*, p. 9). As a high-ranking member of King Shaddai's court, Diabolus's holdings brought enormous wealth and 'an income that might have contented his *Luciferian* heart, had it not been insatiable, and inlarged as Hell it self' (*HW*, p. 9). After a treasonous plot that attempts to destroy Emanuel, Shaddai's son and heir, fails, Diabolus and his followers are defeated, convicted of treason, rebellion and conspiracy, banished from the court and held confined in the pits of Hell. From this position they plan to launch a covert attack on Mansoul, motivated by no other reason than 'malice and rage against *Shaddai*, and against his son', 'considering that that Town was one of the chief works, and delights of King *Shaddai*' (*HW*, p. 10). The people of Mansoul must fall by means of their own free will. As befits their innocence, the people of the town live in a prelapsarian state of virtue and purity and are shown to be easy prey. Accordingly, they are amenable to Diabolus's smooth and silky rhetoric and are encouraged to commit 'Fraud, Guile, and Hypocrisy'. In effect, they are strangers 'to lying and desembling [sic] lips' and ripe for manipulation (HW, p. 13). The end result is that the town is occupied by Diabolus's forces and its government is either suborned or replaced. Diabolus quickly appoints a new Lord Mayor – Lord Lustings – and a new Recorder – Mr Forget-good. The reason for this is made clear enough in the text: 'For who doth not perceive but when those that sit aloft, are vile, and corrupt themselves; they corrupt the whole Region and Country where they are' (HW, p. 25).

King Shaddai responds immediately with force commensurate to the task. An army is assembled with four great captains: Conviction, Judgment, Execution and the leader, Boanerges. In their determination and commitment, all four captains would not look out of place in the mid-century New Model Army of Cromwell and Fairfax. This point is made with greater force later in the text when Diabolus stimulates the townsfolk to resist Shaddai's army. Their near-hysterical response to the sight of the formidable military presence, despatched by Shaddai to retake the town, is telling: 'The men that turn the World upside down are come hither . . . The destroyers of our peace' (HW, p. 40). With the use of such descriptive and evocative language Bunyan demonstrates where his loyalties lie. The besieging army, it follows from this, have the sign of God's favour upon them. As Sharrock and Forrest point out in their notes to the passage, the names of the captains echo Mark 3:17 – 'And James the son of Zebedee, and John the brother of James; and he surnamed them Boanerges, which is, "The sons of thunder" ' (HW, 258n). Conviction, Judgment and Execution represent the 'awakening Christian conscience' (HW, 258n). Nor is Bunyan's Shaddai reluctant when it comes to administering correction. In his instructions to Boanerges Shaddai closes his speech to the captain by urging him 'to make use of all of thy cunning, power, might, and force to bring them under by strength of hand' (HW, p. 38). If the cause be righteous, no measure is deemed excessive.

Diabolus's most formidable weapon as a leader is his charismatic rhetoric and his ability to appeal to man's baser instinct and self-interest. Indeed, for Donald Mackenzie 'the flowering of rhetoric [in *The Holy War*] is its triumph'.[4] Despite the best efforts of Boanerges and the other captains, the town cannot be overcome until Diabolus's rhetorical mastery of the citizens is undermined. Pure force is insufficient to the task at hand. Accordingly, the renewed assault takes place with Ear-gate as the principal target: 'For they knew that unless they could penetrate that, no good could be done upon the Town' (HW, p. 50). The captains' recognition that this is a war of hearts and minds, as well as physical force, is crucial to the eventual outcome. Once this has been fully realised the tide begins to turn and the forces of Shaddai make progress. Notwithstanding their advances, however, something more is needed for victory to be assured. After a petition is written to Shaddai, composed by Captain Conviction, Emanuel is despatched at the head of a mighty army to inflict the final blow and bring about the end of the siege. This is a masterly touch, and in a well-drawn confrontation between Emanuel and Diabolus the latter is shown up as an inferior rhetorician and a coward. Emanuel regains the town – not through subterfuge and specious rhetoric – but by means of love and sacrifice: 'I gave body for body, soul for soul, life for life, blood for blood, and so redeemed my beloved *Mansoul*' (*HW*, p. 75). The battle is duly won.

This, however, is not the end of the matter. When the town is recaptured by Emanuel, and the trials and punishment take place of those who were guilty of treason against Shaddai, a purge of government proceeds. Emanuel restores good governance by having the town of Mansoul 'new modelled'; he then leaves the town to govern itself. This proves to be a mistake: 'in several lurking places of the Corporation' there linger hard-line Diabolonians waiting for their chance. Prominent among these malcontents are 'the Lord Fornication' with the peers Adultery, Blasphemy and Lasciviousness, amongst others (*HW*, p. 161). The town is once more attacked by Diabolus and his followers and a bloody battle for its soul takes place. With Emanuel absent from the siege that takes place in Mansoul, Diabolus's army almost prevails. However, not everything is as it was before. Diabolus's 'outlandish men were not at peace in *Mansoul*, for they were not there entertained as were the Captains and forces of *Emanuel*'. Instead, Diabolus's troops are 'browbeat' by the population and openly reviled (*HW*, pp. 205). On the third day Emanuel returns to take the field, destroys Diabolus's army and slays all of its soldiers (*HW*, p. 222). Emanuel's warning at the text's conclusion is that all should remain vigilant against sin: '*Nothing can* hurt *thee but sin*; *nothing can* grieve *me but sin*; *nothing can make thee base before thy foes but sin*: *Take heed of sin, my* Mansoul.' The citizens of Mansoul, says Emanuel, must 'hold fast till I come' (*HW*, pp. 249, 250).

Politics and religion, 1678–82

The late 1670s and early 1680s witnessed the calling of three parliaments, the temporary failure of censorship with the lapse of the licensing law, the attempt by nonconformists to widen toleration to include moderate dissenters 'and the first use early in 1681 of the terms Whig and Tory to describe politico-religious groupings'.[5] In 1682, the Tory backlash against nonconformists and Whigs, occasioned by the failure of the latter's attempts to exclude the King's brother, James, Duke of York, from the throne, was about to be unleashed. From April 1681 there appeared in the *London Gazette* addresses, driven by the Tory agenda of conformity and loyalty to the crown, warning of the dire consequences that would ensue if the Whigs and the nonconformists prevailed in their attempts to humble royal prerogative by dictating the succession. The language of these addresses was inflammatory to say the least, threatening chaos and the imminent danger of being overwhelmed and enslaved by 'Phanatical, Ambitious and Antimonarchical Parties'. These addresses 'affirmed support for the traditional succession, recalled the spectre of civil war and urged the vigorous execution of the laws against Catholics and dissenters, both of which were represented as threats to public order'. The government 'was determined to turn the public mood firmly against Whigs and nonconformists, a policy that bore fruit'.[6]

Nonconformists henceforth faced a reinvigorated persecution from the triumphant government of the day. From 1678 to 1682 the nation was in the grip of what many perceived as a titanic struggle between emergent Whigs and Tories, impelled by rabid anti-Catholicism on the one hand and a similarly strident fear of evangelical Protestantism on the other. In the words of one historian, 'Whigs thought Tories dupes for popery and arbitrary government. Tories thought Whigs were agents of republicanism and fanaticism.'[7] The detection of the so-called Popish Plot by Titus Oates and Israel Tongue in 1678 proved to be the lightning rod for political and religious turmoil. The spurious and fantastical tale told by Oates to the King – that there was a Catholic conspiracy to assassinate him – would have in all probability been discounted by an investigation. Fortunately for Oates, however, the discovery of the murdered body of Edmund Godfrey – the magistrate to whom Oates first voiced his fears – gave his story a credibility that it did not deserve. A further stroke of luck occurred when seditious comments about the King, in letters written by Edward Coleman to Louis XIV's confessor, were discovered. Coleman had formerly been the Duke of York's secretary.[8]

The King's brother was an open Catholic, exposed as such by his refusal to subscribe to the Test Act in 1673. As the hysteria surrounding the Popish Plot intensified there arose simultaneously a highly organised opposition to James's succession. Fears of a Catholic heir to the throne on the death of Charles II fuelled bigotry and hatred on the part of Protestants and brought back the spectre of Protestant martyrdom so vividly described in Foxe's *Actes and Monuments*, more popularly known as *The Book of Martyrs* (1563). The terms of the debate between Whigs and Tories in the parliaments that followed in 1679, 1680 and 1681 were defined by anti-Catholicism, the extent of royal prerogative and the exclusion from the succession of James, Duke of

York. One of the first eminent casualties of this process was the Earl of Danby, the King's first minister, impeached for treason on the evidence of Ralph Montague, the former ambassador to Paris. Danby had been dealing secretly with Louis XIV to secure financial subsidies for the King. As Edward Vallance has written, 'this . . . put the Commons into a state of near hysteria'.[9] Predictably, when the tables were turned and the King was able to manage Parliament to his will, revenge from the government inevitably followed. The year before the publication of *The Holy War* in 1682 witnessed the beginning of a four-year period where dissenters were ruthlessly persecuted, culminating in the Bloody Assizes of 1685.

Literature played its part in the partisan politics of these years, with many of the major writers of the Restoration period taking sides in the emergence of party politics. With parliaments being called every two and a half years between 1679 and 1716, public participation and representation became an increasingly important factor in the political life of the nation. Mark Knights has recently argued that: 'The period thus witnessed an experiment in representation but also, in the eyes of many contemporaries, one in misrepresentation through slander, political lying, and partisan fictions.'[10] We can see the foundations of this political culture and the languages and forms it generated in the Exclusion Crisis. The most accomplished partisan intervention in literature, and the most brilliant, is John Dryden's satirical defence of the Tory, Anglican and royalist position in *Absalom and Achitophel* (1681). Dryden is an exemplar of the later seventeenth-century writer: a highly educated, politically sophisticated metropolitan who expresses the anxieties of the later 1670s and early 1680s by appealing magnificently to the anxious conservative's fears of a return to the notorious decades of civil war, regicide and republicanism. In engaging with what he sees as the conservative majority, the 'sober part of Israel', Dryden reminds his readers of 'the value of a peaceful reign'. These readers now

> . . . looking backward with a wise afright
> Saw Seames of wounds, dishonest to the sight;
> In contemplation of whose ugly Scars,
> They Curst the memory of Civil Wars.[11]

This was not empty rhetoric. The years between 1640 and 1660 were fresh in the memory of contemporaries. Those decades had witnessed a very bloody civil war that raged intermittently between 1642 and 1651, regicide and an eleven-year rule by republican government. By 1682 the cry for a reinvigorated persecution of those attending conventicles was loudly expressed by conservatives. Anything that threatened traditional views of monarchical power and prerogative in favour of revisiting the values of the mid-century was particularly despised by those that feared a return to 'Plebean Tyrannie'.[12]

Those tumultuous and unprecedented mid-century decades had also witnessed the abolition of the established church and the House of Lords, and rule by a military junta. Many believed in the 1670s and 1680s that Protestant extremism, in the form of a multitude of sects espousing radical ideas, had been allowed free rein. This had led to high taxation in the 1650s, imposed by a deeply unpopular government under the Protectorate of Oliver Cromwell. After the dissolution of the 1681 Oxford Parliament, Bishop Fell wrote to the dissenter, Richard Newdigate, that 'the preservation of the Protestant religion, and established government, is our common care'. This was not, however, best guaranteed by allowing toleration to those who abjured Anglicanism. The bishop goes on to state: 'We remember very well the time, when blood and rapine put on the mark of godliness and reformation; and we lost our king, our liberty and property and religion.'[13] The points that Fell makes here are rendered precisely by the King himself in *His Majesties Declaration to all his Loving Subjects*, after the dissolution of the Oxford Parliament: 'all those [who] consider the Rise and Progress of the late Troubles ... and desire to protect their Country from a Relapse [should remember] that Religion, Liberty and property were all lost when Monarchy was shaken off, and could never be reviv'd till that was restored'.[14] Dryden, Fell and Charles II all equate the indulgence of nonconformity with republicanism and the establishment of an unnatural order. By the early 1680s a tradition had been established by conservative writers and thinkers that nonconformist religious enthusiasm was 'synonymous with early Whiggism'.[15]

Achitophel in Dryden's poem is the Earl of Shaftesbury, Anthony Ashley Cooper, leader of the Whig opposition. A mischief maker, by Dryden's reckoning, Achitophel is keen to revive the Good Old Cause by inspiring the weak-minded to see plots where there are none. In the poet's formulation, 'Plots, true or false, are necessary things, / To raise up Common-wealths, and ruin kings.'[16] In a direct reference to the Popish Plot Dryden argues that the plot – 'the Nation's Curse' – though 'Bad in it self' was 'represented worse'. 'Some Truth there was, but dash'd and brew'd with Lyes; / To please the Fools and puzzle all the Wise.'[17] The author's position throughout this poem is to vilify rebellion against a divinely ordained monarch. Dryden's poem is in many respects an extension of the Tory position as espoused most influentially in the works of Robert Filmer. Filmer's argument that political authority derives its origins from God and was first exemplified in the world by Adam, suits Dryden's message in *Absalom and Achitophel* about the social and political authority of fathers and kings. This is buttressed in Filmer's *The*

Anarchy of Limited or Mixed Monarchy (1648), according to which there is no context in which rebellion against one's monarch can be justified: 'Now if this supreme power was settled and founded by God himself in the fatherhood, how is it possible for the people to have any right or title to alter and dispose of it otherwise.'[18] The King is divinely ordained and an act of rebellion against him is an act of rebellion against God. Dryden's support for royalist politics, in turn supported by an intolerant Anglicanism, relegates all other forms of opposition to sedition. Such, of course, is its purpose.

The politics of *The Holy War*

Bunyan's contribution to the literature of these years, whilst not an actively engaged polemic aimed at ridiculing those whom he sees as threatening, after the fashion of Dryden, nevertheless manages to delineate a politics of opposition that strikes many blows against the intolerant and persecutory mood and temper of political and religious currents in the late 1670s and early 1680s. Literature in the later seventeenth century appealed to readers who were becoming increasingly adept at analysing texts and revealing their political content. One leading historian of the period has recently argued that in order 'for this to happen readers had to read rightly'. They 'were encouraged to learn how to become critics capable of deconstructing a political text in order to learn its true meaning'. As a consequence of this shift in the reception of texts that could be interpreted politically, 'public discourse operated to legitimise or undermine authority and allegiance'.[19] Bunyan was writing *The Holy War* at a time when the pendulum was swinging towards an intensification of persecution, and when complex literary forms such as allegory were effectively being used to convey a political message. Bunyan knew that he was writing for a discerning readership that could interpret his allegory politically. Unlike the very broad appeal of *The Pilgrim's Progress*, *The Holy War* attracted the 'cultivated taste of a more sophisticated elite'.[20]

The Holy War is an allegorical epic that also has elements of 'romance, siege narrative, psychomachia, satire, and – almost – fiction'. As with all satire and allegory the text demonstrates a high level of engagement with contemporary events and topical issues. Some of these include 'the Civil War, the Restoration of Charles II, the Popish Plot and Exclusion Crisis, municipal politics and the Bedford Congregation'.[21] Sharrock and Forrest describe the allegory as having a tripartite function: 'Christian or world history ... the life of the individual soul, and of recent and contemporary English history'. They also mention a possible fourth strain – millenarian history (*HW*, p. xxvi). In *The Holy War* Bunyan participates in the political and religious controversies of these years through the figure of a town under siege. He also 'examined the probable consequences of a Catholic succession'.[22] Bunyan's allegory emphasises throughout the need for diligence, discipline and the maintenance of faith.

The period of relative ease and the gains made in political strength by nonconformists in the later 1670s began immediately to be reversed as soon as Charles II had triumphed over the Whigs. In a letter to Archbishop Sancroft, written by the Bishop of Exeter, we can see the fear and anxiety that was felt by the established church at the growing political and socio-economic advances made by dissenters: 'our corporations and boroughs who have so great a share in the government, are nurseries of faction, sedition and disloyalty ... and we do humbly desire that all the laws regulating corporations particularly that in restraining nonconformists from entering in corporations may be duly put in execution'.[23] *The Holy War* can be – and has been – read as a strident defence of Bunyan's faith in an age of religious and political persecution.[24] Bunyan's narrative responds to attacks on his religion with the language of violent conflict and the necessity of militant and military reaction when the true faith is under siege. This is as true for the individual as it is for the collective entity that is the town of Mansoul. Although he is not normally perceived as a radical, Bunyan was in tune with the views of many Protestants with pronounced anti-establishment views. In the works of Locke, Sidney and Ferguson, for instance 'armed self-defence' was not simply justifiable, but necessary.[25] Nowhere is this more clearly elaborated than in Locke, whose *An Essay on Toleration* (1667) leaves little doubt that arbitrary rule is unnatural to free-born Englishman. Monarchs who promote this agenda 'have forgot what country they are born in, under what laws they live, and certainly cannot but be obliged to declare Magna Charta to be downright heresy'.[26]

The Holy War is also a running commentary on Bunyan's dissatisfaction with the regime of Charles II and that monarch's love – as Bunyan sees it – of a dissolute and ungodly lifestyle. One can see this from the characterisation. In his depiction of the leading followers of Diabolus, Bunyan leaves us in little doubt of his opinions. Lord Lustings's love of unfettered licence is revealed as the birthright of his class when he is tried. He stands condemned by his own words:

> I was ever of opinion that the happiest life a man could live on earth, was to keep himself back from nothing that he desired in the world; nor have I ever been false at any time to this opinion of mine, but have lived in the love of my notions all my days. Nor was I ever so churlish, having found such sweetness in them my self, as to keep the commendations of them from others.   (*HW*, p. 122)

This is not liberty, of course, but licence and libertinism, a culture that dominated the court of Charles II and was most clearly visible in the King

himself. The behaviour of Charles II and his court was well known to contemporaries and was the stuff of gossip. For instance, one contemporary
under interrogation in the aftermath of the Popish Plot felt comfortable
enough to state, as if it were common knowledge, that Charles was a patron
of prostitutes and procurers and was continuously drunk.[27] In *The Holy War*,
Bunyan makes it clear in his marginal notes that a lack of conscience and a
carnal will go hand in glove and that the 'carnal will opposeth conscience'
(*HW*, p. 22).

In the rise and fall of Diabolus, and the emancipation of Mansoul from
diabolic rule, Bunyan elaborates a politics of the will that finds its expression
in the constant need for vigilance and discipline. In moments of political crisis
that bring with it possible threats to his religion, Bunyan can often be found
having recourse to the pen. When this occurs his thoughts on the role of the
will are often close to the surface of the text. In the later 1650s, for instance,
during the protectorate of Richard Cromwell, there was a similar rush to
publication by many that had a vested interest in the future direction of
church and state. In *The Doctrine of Law and Grace Unfolded* (1659)
Bunyan elaborates on 'what is required to sustain the elect in a time of
trial'.[28] Bunyan's reading of covenant theology in this work is not a straightforward exposition of Mosaic Law that stands free from political engagement. On the contrary, he adapts theology to current politics when the need
arises. This was true in 1659 and remained true *c.*1667 when he was once
again urging the elect to stand fast in the face of likely persecution: 'get thy
Will tipt with Heavenly Grace and resolution against all discouragements,
and thou goest *full speed* for heaven; but if thou falter in thy *Will*, and be not
sound there ... be sure thou wilt *fall short at last*' (*MW*, v:165). In *The Strait
Gate* (1676) Bunyan opens the text with the words of Christ as they appear in
Luke 13:24: '*Strive to enter in at the strait gate, for many, I say unto you, seek
to enter in, and shall not be able*' (*MW*, v:167, 71).

Bunyan espouses the need to exercise the will and to strive throughout the
text of *The Holy War*, along with the need for constancy and the right to resist
an ungodly ruler. If physical force is required it should not be stinted. In the
world of the text the use of violence to pursue legitimate ends is not only
needful but necessary. Nor is this a singular event, but a process that is
dependent on context and contingency. Forgiveness for backsliding is a
similarly constant feature of the text; so too, however, is punishment for
those that are unregenerate. *The Holy War* leaves us at its conclusion with
the sentiment that the essential state of man is one of imperfection and an
ongoing struggle to 'await [Emanuel's] final coming' (*HW*, p. xx). That
Bunyan sees this battle as physical and political as well as spiritual is evident
to anyone with knowledge of *The Holy War*'s text and context (*HW*, pp. xvi,

xx). The body, as well as the soul, must join in armed conflict, a rhetorical fictional construct of total war. As his most recent biographer has related, Bunyan's military experience probably influenced the action of *The Holy War* as well as his use of symbols and imagery. Greaves presents us with an analysis of *The Holy War* that draws upon a vast knowledge of nonconformist history and politics in the later seventeenth century to read the allegory in relation to millenarian history and soteriology. Accordingly, for Greaves, the topography of London is probably drawn upon by Bunyan to inspire his description of Mansoul: 'the Tower', we are informed, 'would have been the model for Mansoul's castle'.[29]

Insofar as Greaves's reading of *The Holy War* is an interpretation from history, that history is predominantly millenarian. Bunyan's *The Holy City* (1665) provides the chronological framework: 'the fall and pre-Christian history; Christ and the apostolic church; the church's decline and captivity, followed by a period of altar-work (Wyclif, Hus and the Protestant Reformation) and another of temple-work (the era of gathered churches); Antichrist's fall, the church's emergence from captivity, and the millennium; and finally Christ's return and the last judgement'.[30] The attempt to make analogies between secular history and the events of *The Holy War* is unconvincing, according to Greaves. Yet he admits that there is no denying *The Holy War* contains allusions to some of the key events of the seventeenth century, particularly with regard to plots. The Gunpowder Plot (1605), the Popish Plot (1678) and the Meal Tub Conspiracy, a false plot created by Thomas Dangerfield in 1679 to capitalise on the heightened atmosphere of anti-Catholicism, are all alluded to in the text. Other indications that Bunyan was concerned about secular events are cleverly disguised. Diabolus, for instance, attempts to suborn the citizens of Mansoul by pointing out that life under the rule of Shaddai is far from desirable. Being a subject under Shaddai means being 'inslaved in all places'; 'none in the Universe [are] so unhappy' as the citizens of Mansoul under the rule of Shaddai. In his attempt to rally the citizens into resisting Emanuel's army, Diabolus has recourse to one of the most powerful words in the early modern political lexicon: 'But consider I say, the ball is yet at thy foot, *liberty* you have, if you know how to use it: Yea, a King you have too, if you can tell how to love and obey him' (*HW*, p. 63, emphasis added). Although these words are delivered by Diabolus they contain much that is derived from Whig political writing. Choice is emphasised, as is the need to discern between good and bad kingship. As Milton does with Satan in *Paradise Lost*, Bunyan gives the Devil in *The Holy War* some of the most powerful lines.

The Holy War is a didactic text. Throughout the narrative the residents of Mansoul are given opportunities to exercise their free will. Bunyan then makes clear the consequences after the choice has been made. Emanuel ensures that temptation is never far away. Near the very end of the allegory this is made explicit when Emanuel informs the people of Mansoul that the reason he allows 'Diabolonians *to dwell in thy* walls ... *is to keep thee wakening, to try thy love* [and] *to make thee watchful*' (*HW*, p. 249). In testing times, and in a political world where danger lurks around every corner, Bunyan emphasises that vigilance, discipline and constancy to the Reformed faith are the qualities by which the godly are finally weighed and measured.

NOTES

1. N. H. Keeble, ' "Till one greater man / Restore us ...": Restoration in Milton and Bunyan', *Bunyan Studies*, 6 (1995–6), 6–33 (p. 8).
2. However, for a recent full-length study, see Daniel Virgil Runyon, *John Bunyan's Master Story*: The Holy War *as Battle Allegory in Religious and Biblical Context* (Lewiston, N.Y.: Edward Mellen Press, 2007).
3. *An Account of the Growth of Popery and Arbitrary Government in England* (1677), ed. Nicholas von Maltzahn, in *The Prose Works of Andrew Marvell*, ed. Annabel Patterson *et al.*, 2 vols. (New Haven and London: Yale University Press, 2003), II:225–377 (p. 225).
4. Donald Mackenzie, 'Rhetoric *versus* Apocalypse in *The Holy War*, BS, 2.1 (1990), 33–45 (p. 39).
5. Mark Knights, *Representation and Misrepresentation in Later Stuart Britain: Partisanship and Political Culture* (Oxford University Press, 2005), p. xiv.
6. Richard L. Greaves, *Secrets of the Kingdom: British Radicals from the Popish Plot to the Revolution of 1688–1689* (Stanford University Press, 1992), p. 90.
7. Gary S. De Krey, *Restoration and Revolution in Britain* (London: Palgrave, 2007), p. 149.
8. The classic treatment is by J. P. Kenyon, *The Popish Plot* (1972; London: Phoenix, 2000). For a more recent analysis that sees exclusion as one part of a wider Restoration crisis see Jonathan Scott, *England's Troubles: Seventeenth-Century English Political Instability in European Context* (Cambridge University Press, 2000). For detailed readings of the Plot from a variety of standpoints see also Knights, *Representation and Misrepresentation*; Tim Harris, *Restoration: Charles II and his Kingdoms, 1660–1685* (London: Allen Lane, 2005); De Krey, *Restoration and Revolution*.
9. Edward Vallance, *The Glorious Revolution, 1688: Britain's Fight for Liberty* (London: Little, Brown, 2006), p. 34.
10. Knights, *Representation and Misrepresentation*, p. 3.
11. John Dryden, *Absalom and Achitophel* (1681), in *The Works of John Dryden*, ed. Edward Niles Hooker and H. T. Swedenberg, Jr., 20 vols. (Berkeley: University of California Press, 1956–96), II:7, lines 69–74. All further references to the text are to this edition.
12. *Protestant (Domestick) Intelligence*, 97 (15 February 1681), cited in Greaves, *Secrets of the Kingdom*, p. 91.

13. Quoted in John Spurr, *The Restoration Church of England, 1646–1689* (New Haven and London: Yale University Press, 1991), p. 80.
14. Quoted in Scott, *England's Troubles*, p. 201.
15. Abigail Williams, *Poetry and the Creation of a Whig Literary Culture* (Oxford University Press, 2005).
16. Dryden, *Absalom and Achitophel*, ii:8, lines 84–5.
17. *Ibid.* ii:7–8, lines 108, 113–15.
18. Quoted in Johann P. Somerville (ed.), *Patriarcha and Other Writings* (Cambridge University Press, 1991), p. 138.
19. Knights, *Representation and Misrepresentation*, pp. 7–8.
20. N. H. Keeble, *The Literary Culture of Nonconformity in Later Seventeenth Century England* (Leicester University Press, 1987), p. 143.
21. Beth Lynch, *John Bunyan and the Language of Conviction* (Cambridge: D. S. Brewer, 2004), p. 138; *HW*, p. xx.
22. De Krey, *Restoration and Revolution*, p. 148.
23. Quoted in Douglas R. Lacey, *Dissent and Parliamentary Politics, 1661–1689: A Study in the Perpetuation and Tempering of Parliamentarianism* (New Brunswick, N.J.: Rutgers University Press, 1969), p. 152.
24. Hill, *Turbulent*, p. 241.
25. Scott, *England's Troubles*, p. 203.
26. John Locke, 'An Essay on Toleration', in Mark Goldie (ed.), *Locke: Political Essays* (Cambridge University Press, 1997), pp. 134–59 (p. 136).
27. See Kenyon, *The Popish Plot*, p. 175.
28. David Walker, ' "Heaven is prepared for whosoever will accept of it": Politics of the Will in Bunyan's *Doctrine of Law and Grace Unfolded* (1659)', *Prose Studies*, 21.3 (1998), 19–31 (p. 21).
29. Greaves, *Glimpses*, p. 417.
30. *Ibid.*, p. 426.

9

SHANNON MURRAY

A Book for Boys and Girls: Or, Country Rhimes for Children: Bunyan and literature for children

John Bunyan's work has had a profound and complex influence on the history of children's literature in English, but not in the way he might have expected. For over two centuries, *The Pilgrim's Progress* was essential reading not in the university classroom but in the nursery, adopted by children who, like Louisa May Alcott's Jo March in *Little Women* (1868), revelled in the journey and the adventure of Bunyan's allegory. As a children's book, it was so common that Frances Hodgson Burnett, L. M. Montgomery and Mark Twain could assume a basic knowledge of Christian's journey from the City of Destruction to the Celestial City. Both Montgomery and Twain show their protagonists reading Bunyan, with profoundly different responses. While Emily in Montgomery's *Emily of New Moon* (1923) is proud to have both read and enjoyed Bunyan's allegory (the only book her devout aunts let her read on Sundays), Huckleberry Finn famously judged that the allegory is 'about a man that left his family, it didn't say why. I read considerable in it now and then. The statements was interesting, but tough.'[1]

Frances Hodgson Burnett published her own rewriting – *Two Little Pilgrims' Progress* (1895) – as the journey of two orphans on their way to the Chicago World's Fair of 1893, and Enid Blyton's *The Land of Far Beyond* (1942) is 'a kind of new *Pilgrim's Progress*, in my own words, and with my own quite new ideas'.[2] In novels like *Little Women* (1868), *What Katy Did* (1872), *The Wonderful Wizard of Oz* (1900), *The Land of Far Beyond* and many more, a clever child might detect the characters, concerns, even structural patterns of *The Pilgrim's Progress*.[3] Running through all of these allusions, revisions and adaptations is the belief that Bunyan's allegory – or some mediated version of it – belongs on each child's bookshelf, becoming one of the most important monuments in the history of children's literature.[4]

Bunyan and literature for children

While *The Pilgrim's Progress* was written with a general readership in mind, Bunyan did publish a book meant for young readers: *A Book for Boys and*

120

Girls: or, Country Rhimes for Children (1686). It may be difficult to see at this distance of years how revolutionary that collection of poems was, engaging with its young readers through delight and enticement in an approach that would only truly gain ground in the centuries after Bunyan's death. But the book's eighteenth-century editors altered the work to such a degree that the original was virtually lost until the late nineteenth century, by which time the moment for the verse's power to delight and teach young minds had passed.[5] So Bunyan's voice was heard in the nursery primarily through Christian's journey to the Celestial City.

A Book for Boys and Girls, as the title suggests, is a collection of rhymes written for children, an audience which had only in the seventeenth century been recognised as special in its requirements and capabilities and thus deserving of its own literature. Published in 1686, it is a collection of 74 poems, ranging from 4 to 192 lines long, each working to illustrate some aspect of God's ways to children, but using only those occupations, objects, creatures and experiences that children in rural England would know. Homely and down-to-earth, these poems develop a strategy of pleasing in order to instruct that makes them almost unique among early examples of writing for children.

Before there can be delight and instruction, however, a child must learn to read, so the collection includes a number of prefatory pages giving instruction in basic literacy. 'An help to Children to learn to read English' begins with the alphabet in six different fonts, and then explains vowels, consonants and syllables. On the next page, fifty-eight common children's names, again with syllables separated by hyphens, are listed to allow children to learn to spell aright. These, along with the list of numbers that follows, are offered as 'enough for little children to prepare themselves for the Psalter, or Bible' (*B&G*, p. 196) – or, one presumes, for the poems to follow. In this opening, Bunyan allies himself with the long tradition of hornbooks and battledores which communicated the basic material of literacy and always included the letters of the alphabet, sometimes with accompanying pictures, and some verse like the Lord's Prayer as an example of what one should read once the letters are known.[6] This opening suggests that Bunyan sees his book as something that preliterate children could use to master their letters. The opening poem ends with a quick tour of the kind of fare – primers and hornbooks – that children would regularly encounter, and with encourage-ment for those who are at first slow of study: '*Some Boys with difficulty do begin, / Who in the end, the Bays, and Lawrel win*' (*B&G*, p. 193).

The poems themselves do not reveal a laureate poet, and most leave no doubt that Bunyan's genius was for prose. They are intended as 'country rhimes', perhaps, in several senses, including 'simple' or 'rustic'. The craftsmanship of the poems is varied, ranging from heights (relatively speaking) of rhetorical exuberance to near-doggerel where Bunyan is quite prepared to create a couplet by rhyming a word with itself. The syntax is often inverted – normally for the sake of rhyme – in ways that suggest many readers, if they were indeed just emerging from illiteracy, would need a parent or teacher to guide them.

Like other Puritans, Bunyan saw a special reason for children to learn to read and to interpret rightly what they read: their very souls depended on it. Each Christian had a responsibility to read scripture, so universal literacy became a spiritual requirement for women as well as men, the poor as well as the rich, and the young as well as adults.[7] Unmediated access to the Bible was necessary for the Christian, so the earlier one gained that access, the better. Early examples of literature for Puritan children, however, had more of brimstone than of treacle about them. Joseph Alleine's *Alarum to the Unconverted* (1673), for example, may address very young children, but the reading list he offers them consists wholly of books written for adults, including Bunyan's beloved *The Plaine Mans Path-way to Heaven* (1601). James Janeway's *A Token for Children* (1671) looks at the child's experience, but from what may seem to a twenty-first century audience a morbid perspective; his very popular little book tells stories of thirteen godly children as they cheerfully succumb, one after the other, to disease or death. A similar approach is found in *A Looking-Glass for Children* (1672?) a collection of stories and prison verses compiled by 'H. P.', respectively by the Baptists Henry Jessey and Abraham Chear. Isaac Watts's collection of poems, *Divine Songs*, published after Bunyan's, deals in danger, caution and the threat of hell-fire. The child who does not heed his teachers' or his parents' word, for example, can expect that 'Ravens shall pick out his eyes, / And eagles eat the same'.[8] Against the backdrop of cautionary tales and earnest accounts of blessed early deaths, Bunyan's *Book for Boys and Girls* is refreshingly cheerful in its tone and attractive in its examples.

Indeed, the prefatory poem 'To the Reader' announces the purpose of the collection explicitly in contrast to those '*Ministers*' who have gone before: those that would frighten rather than entice their young readers. The audience of the collection is to be '*Boys and Girls of all Sorts and Degrees*', and Bunyan wryly includes those '*Boys with Beards*' and '*Girls that be / Big as old Women*' among them (*B&G*, p. 190). So his audience is composed of children but also of adults in need of instruction and even those who are wise but who might, if they gave the poems a chance, have their '*Graver Fancies*' taken. The opening poem also sets out the method he will use. Rather than frightening children with 'Thunder-bolts' he will attract them with 'Play-things' (*B&G*, pp. 190–1). His method is to use those things that children know and are naturally pleased with to draw them on to thoughts of God and heaven. Other writers may be using '*better Charge*' – i.e. gunpowder – but too much powder makes the shot go wide (*B&G*, p. 190). Bunyan will start where the children are, with what he sees they already value. Those things then become patterns of higher things. So in the mean, the lowly and the everyday God's work can still be done, and his plan still be seen.

Even more than elevating the everyday, Bunyan offers another way to read God's will. Puritans are invited to read the Book (the Bible) but also to see the world itself (nature) as a book wherein God lays out all one needs to know, could one but read and meditate upon it. His poems offer children a way to read the book of the world, to go to school with spiders and to learn from ants, birds, fish and insects. Just as the verses may help children read well enough to tackle the Bible on their own, so they offer a way to read the world. Through it all one senses, as Graham Midgley suggests, a 'tender and genuine love of children' (*MW*, vi:lvii).

In most of the poems that follow, Bunyan's method recalls the technique of the emblem book. In these immensely popular works, a picture would be accompanied by varying levels of text. Ideally, neither image nor text is more important; each complements the other. The form was developed in continental Europe, where it enjoyed a greater popularity than in England. The first example was the *Emblemata* of Andrea Alciati (1531), who borrowed the term from the Latin meaning 'mosaic',[9] but it was not until Geoffrey Whitney's *A Choice of Emblemes and other Devises* (1586) that the form found its way to England. In the century following, the two most popular English emblem books were George Withers's *Collection of Emblems, Ancient and Moderne* (1625) and Francis Quarles's *Emblems Divine and Moral* (1635). Two thousand copies of Quarles's collection were published in 1639, with another 3,000 in 1640.[10] Bunyan himself shows his debts to the emblem tradition in the Interpreter's house of *The Pilgrim's Progress*, as Christian and then Christiana are shown a variety of scenes and helped to unfold their moral meaning.[11] By the late seventeenth century the taste for emblem books in England had largely passed.[12]

Most of the poems in Bunyan's collection lack accompanying pictures.[13] This may have a practical cause, good illustrators being unavailable or too costly, and it is also possible that Bunyan would have believed the pictures a distraction. Most importantly, the nature of Bunyan's 'emblems' (the continuing use of the term in this context, where there are so few pictures, is somewhat strained) simply made the inclusion of image unnecessary. While Quarles's pictures, for example, offer allegorical figures, Bunyan's emblems explore *only* those things that would be familiar to children in any farm or town in England: eggs, swallows, cuckoos, larks and moles; flies, candles, ants, snails, sun and fish; bell-ringing, looking glasses and paper; music, plums, butterflies and flint. Of the seventy-four poems, perhaps only those on thieves, a fig tree and the apparition of evil spirits might take the child's mind further afield than the next farm. The thief would be known even if not seen, the fig tree was familiar from the Bible and the poem on the apparition of evil spirits tries to persuade children to avoid the fear of unreal things. So the majority of the poems use only the commonplace to urge moral or divine conclusions and in that sense they could also be placed within the tradition of Puritan 'occasional' meditations, such as those written by Joseph Hall or Edmund Calamy. Some poems are indeed expressly identified by Bunyan as 'meditations', such as 'Meditation upon an Egg' (III, *B&G*, pp. 202–3), 'Meditation upon the Peep of Day' (v, *B&G*, p. 205), 'Meditation upon the Candle' (XIII, *B&G*, pp. 210–12) and 'Meditations upon day before Sun-rising' (XVIII, *B&G*, pp. 221).[14]

And yet, Bunyan's collection does not simply conform to the emblematic and meditative tradition. We should also acknowledge its variety, which must have pleased its young readers, especially since the poems do not follow a particular order, but rather shift quite significantly in tone and subject matters. Some poems, such as 'Upon the Ten Commandments' (I, *B&G*, p. 197), 'Upon the Lord's Prayer' or 'Upon the Creed' (x, *B&G*, p. 208) dispense basic religious instructions while others ('Upon the Sacraments', XIV, *B&G*, p. 212) recall catechisms, a tradition used by Bunyan again in Part II of *The Pilgrim's Progress*. 'Upon over-much Niceness' (XII, *B&G*, p. 209–10) gives a simple moral lesson; 'Of Moses and his Wife' (XXXII, *B&G*, p. 236) provides a training in Biblical typology. Graham Midgley has also associated the book with versified fables or moralised dialogues (*MW* VI:xxxviii–xliii). Here, as elsewhere, it is unlikely that Bunyan was consciously working within one particular tradition, but he rather fused several genres that 'call for one thing to set forth another', as he says in the 'Apology' to *The Pilgrim's Progress* (*P'sP*, p. 6). The 'Apology', acknowledges, by contrasting the fisherman's and the fowler's arts, the necessity of adapting techniques for the readers' own good (*P'sP*, p. 2), an attitude Bunyan later adopted towards children in *A Book for Boys and Girls*.

A Book for Boys and Girls and human activities

What we see in Bunyan's little book is a demonstration of how a child might read God's book of the world, and while there are a number of poems that fit neither category, roughly half deal with human subjects of activity and the other half with the natural world. Remarkably few of the poems, however, only eleven of the seventy-four, explicitly identify a child as the subject, and those are interspersed throughout the work. The picture of childhood evoked in these eleven is varied, the typical child being neither a pre-Romantic innocent nor a Calvinist sinner. In two poems that have children interacting with nature, one makes the child an emblem of the vain pursuits of grown men, while in the other the child is a type of the Christ.

In 'Of the Boy and Butter-Fly' (xxi) the opening describes a boy vainly chasing the butterfly that will always escape him:

> Behold how eager this our little Boy,
> Is of this Butter-fly, as if all Joy,
> All Profits, Honours, yea and lasting Pleasures,
> Were wrapt up in her, or the richest Treasures,
> Found in her would be bundled up together,
> When all her all is lighter than a feather.   (*B&G*, p. 223)

In a collection in which the verse tends to be workmanlike rather than graceful, these lines are among the most conspicuously rhetorical, with alliteration and repetition ('all', 'All', 'all her all'), as if the language itself would take flight, although these means are used to conjure an image of false importance. The boy in the next stanza 'hollo's, runs, and cries out here Boys, here', all oblivious to falls, brambles and nettles. The poem, however, deals gently with the foolish boy. Harsh censure is saved for the grown men who ought to know better and yet still chase metaphorical butterflies.

In 'Of the Child with the Bird at the Bush' (xxxi), a child actor again figures in a chase of sorts, but this time the child's intention is to save the flying creature from harm. Here, the child-speaker is a type of Christ, eager to coax the bird to safety and away from thorns, storms, kites and snares, and offering instead warmth, good food, silks, occupation and a palace:

> I'll teach thee all the Notes at Court;
> Unthought of Musick thou shalt play;
> And all that thither do resort,
> Shall praise thee for it ev'ry day.   (*B&G*, p. 235)

How lovely a proposal, to teach music not yet imagined! And yet, in the end, the bird flies away, preferring danger or perhaps not understanding the child's call. The comparison perhaps a little heavy-handedly identifies the child as Christ and the bird as sinners. The bird's own songs are 'foolish Toys / Which to Destruction lead the way' (*B&G*, p. 235). The poem concludes:

> The Arguments this Child doth chuse,
> To draw to him a Bird thus wild,
> Shews Christ familiar Speech doth use,
> To make's to him be reconciled.   (*B&G*, p. 235)

The comparison not only suggests the child's (and by extension Christ's) method, which is to use the familiar to draw the sinner forth, it also mirrors Bunyan's own method throughout the collection. Familiar language and appeals draw the bird, the sinner *and* the child reader. Here the child becomes a figure not just of Christ but also of the poet, who coaxes rather than frightens. However lovely and encouraging the poem, however, the foolish bird ignores the call and flies away. In the end, the focus is on the sinner's ability to make a choice – even the wrong choice – as much as Christ's attractive call.

More common than poems that deal with children are those that look at common man-made objects. Among the three candle poems, the simplest, 'Of the Fly at the Candle' (XXII, *B&G*, pp. 224–5), imagines a fly in a 'Combat with the Candle', but the more it attempts to extinguish the light the more it merely burns itself against a light impervious to its attacks. In 'Upon the Sight of a Pound of Candles falling to the ground' (XLII, *B&G*, p. 245), a wise person who drops candles in the dark is urged to take another candle from above and light it so that he can see to pick the others up. The first lit candle in the comparison is Christ, and while this image of Christ is deeply embedded in Christian tradition, the variation of a theological commonplace shows Bunyan at his most interesting in the collection. The child is invited not just to recognise the comparison but to be delighted in the connection, one that he or she might not have seen before.

It is in 'Meditations on the Candle' (XIII, *B&G*, pp. 210–12) that Bunyan demonstrates his facility with invention, the ability to find not just one but many comparisons for a single subject. A real show-off piece, the poem is sixty-five lines long and offers twenty-one different metaphors, most of which involve the candle's flame as grace, the wick as the soul, the wax as flesh and the surrounding darkness as sin. Here, most comparisons occupy just a couplet, with the observation in the first line and the comparison in the second:

> But Candles in the wind are apt to flare;
> And Christ'ans in a Tempest to despair.
> The flame also with Smoak attended is;
> And in our holy lives there's much amiss.
> Sometimes a Thief will candle-light annoy;
> And lusts do seek our Graces to destroy.   (*B&G*, p. 211)

One can understand F. J. Harvey Darton's suggestion that Bunyan almost tortured his mind to find comparisons,[15] but there is more in this poem of the virtuoso than the tortured mind: how many comparisons can he manage on a candle and still hold the attention of the child? The last comparison introduces a difference, both in form and in matter:

> The man now lays him down upon his Bed;
> The Wick yields up his fire; and so is dead.
> The Candle now extinct is, but the man,
> By Grace mounts up to Glory, there to stand.   (*B&G*, p. 212)

Here, Bunyan identifies the limits of the emblem: a candle is not like a man's life when it is over, because a man can expect a second lighting.

Many of the other man-made objects in the collection – the majority of which come in the second half – are presented as either morally neutral or wholly good. In 'Upon a Sheet of white Paper' (LXX), for instance, the paper can be 'subject . . . unto the foulest Pen, / Or fairest' and it will show freely to its readers anything written on it, whether that be wisdom or blot (*B&G*, p. 267). The looking glass in 'Upon a Looking-glass' (XLVIII) can reflect our faults, but only if we are willing to see them (*B&G*, p. 250). Watches, penny loaves, spectacles and medicine are all offered as only potentially good; what matters is the use to which they are put.

Music for children

Such is the case in the companion poems on musical instruments, which demonstrate a delight in music. Indeed, two poems in the collection are prefaced with simple musical notation. Here is the first half of 'Upon a Skilful Player on an Instrument' (LIX):

> He that can play well on an Instrument,
> Will take the Ear, and captivate the Mind;
> With Mirth, or Sadness: For that *it* is bent
> Thereto as Musick, in it, place doth find.
>   But if one hears that hath therein no skill,
> (As often Musick lights of such a chance)
> Of its brave Notes, they soon be weary will;
> And there are some can neither sing nor dance. (*B&G*, p. 259)

'Upon an Instrument of Musick in an unskilful Hand' (XL, *B&G*, p. 243) suggests a similar idea. There is nothing wrong with the instrument in this analogy, nor is there a fault in good music or in the desire to hear it. Instead, the instrument has the power to provide good, but in an untrained hand, it cannot produce what is wanted. The comparison in this case is to someone new in the church, the 'unlearn'd Novices in things Divine' who 'Abuse the Bible, and unsavoury are' (*B&G*, p. 243). In the earlier poem, the comparison makes a good gospel minister the musician, whose skilful music may nonetheless fall on ears unable to perceive the music. In both, music is to be desired; it is like good gospel preaching; it is like a skilful reading of scripture. Happy though Cromwell and his fellows were to destroy church organs and to rail against profane songs, the issue was not music itself but rather the social and religious abuses with which it was sometimes associated.[16]

Nowhere in the collection is Bunyan's pleasure in music more intriguingly teased out than in 'Upon a Ring of Bells' (XXIX, *B&G*, pp. 231-2). In *Grace Abounding to the Chief of Sinners*, his spiritual autobiography published twenty years before this collection, he had recounted the anxiety he felt at pursuing his delight in church bell-ringing:

> Now you must know, that before this I had taken much delight in ringing, but my Conscience beginning to be tender, I thought that such a practice was but vain, and therefore forced my self to leave it, yet my mind hanckered, wherefore I should go to the Steeple house, and look on: though I durst not ring. But I thought this did not become Religion neither, yet I forced my self and would look on still; but quickly after, I began to think, How, if one of the Bells should fall . . . (*GA*, p. 13).

By the end of the account, the young Bunyan is forced to flee lest the whole steeple fall on him. The combination of the intensity of delight with his novice's anxiety about indulging in vanity culminates in the most memorable image of a sincere lover of religion *and* bells forced to run from an imaginary calamity.

Twenty years later, his long poem on the bell-ringers suggests a milder, more positive view of the value of the bells and their music. Now, instead of being threatened by the steeple's imagined collapse, the speaker *is* the steeple:

> My body is the Steeple, where they hang,
> My Graces they which do ring ev'ry Bell:
> Nor is there any thing gives such a tang,
> When by these Ropes these Ringers ring them well. (*B&G*, p. 231)

The bells are still threatened by naughty boys who would ring badly or for the wrong reasons. Bunyan still takes pleasure in the music of the bells and ends with a fervent desire, should it be appropriate, to continue his enjoyment of that music:

> O Lord! If thy poor Child might have his will,
> And might his meaning freely to thee tell;
> He never of this Musick has his fill,
> There's nothing to him like thy ding, dong, Bell. (*B&G*, p. 232)

The voices of the bells must have room to swing and ring, because it is in silence that the 'tinkling Voice of Vice' (*B&G*, p. 231) is heard. Silence, not music, is the devil's true medium.

A Book for Boys and Girls and the natural world

Human activity and creations occupy about half the collection, but Bunyan shows the strongest appreciation of beauty in his poems of comparison to the natural world and its creatures. Nature is not always benign, of course; some of the liveliest poems in the collection are those in which a natural creature becomes the exemplum for the child to avoid, and Bunyan is at his satirical best in these comparisons. Large-mouthed frogs are hypocrites, overfed swine will have their arrogance corrected by the knife, playful larks are tempted by the fowler-Satan, moles prefer the darkness to the light, and bees (most surprisingly) are like sins, which must be killed before we can safely get the honey. Every creature from the lowly blow-fly to the horse is invoked to demonstrate some danger to the budding Christian child.

The behaviour of some dumb creatures can be emulated as well as avoided, and in this Bunyan has good Biblical precedent to follow. From lions to locusts, Proverbs offers instruction by encouraging examination of the animal world. While neither lions nor locusts were indigenous English species, Bunyan does take two of his subjects from Proverbs – the ant and the spider – as well as the general instruction to look to natural creatures for example. The ant in Proverbs 6:6 is the schoolmaster, the creature best able to instruct the sluggard on good work habits:

> Go to the ant, thou sluggard; Consider her ways, and be wise:
> Which, having no guide, overseer, or ruler,
> Provideth her food in the summer, and gathereth her food in the harvest.

Compare this to Bunyan's poem, 'Upon the Pismire' (XXXIII):

> Must we unto the Pis-mire go to School,
> To learn of her, in Summer to provide
> For Winter next ensuing; Man's a Fool,
> Or silly Ants would not be made his Guide.
> But Sluggard, is it not a shame for thee,
> To be out-done by Pis-mires? Prethee hear:
> Their Works (too) will thy Condemnation be,
> When at the Judgment Seat thou shalt appear.
> But since thy God doth bid thee to her go,
> Obey, her ways consider, and be wise.
> The Piss-ants tell thee will what thou must do,
> And set the way to Life before thine eyes.   (*B&G*, p. 241)

Here the ant is not merely a good example for its industriousness; it is a reproach to humans who must be taught by such a lowly creature. The poem is an adaptation but also a commentary on Proverbs, one that emphasises how base humans must be to need such instruction. Part emblem, part reminder of the scriptural basis for Bunyan's method, the poem counteracts any reluctance on the part of its readers to learn from lowly creatures. The same encouragement to shame or humility is given in the extraordinary dialogue between 'The Sinner and the Spider' (XVII, *B&G*, pp. 214–21), which takes its starting point from Proverbs 30:28 but develops the comparison with the virtuosity of the candle poems. Here, the sinner has trouble accepting advice from the spider, which he variously calls 'venom'd', the 'Dregs', 'Scum' and 'Dross', and threatens to crush beneath his feet. In Proverbs, the comment on the spider is brief, given alongside three others that are 'little on the earth' but are yet 'exceeding wise':

> The ants are a people not strong, yet they prepare their meat in the summer;
> The conies are but a feeble folk, yet make they their houses in the rocks;
> The locusts have no king, yet go they forth all of them by bands;
> The spider taketh hold with her hands, and is in kings' palaces.

Bunyan's poem deals with that last suggestion – we find spiders even in the palaces of kings – and expands on the idea:

> I am a Spider, yet I can possess
> The Palace of a King, where Happiness
> So much abounds. Nor when I do go thither
> Do they ask what, or whence I come, or whither
> I make my hasty Travels ... (*B&G*, p. 219)

The spider has greater freedom than most of us, and therefore greater happiness, but the most important thing is the difference between an ugly spider who 'keep[s] the rules of [his] Creation', and the sinner who is created in God's image but whose sins have made him uglier than the spider (*B&G*, p. 215). A creature of integrity, the spider's instruction increases in length and persuasiveness until in the end the sinner is forced to concede: 'Thou art my Monitor, I am a Fool; / They learn may, that to Spiders go to School' (*B&G*, p. 221). In fact, the spider might even give us the motto for most of the collection:

> I was made for thy profit, do not fear me.
>> But if thy God thou will not hearken to,
> What can the Swallow, Ant, or Spider do?
> Yet I will speak, I can but be rejected;
> Sometimes great things, by small means are effected. (*B&G*, p. 216)

If Bunyan has a favourite part of the book of nature to read and reread it is the sun's position in the sky. Six poems deal with different views of the sky at various times: one before and two just at sunrise, two in the morning (one a 'low'ring' and one a 'fair'), and a final one on sunset. In each, we see a careful reading of the sky and a variety of ways to equate the Sun with the Son. Taken as a sequence, the meditations upon the day show if not a temporal then a spiritual progression from uncertainty, through security, to a warning about the end of life.

In the first – 'Meditation upon Peep of day' (v) – the comparison is with those who are first possessed of grace:

> I oft, though it be peep of day, don't know,
> Whether 'tis Night, whether 'tis Day or no.
> I fancy that I see a little light;
> But cannot yet distinguish day from night.
> I hope, I doubt, but steddy yet I be not,
> I am not at a point, the Sun I see not.
> Thus 'tis with such, who Grace but now possest,
> They know not yet, if they are curst or blest.   (*B&G*, p. 205)

The poem identifies a liminal space, a threshold, over which the new convert must pass but through which he is unsure about his status: saved or not? That space of insecurity – suspecting, hoping, but not yet knowing – interested Bunyan much, both as a Christian and a Christian preacher: those moments of drama even after the 'crisis' of conversion. The simplicity of the shared experience is especially good here: the rising of the sun is recognisable, literally every day, and shared. That same sense of uncertainty about when the day has changed places with night would work as well at the end of the day, but Bunyan, of course wants to illustrate a beginning, not an ending, and the paralleling of simple phrases – 'I hope', 'I doubt' – leaves the speaker in a state of balance, neither in day nor in night.

Although the second poem, 'Upon a low'ring Morning' (xi), would seem to be more threatening than the first, in fact that same sense of balance, of hovering at a threshold, operates in this poem as well. Here the mix of light and dark is caused by clouds that, to the traveller, may threaten 'slabby' rain or snow (*B&G*, p. 209). When, in the poem, it does rain, the speaker changes his attitude towards both rain and the apparently 'low'ring' red of the clouds. The same mixed sky, the comparison tells us, can bring both a 'sense of Grace, and sense of Sin' (*B&G*, p. 209).

The next two poems – 'Upon the Suns Reflections upon the Clouds in a fair Morning' (xv) and 'Meditations upon day before Sun-rising' (xviii) – emphasise greater security (*B&G*, pp. 213, 221). The sun in the clouds recalls the saints in heaven to the speaker in the first, while in the second, the possessors of grace are as eager to see Christ's face as those who look to see the sun rise. The fifth, the most confident, identifies the point at which there is no question any more: the sun has risen, just as the Son has. Not until the last is there a hint of warning: in xxxv, 'Of the going down of the Sun', those who have misspent their summer day are left to mourn the loss of the sun when the day is inevitably over (*B&G*, p. 239). The poems about the sun and the day, taken together, focus on morning, appropriately for poems addressed to those in the first days of life, and on the optimistic idea that, clouds notwithstanding, the sun is there and always rises.

Though they may read neatly as a sequence, no two of these poems are printed together, and so even the most apparently complementary poems are separated rather than grouped. Warren Wooden has argued for a complicated system in the arrangement of verses, concluding that the pattern in the original collection was meant to bring children gradually to an understanding of how to read, a system largely obscured when later editions omitted dozens of the original poems.[17] Such a system for increasing a child's spiritual literacy may underlie the collection, but subjects and comparisons seem more interspersed, chosen for the sake of a pleasing variety for a childhood reader easily bored.

Conclusion: the publication history

Wooden was certainly right about the general effect of the later editions on the reception and readership of Bunyan's little book. The version of the collection under examination here is Bunyan's own, the edition of the poems published in 1686 under the title *A Book for Boys and Girls: Or, Country Rhimes for Children*. From 1701 on, however, this version of the collection virtually disappeared, to be replaced by selected and rearranged versions of the original under new titles. So when George Offor published his edition of Bunyan's works, the collection of children's verse he included was called 'Divine Emblems', and included only forty-nine of the original seventy-four poems. The editor's principle of selection is difficult to determine; forty of the first fifty poems of *Book for Boys and Girls* are included, but only nine of the last twenty-four, which might suggest a simple need for brevity.[18] Poems not conforming to the emblem tradition, such as 'Upon the Ten Commandments' (I, *B&G*, p. 197), 'The awakened Childs Lamentation' (II, *B&G*, pp. 197–202) and 'Upon the Creed' (x, *B&G*, p. 208) are excluded, but so are many ('Upon a Ring of Bells' (xxix, *B&G*, p. 231), 'Upon the Boy on his Hobby-horse' (LXVII, *B&G*, p. 266)) that do. The prefatory 'hornbook' material is missing, as are the last twelve lines of Bunyan's opening.

Whatever the editor's intention, it was this truncated version that survived, first under the title *A Book for Boys and Girls or Temporal Things*

Spiritualized, and from 1724 on as *Divine Emblems or Temporal Things Spiritualized*, the title Offor knew. Not until John Brown's discovery of one copy of the original in the British Library and his subsequent publication of the facsimile edition in 1890 was that full version known. And so it was that the book Bunyan intended for children faded from memory, while *The Pilgrim's Progress* took its place on nursery shelves.

NOTES

1. Mark Twain, *Adventures of Huckleberry Finn* (1884), ed. Sculley Bradley, Richard Croom Beatty and E. Hudson Long (New York: Norton, 1962), p. 83; L. M. Montgomery, *Emily of New Moon* (New York: Frederick A. Stokes, 1923); Frances Hodgson Burnett, *Two Little Pilgrims' Progress: A Story of the City Beautiful* (London: Frederick Warne, 1895).

2. Enid Blyton, *The Land of Far Beyond* (London: Methuen, 1942), 'Introductory note', np.

3. *The Pilgrim's Progress* forms the structural framework for *Little Women*, which begins with the March girls reminiscing about childhood re-enactments of Christian's journey. Chapter headings such as 'Jo's Apollyon' or 'Meg's House of Humiliations' lead Elaine Showalter to argue for the book as a rewriting of Christian's journey from a woman's point of view: *Sister's Choice: Traditions and Change in American Women's Writing* (Oxford University Press, 1991), pp. 51–2.

4. Both Ruth MacDonald in *Christian's Children: The Influence of John Bunyan's 'The Pilgrim's Progress' on American Children's Literature* (Bern: Peter Lang, 1989) and David E. Smith in *John Bunyan in America* (Bloomington: Indiana University Press, 1966) trace Bunyan's influence – both through readings of his actual works and through adaptations – on eighteenth- and nineteenth-century American literature, including that written for children. The Puritan roots of early American settlements may account for the persistent interest.

5. For an account of the publication history of the book, see John Brown's introduction to the facsimile edition, *Book for Boys and Girls or, Country Rhymes for Children* (London: Elliot Stock, 1890).

6. On the history of the hornbook and battledore, see Patricia Demers, *From Instruction to Delight: An Anthology of Children's Literature to 1850* (1982; 2nd edn, Oxford University Press, 2003) and Andrew J. Tuer, *History of the Horn Book* (London: Leadenhall Press, 1896).

7. F. J. Harvey Darton writes about the impulse behind early Puritan books for children in *Children's Books in England: Five Centuries of Social Life* (London: British Library, 1999), pp 51–67.

8. Isaac Watts, Song XXIII, 'Obedience to Parents', in *Divine Songs, Attempted in Easy Language for the Use of Children* (1715), p. 181.

9. Mario Praz, *Studies in Seventeenth Century Imagery* (1939; 2nd edn, Rome: Edizioni di Storia e Letteratura, 1964), p. 18.

10. Rosemary Freeman, *English Emblem Books* (New York: Octagon, 1966), p. 114.

11. Roger Sharrock traces a number of parallels between the images Interpreter presents and specific emblems in a variety of English emblem books that

Bunyan may have known – and may have expected his readers to know; 'Bunyan and the English Emblem Writers', *RES*, 21.82 (April 1945), 105–16.

12. For the early history of the form in England, see Freeman's *English Emblem Books*. Freeman argues that Bunyan's work represents the end of the emblematic tradition.

13. In the Oxford edition a dozen or so simple woodcuts accompany the poems, but these were not added until later eighteenth-century editions.

14. See U. Milo Kaufmann, *'The Pilgrim's Progress' and Traditions in Puritan Meditation* (New Haven and London: Yale University Press, 1966) pp. 118–33. I am indebted to Anne Dunan-Page for pointing out that the pattern of Bunyan's poems follows the principles of the meditative tradition.

15. Darton, *Children's Books*, p. 65.

16. Percy A. Scholes, *The Puritans and Music in England and New England: A Contribution to the Cultural History of Two Nations* (Oxford University Press, 1934), pp. 91–2.

17. Warren W. Wooden, *Children's Literature of the English Renaissance*, ed. Jeanie Watson (Lexington: University Press of Kentucky, 1986), p. 154.

18. Graham Midgley suggests that some of the deleted poems may have appeared 'too gross in their emblems and language to an editor with a less robust and down-to-earth sense of the fitting than Bunyan's'. A delicate sensibility cannot account for all the deletions, however, and Midgley concludes that in the end, perhaps the editor 'simply cut out the poems he did not like' (*MW*, VI:188).

PART III

Readership and reception

10

ANNE DUNAN-PAGE

Posthumous Bunyan: early lives and the development of the canon

Bunyan the outcast

For most of his life, John Bunyan was despised. To clergymen of the Church of England he embodied the worst kind of sectarian fanaticism, and he was repeatedly accused of being a tinker, an 'emblem of lower-class vulgarity, drunkenness and promiscuity'.[1] Charges of ignorance, dishonesty, blasphemy, fanaticism and heresy were levelled against him, and when he challenged the Anglican Edward Fowler his writings were compared to the 'brutish barkings' of a dog. There were concerns that the 'Fury' of such an ignorant 'Pestilent Schismatick' might infect the true doctrine of the English Church and Bunyan's right to preach was quickly challenged.[2]

He had to contend just as much with the dissenters.[3] His dispute with the Quakers began with his first printed works: *Some Gospel-truths Opened* (1656) and his response to its critics, *A Vindication of ... Some Gospel-Truths Opened* (1657). In the eyes of George Fox, one of his later antagonists, Bunyan was a liar and a false prophet whose principles were inconsistent, just as his judgement was erratic.[4] Bunyan's reputation did not improve in 1659 when he was supposed to have supported, in print, the slanders of a Cambridgeshire woman, Margaret Pryor, who accused a Quaker widow of bewitching her and of changing her into a mare (Bunyan's pamphlet on the matter has not survived, if indeed it was ever written). Pryor was soon exposed as a lewd drunkard, the accused woman was acquitted by a jury in fifteen minutes and the accusation of witchcraft was turned against Bunyan.[5] Even the Baptists thought Bunyan to be a traitor. In *A Confession of my Faith* (1672) he had upheld the principle that believers who refused to be re-baptised as adults should nevertheless be welcomed into a church. The Bedford congregation he led was a mixed assembly favouring 'open communion', and such communities were never really considered to be fully-fledged Baptist churches. Despite their differences, these attacks suggest the same sense of danger, even of scandal, that surrounded the person and the writings of John Bunyan. For some, he was an unauthorised lay preacher spreading the fancies of his deluded imagination; for others, he was a misfit in his own community.

The 1692 folio

Conversely, Bunyan had his admirers. They included the Congregationalist ministers John Owen, who is reported to have envied Bunyan's talents as a preacher, and George Cockayne, whose London church was in close contact with Bedford. There was also John Gibbs, a Baptist minister from Newport Pagnell, and Charles Doe, a comb-maker and bookseller from Southwark, who became acquainted with Bunyan about two years before the author's death. Bunyan and Doe developed a relationship which a later commentator compared, perhaps with an excess of enthusiasm, to that of Boswell and Johnson.[6]

And yet one cannot escape the feeling that few of Bunyan's friends sided with him in his lifetime, at least in print, contributing to the impression that he was often somewhat isolated and marginalised. When some of his colleagues came to his rescue, such as his predecessor in Bedford, John Burton, it was generally to introduce his works, and to refute the accusation that his background was low and his education poor, rather than to mount a full-length defence of his principles. Burton wrote that Bunyan was 'one, who hath neither the greatness nor the wisdom of this world to commend him to thee' (MW, I:11). Henry Denne, in his answer to Thomas Smith, who had challenged Bunyan's right to preach, vindicates the legitimacy of the tinker in a short preface, but the bulk of his argument refutes Smith's (not Bunyan's) contention with the Quakers.[7] Similarly 'I. G', perhaps John Gibbs, in his preface to A Few Sighs from Hell (1658), is mostly concerned that 'prejudice' and 'censures', especially concerning the accidents of Bunyan's birth and education, will prevent his works from being accepted among believers. Yet again, this is essentially an introduction to the treatise, not a comprehensive endorsement of Bunyan, and the author is even careful to warn prospective readers that they might indeed find in the following pages material seemingly 'doubtful', 'grievous' and 'offend[ing]' (MW, I:231–44). George Cockayne composed a preface for The Acceptable Sacrifice (1689), dated about a month after Bunyan's death. The work begins by commending Bunyan 'Now with God, reaping the Fruit of all his Labour, Diligence and Success in his Masters Service' but once more fails to deliver the long-awaited apologia (MW, XII:7).[8]

Three years later, however, Charles Doe was responsible for launching some of his friend's works in folio, marking a new departure in the history of the author's reception. W. R. Owens has convincingly argued that the canonisation of Bunyan as a theologian dates from this 1692 edition, for publication in folio was traditionally reserved for the works of established divines and Biblical commentators, most of them university men.[9] It was decidedly not for tinkers. The volume, issued by William Marshall, was nonetheless published with the subscription of some 400 patrons, 30 of whom were ministers (Bunyan, *Works*, sig. 5U1r). It cost ten shillings unbound, twelve shillings bound. Originally advertised for February, it was issued in the autumn.[10] There are twenty-two of Bunyan's theological works in the book, ten of which had been published before, with twelve more printed from original manuscripts. There was not a word of Bunyan's fiction.

This thick volume is introduced by John Sturt's engraved oval portrait of Bunyan, together with a eulogy of the author by two ministers: Ebenezer Chandler, Bunyan's successor in Bedford, and John Wilson, from Hitchin. The book closes with an elaborate index, a catalogue of Bunyan's works, a list of no fewer than thirty reasons why readers should buy the book and a concluding piece entitled *The Struggler* (reproduced in *MW*, XII: 453–60). In this last item, Doe records how he 'struggled' over the publication of the folio, the vocabulary paralleling his description of Bunyan as 'struggling' with himself and with others.

First of all, the folio was meant to save Bunyan's work from the oblivion that could easily engulf material published in a more ephemeral manner. Doe, Chandler and Wilson saw themselves as links in a chain of editors working to make Apostolic and Christian writers available to contemporary readers. They remark time and again on the difficulties of procuring Bunyan's works in single copies, and express an anxiety that some of his most valuable pieces might rapidly sink into oblivion: '*The reason why there are so many Treatises put into one Volume, (some Printed before, others not,) is, that they may be preserved to future Ages, fearing that their continuing single, or the rest being Printed so, may hazard their being lost*' (Bunyan, *Works*, sig. A2v).

Second, in their eulogy, Chandler and Wilson attempt to moderate the image of their author as a religious radical. Taking care not to alienate potential readers inclined to suppose that Bunyan's lack of education rendered his preaching and writing worthless, or at least of doubtful value, they also strive to accommodate those who revered him as a visionary tinker. They avoid any suggestion that theological learning can ever be dispensable, and emphasise the point by inserting the occasional Latin phrase or motto. Bunyan emerges from their work as orthodox in matters of doctrine and in his commitment to unity, but Chandler and Wilson go so far as to suggest that the divine inspiration which the author of *The Pilgrim's Progress* claims in his 'Apology' to the allegory came ultimately to him as a result of hard work: '*so the Author's Knowledge, and insight into Gospel Mysteries, was given to him by God himself; we don't say, by immediate Inspiration, but by Prayer and Study, without any other external Helps'* (Bunyan, *Works*, sig. A1r). Among the particular examples cited to illustrate Bunyan's studious nature are the special care he took in preparing his sermons and his diligence in matters pertaining to Church discipline, such as administering the Lord's Supper, pronouncing admonitions or excommunications and filling up vacancies. In other words, the twenty-two works that were first presented to the world in 1692 appeared prefixed with an image of Bunyan as a 'usefull', 'accomplisht' and serious man, as far from the misguided pseudo-prophet of the seventeenth century as from the inspired genius of the Romantic era.

Finally, the folio was intended to serve as a practical tool for ministers and their churches. This is especially evident in what may seem, at first sight, a curious detail. In *The Struggler*, Doe devotes a considerable amount of space to the usefulness of the index that accompanies the folio, painstakingly explaining his system of references and cross-references, showing where and why a reader should search for a particular word or its synonyms (*MW*, xii: 458–60). The index encompasses important theological notions, controversies, cases of conscience and instructions on how to minister in a church, but it offers even more than that. Doe turns it into a compilation of types, metaphors and similes for ministers to peruse when composing their own sermons. It is an inexhaustible thesaurus of beasts, gems, plants, elements and astronomical notions; of legendary creatures and Biblical places; of crystal, glass, gold, stones, fruit, seeds and sticks; of rivers and wilderness, cities, gates, streets and walls.

The importance of the index to Doe's view of the folio is clear from two copies now in the Angus Library of Regent's Park College, Oxford. In these the title takes only about half the folio page. Underneath, and separated by a horizontal line, there is the following note, where the first two words are handwritten and the rest are printed: 'This index Is presented to Mr ... Of ... In ... By *Charles Doe* and *William Marshall*, because of his good Will in subscribing to the Printing of this *Folio*, 1691.' Evidently the gaps were left so that a name, town and county could be inserted. Marshall and Doe surely intended that some copies of the index, but not all of them, should be sent to their most eminent patrons as a particular mark of esteem.[11] Since all Doe's writings (not only the index itself, but also the catalogue, the list of reasons and *The Struggler*) come *after* the general title page for the index, it was also perhaps intended that all this material be presented to patrons as a good piece of self-advertisement on Doe's part.

Doe took pride in compiling writings and tables that could serve as an invaluable tool for ministers and spread wide the seeds of his chosen author's wisdom. No doubt he was very gratified that some churches subscribed to the folio, such as Bristol and Canterbury.[12] In the eighteenth century William Carr, pastor of a church meeting at Hamsterley and Cold Rowley (County Durham), recorded that 'Bunions folio' was among a small library 'given to the ministry of our Church'. The folio then passed on to Carr's successor, Isaac Gardner, who emphasises the communal ownership of the volume, since it 'belonges to ye Church'.[13]

As a commercial enterprise, the first Bunyan folio was a failure, but it succeeded in making its author well known. Eight years after its publication, in 1700, the London audiences that gathered to see the first performances of William Congreve's *The Way of the World* were expected to recognise a satirical reference to the entertainment value of '*Bunyan's* Works', possibly an allusion to the folio whose full title is *The Works of that Eminent Servant of Christ, Mr John Bunyan*.[14] No second volume would appear for another forty-five years. Perhaps this was due to a lack of business acumen, the folios of dissenters being rarely issued by a single publisher. There were also signs that Doe and Marshall had fallen out.[15] Perhaps, given the disarray of the dissenting community in the early 1690s, the publication of Bunyan's works was simply untimely.[16] By 1708, the idea of a second folio seems to have been abandoned, and it was proposed to publish instead Bunyan's most valuable pieces in octavo 'on a beautiful Letter and good Paper', for which only 100 subscribers were needed.[17]

There are also signs that both Ebenezer Chandler and Doe were controversial figures, not above using Bunyan's name to suit their own needs. Chandler, for instance, was a moderate in doctrine and was passionately opposed to the drift he observed among some dissenters towards 'Antinomianism', the belief that the moral law was not binding for the elect. In 1692, he publicly attacked the Antinomian preacher Richard Davis, the pastor of a neighbouring Independent church in Rothwell.[18] Engaged in such a battle, Chandler might well have wished to construct an image of Bunyan as a famous, reputable and balanced minister, a figure behind whom he and the dissenting community could unite.

Doe had darker shadows in his biography. First a General Baptist, then an 'open' communion Baptist, it was never clear exactly when he had switched sides and embraced Calvinism. When he was not selling or publishing Bunyan's books, he collected accounts of miraculous cures. In the narrative of his conversion he recalls how his wife was cured of a raging toothache by the power of prayer alone.[19] In 1695, he added four short narratives of miraculous cures to the second edition of William Eyre's *Vindiciæ Justificationis Gratuitæ*, and in 1705, he published *a Narrative of the Miraculous Cure of Anne Munnings*, this time presenting himself as the chief instrument of the cure. These stories, each one presented with careful exposition of God's providential mercy, might well have been frowned upon by orthodox members of the godly community, but they nonetheless proved very popular. Doe's activities in the book trade, including his championship of Bunyan, had perhaps as much to do with his need to supplement the income from his comb-making business as with spreading God's word.

Establishing the canon

The folio shows clear signs of an attempt to construct an ideal set of writings by Bunyan. Doe limited the accompanying catalogue to precisely sixty works on the grounds that Bunyan was sixty years of age when he died. Doe proudly announces this coincidence, which he thinks very felicitous, on the title page of the folio, and lists the works, in chronological order, at the end of the volume. This meant giving Bunyan's œuvre a slight twist, and by comparing the works actually printed with those announced on the title page and the final catalogue one can sense the fluidity of the canon at this early stage, for there are several revealing discrepancies. In the final catalogue, Doe apparently forgets that *The Saints Privilege and Profit* has been printed in the volume; he also includes one work twice, first under its title (*The Saints Knowledge of Christ's Love*) and then under its subtitle (*The Unsearchable Riches of Christ*). Two manuscript broadsides are listed, *Of the Trinity and a Christian* and *Of the Law and a Christian*, which increases the number of manuscripts cited to twelve, whereas the title page (and the original advertisement for the folio) mentions only ten. Doe obviously managed to procure the two broadsides between his initial prospectus and the final printing.

The boundaries of the canon can also be seen to be shifting in other ways. One work, *Election and Reprobation* (also known as *Reprobation Asserted*) is almost certainly not authentic.[20] Doe also lists four more works to bring the total to sixty, but he prints none of them and two were never found nor published: 'A Christian Dialogue' and 'A Pocket Concordance'. The two others were printed later; Doe published *The Heavenly Foot-man* in 1698 but *A Relation of the Imprisonment of Mr John Bunyan* had to wait until 1765. As for Bunyan's pamphlet accusing the Quakers of witchcraft, Doe either chose to suppress it or was not aware of its existence.

At the end of the first edition of *The Heavenly Foot-man*, Doe inserted a new and lightly corrected catalogue of Bunyan's works. Things were still very mobile. He reinstated *The Saints Privilege and Profit* and removed the two-fold listing of *The Saints Knowledge of Christ's Love*. This catalogue was reprinted in the second edition of 1700 and was very slightly altered for the fourth in 1708. There are now two separate works of poetry (*Ebal and*

Gerizzim and *Prison-Meditations*) listed as one item, and a spurious work, *Hearts-Ease in Heart-Trouble*. This would prove to be Doe's most enduring mistake since it continued to be printed as an authentic work of Bunyan well into the twentieth century. It was actually the work of an ejected minister from Dartmouth, James Birdwood, and the mistaken attribution almost certainly owes something to a simple confusion of two authors whose initials were JB. Only between 1698 and 1708 did Doe become convinced that the work was canonical.

After Doe, the task of publishing Bunyan's work passed to Samuel Wilson, the grandson of the Hitchin pastor who had co-authored the 1692 preface. Wilson's folio appeared in two volumes in 1736 and 1737.[21] The title page of the first volume does not claim to be an entirely new edition but simply the 'second edition' of the folio 'with additions'. These comprise a preface by Samuel Wilson, a Life of Bunyan with his deathbed sayings, two treatises (*A Vindication of Some Gospel-Truths Opened* and *A Caution to Stir Up Against Sin*) together with an engraving of the House of the Forest of Lebanon. The second volume is an apparently haphazard choice of works from Doe's catalogue. Wilson, however, was in one sense more discerning than his predecessor (and indeed many of his successors) for he dropped the spurious *Election and Reprobation* and *Hearts-Ease*, but he added one title never mentioned by Doe, *An Exhortation to Peace and Unity*. This is a short work and certainly spurious, prefixed to the second edition of the *Barren Fig-Tree* (1688), perhaps, Graham Midgley suggests, introduced there at the last moment to capitalise on Bunyan's growing fame (*MW*, v:7). Sharon Achinstein has recently argued it could be read as a document supporting the Jacobite cause. In 1853, George Offor still included it in his standard edition, although he had 'serious doubt' about its authorship.[22]

Bunyan's canon owes much to Doe and Wilson, but neither had an entirely error-free vision of his œuvre. Arguably, we still do not have one. What we do know is that three spurious works (*Election and Reprobation, An Exhortation to Peace and Unity* and *Hearts-Ease*) entered the canon early on and profited from the endorsement of early editors. Second, that crucial works such as *A Defence of the Doctrine of Justification, by Faith in Jesus Christ* (1672), *A Treatise of the Fear of God* (1678), *The Greatness of the Soul* (1682), *Questions about the Nature and Perpetuity of the Seventh-Day-Sabbath* (1685), *A Discourse of ... the House of God* (1688) were in danger of being lost, as they did not appear in collected works before the 1780s, some hundred years after their first publication. A similar fate befell Bunyan's first prison poetry, *Profitable Meditations* (1661), which was lost until 1860 when J. Camden Hotten, a bookseller from Piccadilly, found a copy. Third, the early friends and editors were only partly successful in establishing Bunyan's legacy.

The collected works had a confined readership. Most of Bunyan's early readers knew his works through cheap editions of single titles that give a very partial image of the complete œuvre. The success of *The Pilgrim's Progress* never flagged from its first edition onwards. The eighteenth century was also kind to *Grace Abounding*, but even more so to *The Holy War*, with more than fifty British editions (a third of which were Scottish), a surprising turn of fortune for an allegory which had not been especially popular before Bunyan's death, and one that remains so far unexplained. Conversely, the number of recorded eighteenth-century editions of *The Life and Death of Mr Badman* is low. Bunyan's *A Few Sighs from Hell* and *Come, and Welcome, to Jesus Christ* remained bestsellers, together with *The Doctrine of the Law and Grace Unfolded*, *The Barren Fig-Tree* and *Solomon's Temple Spiritualiz'd*. There were, however, titles that readers purchased with even greater avidity and they were all spurious: *A Dialogue between a Blind Man and Death*, *Meditations on the Several Ages of Man's Life*, *Scriptural Poems*, *A Race for Eternal Life*, *Rest for a Wearied Soul*, *The Riches of Christ* and *The Visions of John Bunyan*. The eighteenth century produced a conflict between the 'canonical' Bunyan of the expensive collected works and the bogus Bunyan of the cheaper prints, writer of doggerel, visions and meditations.

Early lives

Bunyan died on 31 August 1688 at the London house of the grocer John Strudwick, a deacon of George Cockayne's church. For the last ten years of his life, both Bunyan and Ponder had complained about pirated editions, but no sooner was Bunyan's body deposited in Bunhill Fields than more or less reliable commentators began publishing spurious material. The earliest of these, as we have seen above, was possibly *An Exhortation to Peace and Unity*. The same year, Bunyan's supposed deathbed sayings were published. This was a series of aphorisms on sin, affliction, repentance, prayer, the Lord's day, love of the world, suffering, death and judgement, Heaven and Hell, all far too formal to have been genuine utterances, but which were in keeping with the popularity of the last sayings of famous dissenters that had appeared throughout the Restoration, often in broadside format.[23] These were popular and reprinted both by Samuel Wilson and George Offor.

A cluster of publications, immediately preceding or following the 1692 folio, indicates that the compilation or publication of a Bunyan biography was rapidly beginning to seem a potentially lucrative venture. In Richard Greaves's phrase, 'Bunyan's name had acquired the status of a well-known brand, the use of which enticed people to purchase products associated with his name.'[24] For all the wealth of information provided in the folio, it did not disclose many details about Bunyan's life, leaving others (most notably Robert Ponder, the son of Nathaniel) to tap this rich vein and turn Bunyan's biography into popular lore. The seventh edition of *Grace Abounding* (1692) was published by Robert Ponder with 'The Continuation of Mr Bunyan's Life' (sometimes attributed to Cockayne), 'A brief Character of Mr John Bunyan', a postscript, and a catalogue of Bunyan's works that could rival Doe's.[25] Soon afterwards, the spurious third part of *The Pilgrim's Progress* (1693) appeared with an anonymous 'An Account of the Life and Actions of Mr. John Bunyan', a forty-two-page biography supplemented by a short elegy. The unknown author, finding much 'Flattery and Glozing' in the work of biographers keen to 'insinuate' themselves into the favour of the deceased's relations, purports to give his candid version of Bunyan's life, with '*every thing in its proper shape*'.[26]

'The Continuation of Mr Bunyan's Life' claims to lengthen Bunyan's autobiography, 'since there yet remains some what worthy of Notice and Regard, which occurr'd in the last Scene of his Life'.[27] It concentrates on episodes not dealt with in *Grace Abounding*. We learn about the building of the new Bedford meeting-house (which in fact saw the light only in 1707), of Bunyan's travels to London, of his family 'discipline' and of the circumstances of his sudden death in London. The writer claims to recall Bunyan's dying words, in the conventional form of a deathbed scene: '[He] fell sick of a violent Feavor, which he bore with much constancy and patience, and expressed himself, as if he desired nothing more than to be dissolved, and to be with Christ ... esteeming Death as gain, and Life only a tedious delaying felicity expected.'[28] The famous '*brief Character*' concentrates on Bunyan's physique: 'As for his Person he was Tall of Stature, strong Boned, though not corpulent somewhat of a Ruddy Face, with Sparkling Eyes, wearing his Hair on his upper Lip, after the Old *British* fashion; his Hair Reddish.'[29] The 'Continuation' was for a long time favoured as the most genuine account of Bunyan's life. It still supplemented *Grace Abounding* in Offor's edition.

'An Account of the Life and Actions of Mr John Bunyan' is both much longer and far less reliable, cribbing entire sections from *Grace Abounding*. Just like his predecessor, however, the author contends that Bunyan's biography is somehow defective, or at the very least incomplete, and that his friends have been deficient in their duty of memory.[30] Scholars have long discarded this account as a reliable guide to Bunyan's biography, for most of the information it gives not derived from *Grace Abounding* is wrong or impausible. Thus it claims that Bunyan's father taught him 'many Psalms, Graces, and Prayers by heart, to season him in his Infancy' (whereas Bunyan himself reports that his father was a poor Christian), that his gambling forced him to choose a poor wife and that he was present at the siege of Leicester during the Civil War.[31]

The veracity of some other added material is more difficult to determine. Some may be authentic, while some may simply reflect the ingenuity of an editor who knew, by 1693, the kind of thing that readers wanted to hear about John Bunyan. In *Grace Abounding*, for example, Bunyan mentions his time at a local school and says that he 'did soon loose that little [he] learned, even almost utterly' (*GA*, p. 5). The author of the 'Life' suggests that Bunyan means he lost the ability to read and therefore lapsed into illiteracy.[32] Bunyan's early dreams are then carefully recorded, with more details than in *Grace Abounding*, some of them lurid in ways that tellingly suggest a desire to invent spurious and sensational material to meet an avid demand: 'generally these Dreams were about evil Spirits, in monsterous shapes and forms, that presented themselves to him in threatning postures, as if they would have taken him away, or torn him in pieces: At some times they seemed to belch flame, at other times a contigeous smoak, with horrible Noises and Roaring.'[33] Finally, a long passage is devoted to Bunyan's arrest in 1660 for illegal preaching: 'Then a Constable was ordered to fetch him down [from the pulpit], who coming up, and taking hold on his Coat, no sooner did Mr *Bunyan* fix his Eyes stedfastly upon him, having his Bible then open in his hand, but the Man let go, looked pale, and retired.'[34] Bunyan the illiterate tinker, pursued by nightmarish monsters, kept at bay the forces of Antichrist with a sharp eye and a Bible. From then on, historical accuracy seemed to matter less than the image of a blessed and impoverished holy man whose wisdom could be bought for a few pennies.

In the meantime, Charles Doe seems to have realised he was missing an opportunity to give a more authentic record of Bunyan's life to the world. In 1700, he accordingly published the second edition of *The Heavenly Foot-Man* with an anonymous 'The Life and Death of Mr *John Bunyan*'. Although much of this is a summary of *Grace Abounding* in the third person, it includes details which first appeared in 'A Continuation' and 'An Account of the Life'. It adds, however, an interesting anecdote for the history of dissent. The writer dates his encounter with Bunyan from the time when the author was in prison and therefore provides a precious eye-witness account of Bedford jail. He records that about sixty dissenters were sharing the space with Bunyan, who was preaching on a regular basis. We also learn that Bunyan's prison 'library' comprised a Bible and Foxe's *Actes and Monuments* (1563); it seems that he had also learned to make shoelaces to support his family.[35] However, this biographer is at times no more accurate than his predecessors. He seems convinced that Bunyan's parents were godly and, like the author of 'An Account of the Life', he announces that Bunyan had forgotten for a while how to read and write. He also repeats the false claim that Bunyan was present at the siege of Leicester, while advancing the date of his baptism to

1653, rather than 1655.[36] It seems that Doe's endorsement gave credit to this account, for it is the one that Samuel Wilson chose to reproduce as an introduction to the 1736 folio.

Accounts of Bunyan's life by more or less reliable and contemporary observers began appearing as early as 1692, in the wake of the first folio. The readership's demand for details about Bunyan's life, to supplement *Grace Abounding*, must have been soaring, encouraging the publication of rival accounts. This had consequences for the reception of Bunyan's genuine autobiography. The vast majority of the eighteenth-century English (but not Scottish) editions of *Grace Abounding* abandon Bunyan's original subtitle, *A Brief and Faithful Relation of the Exceeding Mercy of God in Christ to his Poor Servant John Bunyan* and replace it with a simpler and more eye-catching phrase, *A Faithful Account of the Life and Death of John Bunyan*, sounding an echo of his own *Life and Death of Mr Badman*. For some, Bunyan the theologian was less appealing than Bunyan the wretched sinner who was 'miraculously' converted. In order to emphasise the extraordinary nature of that experience, Bunyan's early biographers exaggerated the meanness of his social condition, his lack of education and the enormity of his sins. This is ultimately how he is represented, as he was before his conversion, by John Ryland, a minister from Southampton, in the first volume of the octavo edition that John Hagg published in the early 1780s: 'No man of common sense and common integrity can deny that Bunyan, the tinker of Elstow near Bedford, was a practical atheist, a worthless contemptible infidel, a vile rebel to God and goodness, a common profligate, a soul-despising, a soul-murdering, a soul-doming, thoughtless wretch as could exist in the face of the earth.'[37] Even in his most self-lacerating moments, Bunyan had never gone that far.

Conclusion

The course of Bunyan's early reception is essentially the story of his transformation into the pastoral giant of the eighteenth century. He was given an air of respectability, indeed of holiness, to appeal to the greatest number of readers. Bunyan's legacy was claimed by friends, colleagues and editors who had competing motives and were sometimes embroiled in personal and professional controversies to which Bunyan could lend some posthumous authority on one side or the other. The editors of the collected volumes and those of spurious single works built up the legendary Bunyan not as the enthusiastical Anabaptist firebrand who challenged the Restored ecclesiastical authorities, not as a serious 'divine' in the sense of a meaty theologian, but as a champion of practical theology, as useful to the Baptist minister as to the doubting Christian.

Nonetheless, Bunyan's heritage proved too rich and complex to be easily controlled by those who appointed themselves the guardians of his legacy. As readers began to forget about Bunyan's fiercest controversies, they became fascinated by the minutiae of his personal life and eager to hear time and again of the miraculous conversion of an illiterate sinner. In studying Bunyan's early reception, there is no need to undermine the role of the early editors and friends who helped to fix the canon, even if they were not above using Bunyan's name to acquire personal or professional profit. Nor should one discredit the myriad of lesser-known or anonymous writers who exploited the intense curiosity about the man and his work. Together, they kept Bunyan's memory and work alive until the Romantics and the Victorians transformed the tinker of Bedford into one of the great icons of the nineteenth century.

NOTES

1. Christopher Hill, 'Bunyan's Contemporary Reputation', in Anne Laurence, W.R. Owens and Stuart Sim (eds.), *John Bunyan and His England, 1628–1688* (London and Ronceverte, W.Va.: The Hambledon Press, 1990), pp. 3–15 (p. 4).
2. Anon., *Dirt Wipt Off* (1672), sig. A4r, pp. 1–2; see also Thomas Smith, *The Quaker Disarm'd* (1659).
3. Ted L. Underwood, ' "It pleased me much to contend": John Bunyan as Controversialist', *Church History*, 57 (1988), 456–69. On Bunyan's reputation, see W.R. Owens, 'The Reception of *The Pilgrim's Progress* in England', in M. van Os and G.J. Schutte (eds.), *Bunyan in England and Abroad* (Amsterdam: Vrije University Press, 1990), pp. 91–104; N.H. Keeble, ' "Of him thousands daily Sing and talk": Bunyan and his Reputation', in Keeble (ed.), *Conventicle*, pp. 241–63; Greaves, *Glimpses*, pp. 610–34; W.R. Owens and Stuart Sim (eds.), *Reception, Appropriation, Recollection: Bunyan's 'Pilgrim's Progress'* (Bern: Peter Lang, 2007).
4. George Fox, *The Great Mistery of the Great Whore Unfolded* (1659), pp. 8–14.
5. James Blackley *et al.*, *A Lying Wonder Discovered* (1659). On the episode, see Margaret J.M. Ezell, 'Bunyan's Women, Women's Bunyan', in Vera J. Camden (ed.), *Trauma and Transformation: The Political Progress of John Bunyan* (Stanford University Press, 2008), pp. 63–80.
6. Brown, *Bunyan*, p. 369.
7. Henry Denne, *The Quaker No Papist* (1659), sig. A2r–A2v.
8. Perhaps only once did Bunyan need – and expressly ask for – the help of a renowned London name, and that was refused to him. He called for the support of John Owen in the controversy that opposed him to the 'closed-communion' Baptists in 1672–3. For some reason, possibly because he did not wish to be involved in a controversy that was best kept within the Baptist community, Owen denied Bunyan his public support; see Greaves, *Glimpses*, p. 297.
9. W.R. Owens, 'Reading the Bibliographical Codes: Bunyan's Publication in Folio', in N.H. Keeble (ed.), *John Bunyan: Reading Dissenting Writing* (Bern: Peter Lang, 2002), pp. 59–77.
10. See Marshall's advertisement at the end of John Owen's *A Guide to Church-Fellowship* (1692).

11. Angus Library FPC-B.4. The name 'John Carter', one of the honoured subscribers, is inserted in one of the copies.

12. See Marshall's subscription proposal quoted by Owens, 'Reading the Bibliographical Codes', p. 65.

13. 'Records of the Church of Hexham, Hamsterley and Cold Rowley', fols. 110, 126 (all MSS cited with permission of the Angus Library, Regent's Park College, University of Oxford).

14. William Congreve, *The Way of the World* (1700), p. 34. The word 'Works' is capitalised in the original.

15. Owens, 'Reading the Bibliographical Codes', pp. 75–6.

16. Most of the folios printed by subscription were issued by two to six men who shared the financial burden, see Sarah L. C. Clapp, 'Subscription Publishers Prior to Jacob Tonson', *The Library*, 4th ser. (1932), 158–83. I owe this reference to Owens, 'Reading the Bibliographical Codes', p. 64.

17. *The Heavenly Foot-Man*, 1698, 4th edn (1708), p. 23.

18. See Davis's attacks against Chandler in *Truth and Innocency Vindicated* (1692).

19. Charles Doe, *A Collection of Experience of the Work of Grace* (1700), pp. 47–9.

20. Richard L. Greaves, *John Bunyan and English Nonconformity* (London: Hambledon Press, 1992), pp. 185–91.

21. There was a third English folio in 1767, with a preface by the Methodist George Whitefield, a Scottish folio in 1771, and in the early 1780s John Hagg published the most complete collection to date, in six octavo volumes.

22. George Offor (ed.), *The Works of John Bunyan*, 3 vols. (Glasgow, Edinburgh and London: Blackie, 1852–3), II:742; Sharon Achinstein, 'Bunyan and the Politics of Rememberance', in Camden (ed.), *Trauma and Transformation*, pp. 135–52 (pp. 148–51).

23. See for instance *Old Mr Edmund Calamy's Former and Latter Sayings upon Several Occasions* (1674), *The Sayings of that Reverend and Great Preacher Mr S. Charnock* (1680), *Most Holy and Profitable Sayings of that Reverend Divine, Doctor Tho. Goodwin* (nd), *Mr Janeway's Sayings Not long before his Death* (1674), *The Golden Sayings, Sentences and Experiences of Mr Vavasor Powell* (nd).

24. Greaves, *Glimpses*, p. 618.

25. *Grace Abounding*, 1666, 7th edn (1692), pp. 157–74.

26. 'An Account of the Life and Actions of Mr John Bunyan', *The Pilgrim's Progress: The Third Part* (1693), p. 4.

27. 'The Continuation', *Grace Abounding* (1692), p. 158.

28. *Ibid.*, p. 169.

29. *Ibid.*, pp. 170–1.

30. 'The Life and Actions', p. 4.

31. *Ibid.*, pp. 6, 16–18.

32. *Ibid.*, p. 17.

33. *Ibid.*, p. 10.

34. *Ibid.*, p. 33.

35. 'The Life and Death of Mr *John Bunyan*', *The Heavenly Foot-Man* (1700), pp. 126–7.

36. *Ibid.*, pp. 110, 131, 123.

37. *The Whole Works of that Eminent Servant of Christ*, ed. John Hagg, 6 vols. (nd), I:iii.

11

EMMA MASON

The Victorians and Bunyan's legacy

Little Nell's journey out of London into the Midlands in *The Old Curiosity Shop* (1841) might easily be read as a progress from the Slough of Despond into the Celestial City. Accompanied by her grandfather, Nelly Trent cheerfully engages on her pilgrimage, her path illuminated by the 'full glory of the sun' and decorated by scores of new-build churches, 'erected with a little superfluous wealth, to show the way to Heaven'. Forging her way through 'the haunts of commerce and great traffic' (symbols that, if granted capital letters, would be happy in the company of Bunyan's Talkative or Giant Despair), Nell arrives at Dickens's rendering of the Wicket Gate, a turnpike framed in a pastoral setting. From here, the narrator claims

> the traveller might stop, and – looking back at old Saint Paul's looming through the smoke, its cross peeping above the cloud (if the day were clear), and glittering in the sun; and casting his eyes upon the Babel out of which it grew until he traced it down to the furthest outposts of the invading army of bricks and mortar whose station lay for the present nearly at his feet – might feel at last that he was clear of London.

Stopping here for breakfast, Nell and her grandfather are momentarily content, surrounded by 'the singing of the birds, the beauty of the waving grass, the deep green leaves, the wild flowers, and the thousand exquisite scents and sounds that floated in the air', a scene in which Nell recalls her

> old copy of the Pilgrim's Progress, with strange plates, upon a shelf at home, over which she had often pored whole evenings, wondering whether it was true in every word, and where those distant countries with the curious names might be. As she looked back upon the place they had left, one part of it came strongly on her mind. 'Dear grandfather,' she said, 'only that this place is prettier and a great deal better than the real one, if that in the book is like it, I feel as if we were both Christian, and laid down on this grass all the cares and troubles we brought with us; never to take them up again.' 'No – never to return – never to return' – replied the old man, waving his hand towards the city. 'Thou and I are free of it now, Nell. They shall never lure us back.'[1]

Like Nell, many Victorian readers sympathetically received Dickens's depiction of *The Pilgrim's Progress* as a redemptive, salvific and consolatory evangelical narrative. While modern critics find scenes such as the one quoted above suspiciously sentimental, and encourage a hermeneutic that looks for a subtext that undercuts the reassurance Bunyan offered contemporary readers, the Victorians consumed pilgrimage narratives, a genre for which Bunyan's text was the central template, in huge numbers. *The Pilgrim's Progress* was a particular favourite in the nineteenth century, primarily because of the way the narrative lent itself to a Victorian obsession with exploring the personal truths of individual subjectivity. Numerous episodes in Bunyan's pilgrimage narrative – in the Slough of Despond, Doubting Castle, the crossing of the river, for example – speak to a Victorian sense that the journey to grace was marked by personal struggle and temptation, trials that were overcome through self-analysis as much as Biblical study. As Roger Sharrock argues, Bunyan's imagination is as dependent on the affective, social and psychologised as it is on the allegorical, moral and symbolic, and *The Pilgrim's Progress* and *Grace Abounding* alike are both self-consciously creative, encouraging forwarded moments of awakening in which the reader sees the world 'with new eyes' to read as he or she 'never did before' (*GA*, p. 17).[2] This chapter traces the impact of Bunyan's work on the Victorians, first by addressing its broad, cross-class appeal, one that is testified to by the multiplicity of editions of his work reproduced in the period. Following from this, the discussion turns to Bunyan's reputation and politicisation in the nineteenth century, both invariably emotionalised by admirers as they referenced, quoted and absorbed his work into Victorian novels and biographies of Bunyan himself. The chapter closes by focusing on the way two writers – Charles Dickens and L. Frank Baum – translate Bunyan's allegory into their popular fictions, texts that rely on their readers' familiarity with and affection for Bunyan's devotional writing.

Mass-market Bunyan

A key argument for Bunyan's popularity adduced by nineteenth-century commentators was his appeal to all classes. In 1876, the Dean of Chester, J. S. Howson, announced that *The Pilgrim's Progress* provided 'common ground for persons of the highest education, and for those whom we commonly term the working classes'.[3] As Mary Hammond argues, the market for cheap and morally useful literature opened up during the nineteenth century, and Bunyan's works were published with increasingly heavy frames of footnotes and chapters of didactic exposition in an attempt to control an author read by so many.[4] The myriad of editions of *The Pilgrim's Progress* also attests to its broad reach; the reader who wanted to invest in an expensive edition would have purchased James Nisbet and Co.'s leather-bound, gilt-edged illustrated copy or Cambridge University Press's pocket-book version; while the reader who required a cheaper, thin-papered copy might have sought William Mason's reissue (ideal as an option for a Sunday School prize) or the Reverend James Black's late-century devotional exposition.[5] Even as an increasingly secularised nineteenth-century readership turned towards newspapers and novels, Bunyan remained popular. His work was reinterpreted as a psychological study (in J. A. Kerr's book of 1887, *The People of the Pilgrimage: An Expository Study of 'The Pilgrim's Progress' as a Book of Character*); as a textbook to teach shorthand (in Pitman's 1891 edition); as what would now be called a coffee-table book (Pearson's 1898 illustrated copy); and as a historic classic (Elliot Stock's 1895 facsimile).[6]

As early as the 1780s, Bunyan had become, alongside the Bible, staple reading. Countless popular illustrated editions targeted those unable to read, and the allegorical form of *The Pilgrim's Progress* in particular worked successfully in pictorial form.[7] Commenting on the visual aspect of Bunyan's narrative, the radical weaver and writer, Samuel Bamford, wrote in his memoirs:

> The first book which attracted my particular notice was 'The *Pilgrim's* Progress' with rude woodcuts; it excited my curiosity in an extraordinary degree. There was 'Christian knocking at the strait gate', his 'fight with Apollyon', his 'passing near the lions', his 'escape from Giant Despair', his 'perils at Vanity Fair', his arrival in the 'land of Beulah', and his final passage to 'Eternal Rest'; all these were matters for the exercise of my feeling and imagination.[8]

Bamford's testimony reveals more than the status of illustrated copies of *The Pilgrim's Progress*. First, it points towards Bunyan's reputation at the turn of the century; and second, it is suggestive of Bunyan's politicisation in the long nineteenth century. While an older Coleridge would eventually denounce the Bunyan of the 'Conventicle' and favour the Bunyan of 'Parnassus', the younger and more politicised poet joined Blake and Wordsworth in heralding him as part of a radical seventeenth-century movement connected to the English Revolution as their poetry had been to the French Revolution.[9] Many readers, however, were uncomfortable with the politicisation of Bunyan. Walter Scott's review of Robert Southey's *The Pilgrim's Progress, with a Life of John Bunyan* (1830) betrays an eagerness to separate Bunyan's politics from his religious beliefs and urges readers to assess his work for its individual aesthetic rather than its didactic content. As Scott declared: 'In an evil hour were the doctrines of the Gospel sophisticated with questions which should have been left in the schools ... Many are the poor creatures whom such questions have driven to despair and madness, and suicide; and no one ever more narrowly escaped such a catastrophe than Bunyan.'[10]

A political and spiritual guide

For Scott, Bunyan was saved from the immoderate emotions of religious enthusiasm partly by his 'Romantic' genius and partly by the mental and physical exhaustion of serving a prison sentence. Incarceration, Scott assumes, would have knocked any political or religious pretensions out of a once unruly Bunyan. Thomas Macaulay, on the other hand, views Bunyan as a thoroughly radicalised social commentator; Faithful's martyrdom, for example, becomes an observation on state trials under Charles II, while Greatheart is understood to be modelled upon those who led the armies at Naseby and Worcester.[11] As C. Stephen Finley argues, Macaulay believed that Bunyan's achievement was to present political ideas through personal suggestion, and the Slough of Despond, the Delectable Mountains, Giant Despair were all 'forms of life, words that carried within them the charge of psychological verities'.[12] For Macaulay, Bunyan 'gave to the abstract the interest of the concrete', so granting Victorian readers a one-way ticket back to an old dissenting tradition under attack from high church reform on the one hand and an escalating preference for Latitudinarianism on the other.[13] Bamford, for example, directly associated Bunyan with the radical militancy he turned to while fighting for working-class rights in the early nineteenth century; so did the Chartist leader, Thomas Cooper, who labelled *The Pilgrim's Progress* the 'book of books'.[14] Political radicals deemed Lord Hategood and Giant Despair to be hostile, bullying and destructive images of bourgeois oppression in the period, and in 1839, Bunyan's allegory was serialised in the Chartist journal, *The Northern Liberator*, as *The Political Pilgrim's Progress*.[15] Not only did Bunyan's Puritan activism establish him as a model of reform, but his emphasis on the Bible over other kinds of education also appealed to a readership alienated by elitist conceptions of schooling. As Bunyan claims in *Solomon's Temple Spiritualiz'd*, 'my Bible and Concordance are my only library in my writings' (*MW*, VII:9), a sentiment echoed in *Grace Abounding*, wherein the reader is informed that if Greek were required to read the Bible 'then but a very few of the poorest sort should be saved' (*A Relation of the Imprisonment of Mr John Bunyan, GA*, p. 111).

No wonder Christopher Hill and E. P. Thompson both view Bunyan's works as the foundation of the radical dissenting tradition. For Thompson, *The Pilgrim's Progress* is, with Tom Paine's *Rights of Man* (1791), 'one of the two foundation texts of the English working-class movement', embodying as it does 'the slumbering radicalism which was preserved through the eighteenth century, and which breaks out again in the nineteenth century'.[16] Bunyan's sense that each individual should read and interpret scripture from a specific and particularised viewpoint was in itself a political assertion, although as a writer who appears not to have formally joined any political movement, his presence in Victorian households did not necessarily mark him as a nonconformist. His belief that the Bible was the Word of God stood in direction opposition to the dissenting, Quaker-driven understanding of scripture as a kind of non-specific light within. As Andrew Bradstock argues, even as Bunyan 'saw a vital role for the Spirit in applying Scripture to the human heart', he 'understood salvation to be dependent upon the literal, historical birth, death, resurrection, and second coming of Jesus of Nasareth as related in the Bible'.[17] In both *The Pilgrim's Progress* and *Grace Abounding*, Bunyan's sense that specific Biblical verses can now unsettle and now console makes exegesis a devotional practice that must be led by conviction and faith in the face of extreme doubt and fear. Turn, for example, to his *A Few Sighs from Hell, or the Groans of a Damned Soul* (1658), where Bunyan reflects on 2 Timothy 3:16–17 to assert: 'Do but mark the words. *All scripture is profitable*, Mark. *All*, take it where you will, and in what place you will' (MW, 1:324).

While the Victorian crisis of faith has been much overplayed by literary critics and historians alike, there is no question that countless readers found profound comfort in Bunyan's assertion that every word of the Bible was essential to their religious journey. His work encouraged readers to make sense of scripture, not by comparing it to other abstract philosophies or scientific theories, but by personal, subjective interpretation. As Macaulay notes, 'the allegory of Bunyan has been read by many thousands with tears', and this kind of emotional response is characteristic of Victorian readings of Bunyan.[18] J. A. Froude, for example, suffocated by the endless doctrinal debates with which he had concerned himself as an associate of the Oxford Movement, found in Bunyan's writing a revelatory clarity that he presents entirely as an emotional experience that moved him mentally and physically. In his 'English Men of Letters' study of Bunyan, Froude declared *The Pilgrim's Progress* to be 'the true record of the genuine emotions of the human soul': 'to such a record', he wrote, 'the emotions of other men will respond, as one stringed instrument vibrates responsively to another'.[19] Quick to frame his religiously affective connection with other men as 'masculine', 'strong' and intellectual, Froude champions Bunyan as a muscular barricade behind which believers might be protected from the anxiety of secularisation, his doctrine that of 'the best and strongest minds in Europe ... it was a fire from heaven shining like a sun in a dark world'. Yet for an ultimately always gloomy Froude, this 'fire has gone out; in the place of it we have but smoke and ashes'.[20] He therefore turns to Bunyan as an Old

Testament father with the singular potential to resuscitate a dying Christianity that tolls 'in a modern ear like a cracked bell', convulsing in its final 'spasmodic' 'agonies of death'.[21]

Froude's contemporary, William Hale White, similarly invested in Bunyan as a spiritual guide who would help him work through his lingering commitment to a Calvinist nonconformism, even as he underwent a severe loss of faith. His *Autobiography of Mark Rutherford* (1881), for example, is an imitation of *Grace Abounding* in reverse, the journey presented being one of de-conversion during which Hale White is delivered from grace into sin. Similarly, his account of *The Pilgrim's Progress* in his book *John Bunyan* (1905) focuses on the Slough of Despond, Doubting Castle, the River of Death, the Valley of the Shadow of Death and the struggle with Apollyon, all scenes that, as Vincent Newey suggests, bring into focus themes of suffering, vulnerability and futility.[22] As Hale White asks in the *Autobiography*: 'Why this ceaseless struggle, if in a few short years I was to be asleep for ever?', a fear that grasps him 'with such relentless tenacity' that he becomes 'passive' in its 'grasp'.[23] This psychomachic monomania is temporarily relieved by a Wordsworthian and near pantheist dependence on the salvation offered by nature, as we see in *Mark Rutherford's Deliverance* (1885), but it is Bunyan's ability to search for and find solace in hope, if not faith, to which Hale White seems able to return even in his darkest moments. John Ruskin too regarded Bunyan in similar terms, finding in him a model, not only of faith and feeling, but also of hermeneutical precision and habitual application to the 'spiritual meaning of things'.[24] At first repelled by the torment that marked the copy of *Grace Abounding* his mother secretly slipped into his bag as a young man, Ruskin soon came to rely on Bunyan's work, regarding it, as he reveals in *Modern Painters*, as almost interchangeable with the Bible.[25]

Ruskin's *Modern Painters* is just one of hundreds of Victorian pilgrimage narratives in the period, however. While a template for the Christian pilgrimage can be sought in Augustine or Chaucer, *The Pilgrim's Progress* offered an accessible and sympathetic format to innumerable writers, including William Cowper, Thomas Carlyle, Charles Kingsley, Charlotte Brontë, George Eliot, Mrs Humphry Ward, as well as Southey, Ruskin, Hale White and Dickens. For Victorian novelists in particular, Bunyan's intensely introspective and self-conscious characters are not unlike the psychologised individuals that populate nineteenth-century fiction. As Sharrock argues, *The Pilgrim's Progress* is a stylistic hybrid of allegorical exposition, medieval morality play and prose fiction, an ideal medium for exploring social as well as spiritual life.[26] Writers such as George Eliot even took the idea of Bunyan's holy call to the good life and secularised it, sending *Middlemarch*'s (1874) Dorothea Brooke on a humanitarian pilgrimage that remains coloured by a spiritual ontology inherited from *The Pilgrim's Progress*.[27] Charles Kingsley also assimilated Bunyan's text into his own writing as one that spoke more directly to a contemporary concern with the impact of culture and society on the individual's personal relationship with God. In his introduction to Charles H. Bennett's 1860 illustrated edition of *The Pilgrim's Progress*, Kingsley heralds Bunyan's ability to combine the moral with the aesthetic, but fears that his Puritanism threatens the personal by focusing on it too much. In *Yeast* (1851), *Alton Locke* (1850), *Two Years Ago* (1857) and even *The Water-Babies* (1863), Kingsley draws on Bunyan's quest narrative, but uses it to structure a journey of political, scientific, philosophical and emotional discovery, as well as one of spiritual joy. As Norman Vance argues, Bunyan's Biblical construction of the pilgrim as a stranger or exile offered writers a paradigm that augmented secular portrayals of the traveller or wanderer, which might have otherwise appeared shallow and one-dimensional. Thomas Hardy, for example, often loads his characters' quests with a religious symbolism borrowed from Bunyan that cushions their inevitable disappointments. Jude's scholarly pilgrimage towards Christminster, for example, is granted a poignant depth by the spiritual emptiness and disappointment he encounters on reaching his Beulah; while Faintheart's impotent mission to attract a lover in Hardy's poem, 'Faintheart in a Railway Train' (1920), betrays the consequences of concerning oneself with entirely secular objectives.[28]

Dickens and Baum

Involving oneself with secular achievement at the expense of the religious life is a problematic that obsessed Dickens, a writer who, as Newey claims, 'is the one most variously in touch with Bunyan' of all nineteenth-century authors.[29] Yet Dickens's good 'Christian' characters are often closer to Bunyan's Ignorance than to Christian; they are 'secular pilgrims', as Barry Qualls labels them, who escape judgement through benevolence and charity.[30] Dickens's current status as a warm-hearted but straight-thinking secular novelist derives, once again, from modern literary criticism's distrust of all things Christian, and yet his contemporary audience regarded him as a key defender of a New Testament Christianity under attack from sombre high and low church evangelising. Richard Henry Horne even considered Dickens a representative 'spirit of the age' due to his capacity for a particularised form of observation learned from gospel parables and a careful reading of *The Pilgrim's Progress*.[31] Constructing himself, like Froude's Bunyan, as a manly and forthright voice of the period, Dickens was free liberally to declare that 'the spirit of Christianity' was love and community while rejecting what he regarded as the hypocritical orthodoxy – that 'too tight a hand' – of the established church.[32] Some of his most sinisterly cartoonish characters – Mrs Jellyby, Mrs Barbary, Reverend Stiggins, Mrs Clennam – are blatant echoes of Bunyan's more shady cast members and Sharrock even describes Mr Worldly Wiseman as 'Podsnapian' after *Our Mutual Friend*'s John Podsnap.[33]

Yet Dickens's experience of Bunyan's writing was always compromised by his distrust of evangelicalism. When Dickens was five, his family moved to Chatham and despite their nominal Anglican sympathies began to attend a local Baptist church overseen by their neighbour, Reverend William Giles. Dickens loathed the endless sermons he endured there, writing that he felt 'steamed like a potato in the unventilated breath of Boanerges Boiler', horrified by what he understood to be a cruel and judgemental Old Testament Christianity.[34] His suspicions were confirmed when the MP Sir Andrew Agnew attempted to pass the Sabbath Observances Bill in Parliament on behalf of the Society for Promoting Due Observance of the Lord's Day. This puritanical Bill legislated against Sunday amusements specifically enjoyed by the working classes – concerts in public parks, visits to coffee- and tea-shops, circuses, fairs, picnics and so on – while refusing to comment on the private leisure pursuits of the middle and upper classes. Like temperance reforms, aimed at the 'abuse' of drink by the poor rather than the high consumption of alcohol by the rich, these Sabbatarian attempts at controlling social behaviour emerged from a harsh evangelicalism Dickens targeted in *Sunday under Three Heads* (1836), a direct attack on the class prejudices of the Sabbath Observances Bill.[35]

Dickens's virulent critique of puritanical evangelising is at its height in his portrayals of numerous incorrigible clergyman, fashioned in the same mould as Mr By-Ends, The Flatterer, Timorous and Pliable. Reverend Stiggins, for example, also known as the Reverend Gentleman with the Red Nose, drunkenly advocates temperance throughout *The Pickwick Papers*; Melchisedech Howler, similarly inebriated, rants about the end of the world in *Dombey and Son*; and Reverend Chadband preaches the 'spiritual profit' of 'moderation' while gorging himself at the Snagsbys' dinner party in *Bleak House*. Chadband is a typical Dickensian clergyman, 'attached to no particular denomination', and, like Formalist and Hypocrisy, having 'nothing so very remarkable to say on the greatest of subjects'.[36] Lacking any kind of sustained conviction or integrity, Chadband symbolises that 'indolent temporizing' that formed the rotten core of the established church for Dickens, a manipulative and bankrupt institution whose 'dark and dingy' buildings blackened the sky-scape of Britain, suffocating its inhabitants with 'an air of mourning' and 'death'.[37] We might even see in *Great Expectations*' Mrs Joe, who has 'an exquisite art of making her cleanliness more uncomfortable and unacceptable than dirt itself', a legatee of Talkative. Dickens's 'godly' characters, like Bunyan's more superficial believers, are often more unnerving than his most malevolent villains.[38]

Along with Walter Scott, Dickens also distrusted any kind of overtly introspective faith, despising what he called 'the stern and gloomy enthusiasts' who made 'earth a hell, and religion a torment'.[39] His attitude to the New Testament – a book 'accessible to all men', he said – is illustrated in his beginner's guide to the Gospels, *The Life of Our Lord* (1846), or 'The Children's New Testament'.[40] Written for his children (and not for publication), Dickens's account offers a sentimentalised, rather than theologically or doctrinally consistent depiction of Christ, praising him as one 'full of compassion' and teaching 'people how to love God' through example rather than dogma.[41] Omitting the more supernatural events of the Gospels (such as the Virgin Birth), the guide functions as a Bunyan-like moral guide to life rather than as a religious manual, instructing its readers to 'Remember! It is Christianity *to do good* always – even to those who do evil to us. It is Christianity to love your neighbour as yourself, and to do to all men as we would have them do to us. It is Christianity to be gentle, merciful, and forgiving and to keep those qualities quiet in our own hearts.'[42] This could also be a description of the angelic Little Nell, a self-confessed pilgrim, whose own journey through the Valley of the Shadow of Death is sweetened by her belief that she has saved her grandfather, a confession she frames in terms of Puritan deliverance:

> the child herself was sensible of a new feeling within her, which elevated her nature, and inspired her with an energy and confidence she had never known. There was no divided responsibility now; the whole burden of their two lives had fallen upon her, and henceforth she must think and act for both. 'I have saved him', she thought. 'In all dangers and distresses, I will remember that.'[43]

Dickens's Scrooge wanders through his own Valley of the Shadow of Death towards the end of *A Christmas Carol* (1843), anticipating his redemption as the Ghost of Christmas Yet To Come arrives, but being led astray by vanity, just as Christian is drawn into Doubting Castle by Vain-confidence.[44] *A Christmas Carol*'s at once melodramatic and tacitly homiletic narrative is as much one of religious exhortation, or 'reclamation' as the Ghost of Christmas Past calls it, as *The Pilgrim's Progress*.[45] Like Christian's journey, Scrooge's psychodrama is compulsory, painful, overpowering and transformative, and makes most sense, Newey argues, 'against the backcloth of Puritan conversion narrative and spiritual autobiography'.[46] While Dickens ultimately replaces revealed religion with a liberal, gospel-led humanism, he uses Bunyan's focus on inward sin as a way to comment on Scrooge's failure to respect or engage with the family, charity, fairness to others and basic practices of goodness and kindness. As Help assists Christian in the aftermath of his scripturally laden dream, so Marley's Ghost spells out to Scrooge the allegorical message of the 'quaint Dutch tiles, designed to illustrate the Scriptures' that pave his fireplace, Dickens, like Bunyan, advocating, not a dogmatic journey into grace but one facilitated by self-learning, example and dialogue.[47]

Bunyan, then, is not only endlessly quoted by the Victorians, he also haunts the plot-lines, pedagogies and affective subtexts of their literature. To conclude, we might briefly turn to a final exponent of Bunyan's work, the late Victorian, L. Frank Baum, whose *The Wonderful Wizard of Oz* (1900) begins, like *The Pilgrim's Progress*, just off the beaten track.[48] Just as Bunyan's gold-paved road leads directly to the Celestial City, so Baum's yellow-brick road leads to the Emerald City, the travellers upon both being engaged in a psychological quest where they attempt to conquer spiritual and emotional inadequacy. As J. Karl Franson argues, Baum appears to have drawn heavily on *The Pilgrim's Progress* for the structure, imagery, diction and narrative of his story, the two texts sharing allegorical characters, wasteland settings, dream-like realities and a reliance on supernatural intervention.[49] Compassionate and determined, and yet separated from their families, Christian and Dorothy both lead a group of pilgrims into a city, and both attempt to dissuade their companions from the temptations of those whom they meet on the way.[50] Bunyan's Madame Bubble, witch-like and torturous but captivating and seductive, seems to have been fractured by Baum into his four witches of Oz; while the Scarecrow, Tin Man, Lion, Wizard and Kalidahs are recognisable in Mr Feeble-Mind, Mr Great-Heart, Mr Fearing, Ignorance and Apollyon.[51] As Franson suggests, the course of each pilgrimage also holds several parallels. Dorothy and Christian each find sustenance in the form of fruit trees by rivers; they are both imprisoned, Christian in Doubting Castle, Dorothy in the castle of the West Witch; both are given tinted glass through which to view the dazzling gleam of Zion and the Emerald City, and both are repelled by the iniquity of consumption and deception at Vanity Fair and the festivities being held in Emerald City. While *The Wonderful Wizard of Oz* ultimately breaks away from Bunyan's narrative, most notably in its embodiment of goodness in a female figure (Glinda the Good Witch) rather than Christ, it is nevertheless heavily dependent on overtly religious episodes borrowed directly from a story as familiar as the Bible to Baum's nineteenth-century generation.[52]

NOTES

1. Charles Dickens, *The Old Curiosity Shop* (London: Penguin, 2000), pp. 123–5.
2. See Roger Sharrock, *John Bunyan: The Pilgrim's Progress* (London: Edward Arnold, 1966), pp. 9–23.
3. Quoted in Mary Hammond, '*The Pilgrim's Progress* and its Nineteenth-Century Publishers', in W. R. Owens and Stuart Sim (eds.), *Reception, Appropriation,*

Recollection: Bunyan's 'Pilgrim's Progress' (Bern: Peter Lang, 2007), pp. 99–118 (pp. 99–100).

4. *Ibid.*, p. 103.
5. *Ibid.*, pp. 103–6.
6. *Ibid.*, p. 116.
7. Nathalie Collé-Bak, 'The Role of Illustrations in the Reception of *The Pilgrim's Progress*', in Owens and Sim (eds.), *Reception*, pp. 81–97.
8. Quoted in Patricia Anderson, *The Printed Image and the Transformation of Popular Culture, 1790–1860* (Oxford: Clarendon Press, 1991), p. 40.
9. Samuel Taylor Coleridge, *Lectures 1808–1811: On Literature*, ed. R. A. Foakes, 2 vols. (Princeton University Press, 1987), II:102–3.
10. Walter Scott, '*The Pilgrim's Progress* [ed. Robert Southey]', *The Quarterly Review*, 43.86 (1830), 469–94; and see David Walker, 'Bunyan's Reception in the Romantic Period', in Owens and Sim (eds.), *Reception*, pp. 49–67.
11. Thomas Babington Macaulay, 'Southey's Edition of the *Pilgrim's Progress*', *The Edinburgh Review*, 54.108 (1831), 450–61.
12. C. Stephen Finley, 'Bunyan among the Victorians: Macaulay, Froude, Ruskin', *Literature and Theology*, 3.1 (1989), 77–94 (p. 78).
13. Thomas Babington Macaulay, *Critical and Historical Essays*, 2 vols. (London: J. M. Dent and Sons, 1907), II:403.
14. Andrew Bradstock, 'John Bunyan', in Rebecca Lemon, Emma Mason, Jon Roberts and Christopher Rowland (eds.), *The Blackwell Companion to the Bible in English Literature* (Oxford: Blackwell, 2009), pp. 286–96 (p. 288).
15. Norman Vance, 'Pilgrims Abounding: Bunyan and the Victorian Novel', in Owens and Sim (eds.), *Reception*, pp. 69–79 (p. 73).
16. See Hill, *Turbulent*; and E. P. Thompson, *The Making of the English Working Class* (Harmondsworth: Penguin, 1968), p. 34.
17. Bradstock, 'John Bunyan', p. 289.
18. Macaulay, *Critical and Historical Essays*, II:400.
19. J. A. Froude, *Bunyan* (London: Macmillan, 1880) p. 16.
20. *Ibid.*, pp. 55–6.
21. *Ibid.*, p. 29; and J. A. Froude, 'Condition and Prospects of Protestantism', *Short Studies on Great Subjects*, 4 vols. (New York: Charles Sribner's Sons, 1868–83), II:127, 130, quoted in Finley, 'Bunyan among the Victorians', p. 81.
22. Vincent Newey, 'Bunyan's Afterlives: Case Studies', in Owens and Sim (eds.), *Reception*, pp. 25–48 (p. 41).
23. William Hale White, *The Autobiography of Mark Rutherford, Dissenting Minister*, ed. William S. Peterson (Oxford University Press, 1990), p. 90.
24. John Ruskin, letter to W. J. Stillman, 1851, quoted in Finley, 'Bunyan among the Victorians', p. 84.
25. Finley, 'Bunyan among the Victorians', p. 82.
26. Sharrock, *John Bunyan*, p. 12.
27. Newey, 'Bunyan's Afterlives', pp. 38–9.
28. Vance, 'Pilgrims Abounding', p. 77.
29. Newey, 'Bunyan's Afterlives', p. 35.
30. Barry Qualls, *The Secular Pilgrims of Victorian Fiction* (Cambridge University Press, 1982).
31. Richard Henry Horne, *A New Spirit of the Age* (London: Smith, Elder, 1844).

32. Charles Dickens, 'The Sunday Screw', *Household Words* (22 June 1850), in *Dickens's Journalism: 'The Amusements of the People' and Other Papers: Reports, Essays and Reviews, 1834–1851*, ed. Michael Slater (London: J. M. Dent, 1997), pp. 249–57 (pp. 250, 256).

33. Sharrock, *John Bunyan*, p. 25.

34. Charles Dickens, 'City of London Churches', in *The Uncommercial Traveller and Reprinted Pieces, etc.* (Oxford University Press, 1958), pp. 83–93 (p. 83).

35. See Paul Schlicke, *Dickens and Popular Entertainment* (London: Unwin Hyman, 1988), pp. 198–200.

36. Charles Dickens, *Bleak House* (London: Penguin, 2003), pp. 313, 303.

37. Charles Dickens, letter to Miss Burdett-Coutts (22 August 1851), in *The Letters of Charles Dickens*, ed. Graham Storey *et al.*, 12 vols. (Oxford: Clarendon Press, 1988), VI:466; and *Our Mutual Friend* (London: Penguin, 2004), p. 450.

38. Charles Dickens, *Great Expectations* (London: Penguin, 1985), p. 54.

39. Charles Dickens, *Sunday Under Three Heads; As It Is, As the Sabbath Bills Would Make It, and As It Might Be* (London: Chapman and Hall, 1836), p. 34; Richard Kingston, *Enthusiastic impostors, no divinely inspir'd prophets. Wherein the pretended French and English prophets are shewn in their proper colours* (1709), p. 114.

40. Dickens, letter to the Reverend David Macrae, 1861(b), in *Letters*, XI:557.

41. Charles Dickens, *The Life of Our Lord* (Oxford: Albion Press, 1987), p. 27.

42. *Ibid.*, p. 79.

43. Dickens, *The Old Curiosity Shop*, p. 325.

44. Vincent Newey, *Scriptures of Charles Dickens: Novels of Ideology, Novels of the Self* (Aldershot: Ashgate, 2004), p. 36.

45. Charles Dickens, *A Christmas Carol* (London: Penguin, 2003), p. 56; and Newey, *Scriptures of Charles Dickens*, p. 17.

46. Newey, *Scriptures of Charles Dickens*, p. 19.

47. Dickens, *A Christmas Carol*, p. 43; Newey, *Scriptures of Charles Dickens*, p. 23.

48. J. Karl Franson, 'From Vanity Fair to Emerald City: Baum's Debt to Bunyan', *Children's Literature*, 23 (1995), 91–114.

49. *Ibid.*, p. 92.

50. *Ibid.*, p. 95.

51. *Ibid.*, pp. 96, 99.

52. See Paul Nathanson, *Over the Rainbow: The Wizard of Oz as a Secular Myth of America* (Albany: State University of New York Press, 1991).

12

ISABEL HOFMEYR

Bunyan: colonial, postcolonial

In the wake of Barack Obama's nomination as President Elect of the USA in November 2008, tributes poured in from across the world. One, entitled 'Pilgrim's Progress', came from Tolu Ogunlesi, a Nigerian poet. The poem begins by depicting a cacophonous media spectacle, rather like an electronic Vanity Fair. Journalists and media pundits constitute 'an army of voluble blackberries'. Those of a left-wing persuasion translate 'King into textese'; the right comprises a 'Klan of epithet dealers'. Into this noisy arena walks Obama. He belongs to neither camp and is further set apart from the predominant whiteness of the gathering with its 'star-spangled genes'. The poem continues:

> He will not be one of them. Nor one of us.
> He will simply be the sepia-toned pilgrim . . .
> He himself will be naked
> To be clothed by all who see or hear of him.[1]

Obama will belong to none, yet all will claim him. He will be the screen on to which everyone will project their own particular desires.

To elucidate this process, the poem introduces the figure of Bunyan's pilgrim, another international icon who has been claimed by a range of different publics. Like Obama, the pilgrim has functioned as an empty cipher which audiences could fill with their own agendas. Readers as diverse as Jamaican Baptists and persecuted Christian converts in Madagascar have claimed the text as their own.[2] The text's episodic structure allows readers to select the bits which serve their purposes while its allegorical architecture permits a wide range of interpretations. Thanks in large part to this mode of reception, *The Pilgrim's Progress*, the only work of Bunyan that really proved portable, has become one of the most widely distributed English texts. Spread mainly by the Protestant mission movement and translated into 200 languages worldwide, the text is a world bestseller.[3]

Yet, oddly enough, this worldwide distribution has not registered itself strongly in Bunyan scholarship, which until very recently remained resolutely national in orientation and focused on seventeenth-century England. In this dispensation, Bunyan's transnational presence has been of little consequence. This model of examining Bunyan within the boundaries of the nation state is a bequest of the writer's entry into the canon of English literature over the course of the second half of the nineteenth century. Before being claimed as a national icon, Bunyan was recognised as an avowedly transnational writer whose international successes were assiduously publicised by his nonconformist supporters in Britain. These Bunyan enthusiasts seized the opportunity to raise the profile of their most beloved writer, who still laboured under the class and denominational prejudice of the Anglican intelligentsia. Publicity in mission publications, exhibitions, local church meetings and lectures raised the standing of Bunyan and created the conditions for him to be claimed by the emerging discipline of English literature. The price of this elevation was the excision of his transnational presence, which had been premised on an evangelical Protestantism and which reached people of different races and cultures. The English literary tradition by contrast was secular, national and 'white', being a project to establish the cultural and racial distinctiveness of Britons. As the 'father of the English novel', Bunyan became studied as a figure of seventeenth-century England. His transcultural reach had to be erased in order for him to emerge as a national figure.[4]

With the marked transnational turn in the academy, this situation is starting to change and there is a growing body of work that seeks to understand Bunyan beyond national boundaries. What are these new approaches and how do they relate to older nineteenth-century understandings of Bunyan's transnationalism?

Nineteenth-century transnational approaches to Bunyan

For dissenters and nonconformists, Bunyan was a cherished icon, and unsurprisingly his work was deeply woven into their everyday lives. At home and at church, through each stage of life, nineteenth-century nonconformists encountered Bunyan in every imaginable media: Sabbath day readings, household performances, jigsaw puzzles, portraits, sermons, hymns, choir services, magic lantern slides, tableaux, postcards, wall charts. One ardent Bunyan fan in Cheshire landscaped his garden as a Bunyan theme park. *The Pilgrim's Progress* was less a discrete book than a total environment, its language as naturalised as that of the Lord's Prayer, its characters as familiar as the figures 'on the Front at Brighton'.[5]

Evangelical in orientation, dissent and then nonconformity expected texts to travel to undertake their work of conversion. Indeed, *The Pilgrim's Progress* itself is imagined in this way, and in the prefatory poem which introduces Part II of the book, Bunyan explicitly urges his book to travel out into the world. The book did indeed circulate very rapidly. Virtually as it was published in England in 1678 and 1684, it moved to Scotland, Wales, Protestant Europe and the New World. Its next fillip came courtesy of the Protestant mission movement. By the late 1700s it had been translated in India and was starting to enter Africa.

Nonconformists back in Britain were keen to publicise the growing international reach of their cherished icon. As Susan Thorne has demonstrated, nonconformists, who still suffered lingering forms of civil disability, seized the international Protestant mission movement as a way of announcing their own successes and elevating their social and political profile.[6] One plank in this broader publicity offensive was provided by Bunyan translations, which were routinely shown in missionary exhibitions, book displays, lectures and press reports.

This activity soon generated a distinctive evangelical and transnational Bunyan historiography which has left two important bequests: firstly it constructed the idea of Bunyan as a universal writer and secondly it led to the formation of various archives which have and will become critical for contemporary transnational histories of Bunyan.

With regard to the trope of universality, nonconformist publicity portrays Bunyan's text as travelling effortlessly through the ether of language and culture across the entire Protestant world. In a trope that Kipling was subsequently to summarise as 'palm and pine',[7] this discourse invokes the idea of diverse societies, cultures and landscapes united by the travels of one text. George Offor (1787–1864), an early Bunyan editor and strong evangelical nonconformist, noted in an introduction to Bunyan's collected works, 'The Pilgrim has been translated into most of the languages and dialects of the world. The Caffrarian and Hottentot, the enlightened Greek and Hindoo, the remnant of the Hebrew race, the savage Malay and the voluptuous Chinese – all have the wondrous narrative in their own languages.'[8] There was inevitably a degree of optical illusion in such claims that everyone read the same text in the same way. Most mission translations were generally based on excerpts or abridged editions which in turn had been suggested by converts who chose them to support their particular interpretations of Protestantism. In some cases, converts edited out the theological explanations with which the text was larded so that the bones of the story would become clearer and be available to be interpreted in keeping with local configurations of Christianity. In other cases, particular sections of the story which proved popular were foregrounded. An episode near the end of Part I where Christian and Hopeful must hand in their certificates in order to gain access to heaven proved especially popular amongst converts. In an imperial situation where literacy was mediated by church and colonial state and was used to exclude and control people, this image of documents as power-laden and being able to offer select entry resonated with the experience of many readers. This section of the story made its way into illustrations in African editions which showed Christian and Hopeful clutching their certificates at the gates of Heaven. European editions routinely illustrated this episode but nowhere does one see any certificates: gaining access to paradise by means of a piece of paper did not accord with the experiences of European Christians.[9] These differences were, however, never played up. Instead, the common reference points in the story were portrayed as a landscape shared by all Protestants across the world. Evangelical theories of reading which held that texts (of the right spiritual persuasion) could exercise magical and transformative effects on readers strengthened this impression.

This idea of Bunyan as universal was taken up by the emerging discipline of English literature, which initially celebrated him as a writer of England and the world. Yet the idea of universality and national particularity did not sit easily together. One critic noted this paradox: the book was 'at once universal and insular'; 'wide as humanity' yet 'narrow in its social outlook'. Speaking at the Bunyan tercentenary celebrations in 1928, the Bishop of Durham said: 'In view of the intensely English tone and temper of the work, it is particularly surprising that it should have commended itself so extensively to foreigners.'[10]

The contradiction itself became most visible in the differing ideas of religion, nationality and race implicit in these two concepts: national particularity and evangelical universalism. For nonconformists, the key to Bunyan was his evangelical message, which in turn assured his universality and his ability to speak to people across the barriers of language, race and culture. For English literature scholars, Bunyan's religious and theological intentions were secondary to his aesthetic literary achievements, which were read within a national frame as evidence of his Englishness. Indeed, his worldwide circulation and his over-association with black colonised societies became something of an embarrassment which compromised the idea of whiteness implicit in the notion of being English.

These tensions became especially apparent in Alfred Noyes's famous attack on Bunyan in 1928. Setting himself up as an intellectual 'writing secular literary criticism', Noyes characterised Bunyan's theology as repulsive and his work as resembling 'the lowest and most squalid levels of the primitive races of Africa'. The author of The Pilgrim's Progress is 'poor Caliban-Bunyan'; his language is 'Hottentotish'.[11]

The tensions around race, nation and religion were finally to be addressed by the expedient of changing the meaning of the term 'universality'. Instead of

the word denoting the literal circulation of Bunyan's text to numerous societies throughout the world, it came to mean an abstract human nature. This
strategy could retain the value-conferring properties of the word whilst also
lifting Bunyan above the colonised societies which threatened to 'contami-
nate' him. Bunyan could emerge as 'white', national and secular (in the sense
that aesthetic rather than theological properties of the text matter most). The
troublesome question of his international evangelical circulation could be
sidelined.[12]

With regard to archives, the Bunyan Meeting House in Bedford became a
significant evangelical site for commemorating Bunyan and curating his
memory. Over the years, the Meeting House has assembled a substantial
collection of translations of *The Pilgrim's Progress*. These are enumerated
in Patricia Hurry and Alan C. Cirket, *Bunyan Meeting Museum Library
Catalogue*, a crucial starting point for anyone interested in a postcolonial
Bunyan.[13] Also important are the Frank Mott Harrison collection and
George Offor collection in the Bedford Public Library which contain important information on translated editions of *The Pilgrim's Progress*.

Taken together, these various traditions of work on Bunyan's transnational
presence are important. They have popularised the idea of Bunyan as universal while also building up archives that document and make visible the
pathways of his circulation. They have also focused attention on Bunyan's
evangelical message as a key element in ensuring his transnational circulation.
However, these historiographies have had less to say on the material trajectories of circulation; how, where, why and when were Bunyan texts circulated. Like all religious enterprises, evangelical understandings tend to
suppress material questions of how media technologies work in favour of
portraying these effects as the miraculous consequences of supernatural
forces. Dominated by evangelical theories of reading which imbue texts
with magical properties, nineteenth-century transnational approaches to
The Pilgrim's Progress show little interest in questions of exactly how, in
what form, through what circuits the text was disseminated. These were
questions that have been taken up by more recent transnational approaches.

Twentieth- and twenty-first-century transnational approaches

The literary academic market is currently crowded with a range of
approaches which seek to understand literary and cultural production outside
the analytical frame of the nation state. There are a range of relatively new
'brands' (postcolonialism, diaspora studies, transnationalism, world literature) which in turn draw on and reconfigure older traditions (world-systems
theory, area studies, women's and ethnic studies, third world studies,

comparative literature). These are all attempts to understand literary forms as emerging in transnational pathways of circulation. Postcolonialism itself pays particular attention to questions of European imperialism: the world in which we live has been shaped by the legacies of imperialism and if we wish to understand literary production, then it must be inserted into this context.

Cross-cutting these developments are other academic currents, namely post-structuralism and postmodernism, which seek to question the basis of the modernity, rationality and individualism which underwrote ideas of national citizenship. Post-structuralism has cross-fertilised well with some versions of postcolonialism, producing a field of study known as colonial discourse analysis, which aims to deconstruct the modes of knowledge and classification through which colonial rule claimed part of its power. How has Bunyan featured in this suite of approaches?

An undoubted pioneer is Tamsin Spargo's *The Writing of John Bunyan*.[14] Using a post-structuralist/postcolonial/gender studies approach, she seeks to deconstruct the 'author function' which has grown up around the name of John Bunyan. As she demonstrates, this name is a way of adjudicating interpretations of the text by allowing those which 'the author' as a sovereign rational individual apparently intended. Her work reveals the 'operations of that name [and] explore[s] the discursive techniques which produced the figure of the author'.[15] She also examines the patriarchal authority invested in Bunyan by focusing on female figures excluded in the seventeenth century and subsequent contemporary critical studies. This strand of her work draws on and extends a tradition of gender studies in Bunyan which explores questions of maleness, femaleness, power and spiritual authority.[16] The final part of Spargo's book examines the use of *The Pilgrim's Progress* in 'imperialist frameworks' and seeks to understand how the text 'enlists and control non-Western, non-Christian subjects'.[17] Spargo's work points to three important avenues: readership and reception, circulation, and translation.

Readership and reception

Questions of readership and reception both within Britain and beyond have become a growth node in Bunyan scholarship. A recent collection by W. R. Owens and Stuart Sim, *Reception, Appropriation, Recollection: Bunyan's 'Pilgrim's Progress'* (2007) demonstrates the continuing 'intense academic interest [in Bunyan], with scholars eager to track down new evidence of his imprint on global culture from a variety of critical perspectives'.[18]

This work on reception follows a variety of routes. One long-standing strand of research focuses on the ways in which Bunyan has been taken up in various genres of English literature, most notably the Victorian and late Victorian novel.[19] Since this work takes place squarely within a national framework, it may appear to have little to do with postcolonialism and transnationalism. However, since postcolonial studies claim all literary production from the beginnings of European imperialism as their field of analysis, these novels would fall within its ambit. One interesting project which could be pursued would be to examine these Victorian novels transnationally and to ask what function the appropriation of Bunyan plays in this context. Much of the plot of *Vanity Fair*, for example depends on developments in India. What might this mean for interpretations of Bunyan's imprint in the novel? Moving into the Edwardian period and beyond, several of John Buchan's novels, especially *Mr Standfast* (1919), are powerfully indebted to Bunyan. An important imperial figure, Buchan (1875–1940) spent time in South Africa and subsequently Canada (where he was Governor-General), and his novels speak to the imperial world often via a Scottish interpretation of Bunyan. Buchan's œuvre points to a strong tradition of colonial settler appropriations of Bunyan's work. James Froude in his 1880 biography noted that Bunyan is a man 'whose writings have for two centuries affected the spiritual opinions of the English race in every part of the world more powerfully than any book or books, except the Bible'.[20] Several decades later another commentator, Alice Law, noted a particular affinity between Britons in the empire and Bunyan:

> it is particularly because we are a nation of pilgrims that Bunyan's great work should especially appeal to us and help us. Travelling as members of our great Empire often must, upon seas and continents on which the banner of Britain flies, from the English home-centre to the outermost circumference and back, one cannot conceive any comparison more suitable or helpful ... than this tinker's masterpiece ...[21]

The imprint of Bunyan on white settler writing and thought has yet to be fully investigated but would form an important part of understanding one dimension of his transnational circulation. It is important to stress that this settler appropriation of Bunyan needs to be understood as discrete from mission uses of the text. There is a tendency in talking about Bunyan in empire to conflate the colonial state, white settler interest and missions and treat these as identical. Hence white settler appropriations of *The Pilgrim's Progress* in English (in which the story was frequently fashioned as an imperial allegory) are construed as similar to the translated versions sponsored by mission organisations.[22] As we discuss in more detail below, mission translations bore the imprint of converts' ideas and opinions and were seldom, if ever, straightforwardly imperial.

Also important as part of postcolonial interpretations of Bunyan would be readings of novels, in previously colonised parts of the world, which use *The Pilgrim's Progress*. A range of African novelists, including the Kenyan Ngũgĩ wa Thiong'o and the Zimbabwean Tsitsi Dangarembga, use Bunyan in their texts.[23] In doing so, their intention is less to subvert a European/imperial Bunyan than to engage with long-standing African interpretations of the text. In *Devil on the Cross* Ngũgĩ seeks to 'convert' the evangelical meaning of Bunyan to African socialist ends, while Dangarembga uses *The Pilgrim's Progress* to provide a gendered critique of masculinist traditions of the African novel. One template for figuring the difficult path of male African elite upward mobility in a colonial context had been drawn from Bunyan. By invoking this template, Dangarembga dramatises the choices that her female protagonists have to make about how to fit, or not fit, into this preordained story.

Another emphasis within the field of readership and reception has been questions of the new audiences that Bunyan acquires alongside changes in printing technologies. This question of 'new readers' is in fact inherent in the original text itself, which spoke to dissenting and nonconformist audiences, many of whom were of uncertain literacy. Bunyan himself was a first-generation literate, and the ideas of literacy that he embodies are embedded in older repertoires of the oral folk tale, the song, the sermon, the dream. As Maxine Hancock points out, reading for Bunyan is a laborious process, 'a physical pilgrimage through print'; a 'slow and persistent toiling towards meaning that reading would have been for readers of Bunyan's social class and educational background'.[24]

As the text travelled, it acquired further 'new readers' in the industrial working classes and communities of mission converts in the Protestant empire. As work on the publishing history of the text itself demonstrates, these different audiences have left evidence of their tastes and preoccupations in the physical appearance of the text itself.[25] Studies by Mary Hammond and W. R. Owens reveal the huge range of different English editions stretching from tract and pamphlet versions up to sumptuous hard-cover tomes. Nathalie Collé-Bak shows how the different traditions of illustration in *The Pilgrim's Progress* point to the different audiences at which the text was aimed.[26]

Circulation

There is a body of work that examines Bunyan's circulation to different parts of the world. This includes David E. Smith, *John Bunyan in America*, as well as discussions of *The Pilgrim's Progress* in Germany, the Netherlands, Sweden and Japan.[27] These works demonstrate the role that Bunyan plays in different intellectual configurations as well as the possible range of interpretations that the text can support. They also point to the critical role of translation in studies of Bunyan's reception, a topic discussed below.

While these studies are important for illuminating Bunyan's role in the 'host' society, they are inevitably captive to the template of the nation state. As a result, these analyses are one-way and end-stopped and cannot tell us what this circulation of *The Pilgrim's Progress* meant for Bunyan's status back home. To understand such issues one must turn to theories of circulation which argue that cultural formations have to be analysed not as part of static entities but as made in processes of mobility, exchange and movement.[28] Seen in a colonial context, and as a considerable body of revisionist scholarship on empire argues,[29] one needs to integrate different parts of the imperial map. One cannot work with notions of 'centre' and 'periphery', in which cultural currents emanate outwards in one direction only. Instead, influences flow in more than one direction at a time while metropole and colony shape each other.

My own work on Bunyan's reception in Africa drew inspiration from this approach and sought to understand the relationship between the wide circulation of *The Pilgrim's Progress* in Africa (where eighty translations were done) and Bunyan's standing back in Britain. Rather than just focus on African appropriations of the text and leave it at that, I felt it important to draw the link back to Britain, not least because without it, the research would be seen as of marginal interest to 'mainstream' Bunyan scholarship. As indicated above, the framework which enabled such an integrated approach was to rethink nonconformity as transnational. The role of nonconformity in buying Bunyan respectability has long been recognised, but such analyses have treated nonconformity as a national phenomenon. As a species of evangelical Protestantism, it was by contrast avowedly transnational in its ambitions. The global reach of the Protestant mission empire was assiduously publicised back home along with Bunyan, one of its key icons. Once seen in this way, it became clear that Bunyan's circulation in Africa and other parts of the mission empire was not some separate and sequestered story but was central to how he was seen back in England.

Drawing on ideas of circulation, I followed a method of keeping my eye on the text in order to understand as precisely as possible how various editions of *The Pilgrim's Progress* were read, produced, taught, disseminated, reinterpreted. I did not conceive these activities as being divided between audiences 'at home' and audiences 'abroad' but rather understood the transnational dissemination of *The Pilgrim's Progress* as one integrated evangelical field. Evangelical distribution is always necessarily experimental as those disseminating texts try and work out what will appeal to the new audiences they are trying to reach, whether these be slum children in the East End of London or Telugu Baptists in South India. The insights gained from these different experiments as well as the responses from the new readers flowed between these different constituencies as missionaries shared ideas and experiences.

This exchange of ideas became especially visible in transnational organisations such as the Religious Tract Society that churned out billions of Protestant texts for worldwide distribution. Large mission organisations which undertook their own textual production also became clearing houses for debate and discussion on which texts worked best. As a text that generally made it into the first top ten texts to be translated by Protestant missionaries, *The Pilgrim's Progress* featured frequently in such debates, with different players putting forward ideas on how to translate (the whole text or an abridgement; only some episodes and if so, which ones; which illustrations worked best; discussions on different visual media – magic lantern, wall chart, postcard). Alongside actual translations themselves, these discussions provide insights into the multifarious ways in which the text was distributed and received. These modes of appropriation varied enormously. In some cases, African mission-educated elites read the text as an allegory on their anti-colonial responsibility to lead the colonised people to freedom. In other instances, non-elite African converts drawn from the ranks of commoners seized the message of the story to criticise their social betters, namely the chiefs who at times persecuted converts.

Translation

With regard to actual translations of *The Pilgrim's Progress*, this is a field that awaits proper investigation since it requires pooling expertise from a wide range of languages. In the cases for which I was able to gather evidence as well as the non-English versions I could read (Afrikaans and Sesotho), it would appear that translation sought to indigenise the text and make it as realistic as possible. Topographical references were translated to suit the physical environment of the reader. Proverbs and names were indigenised while the social marginality of Christian and his colleagues is translated in such a way as to stress a similar tenuousness of African converts, who were often drawn from disadvantaged strata within African society.[30] Despised by their chiefs and rulers for taking up the new religion, they were likewise spurned by racist settler society while being kept in humiliatingly junior positions within the mission establishment itself. Tiyo Soga, who undertook the first Xhosa translation of Part I in 1868, encouraged readers to insert themselves into the text. His introduction gave the following advice:

> Folks! Here is a book for you to examine. The book tells the story of a traveller who walks the road which many of you would like to travel. Accompany the

traveller whilst slowly trying to make acquaintance with each other – stopping to take rest whilst listening to things the traveller tells and reports to you; move along with the traveller to his destination, the end of his journey.[31]

Alongside linguistic analyses of the texts, material practices of translation constitute an important analytical field in understanding Bunyan's transnational circulation. These practices varied enormously. At one extreme, one could have a white male missionary undertaking a solo translation. On the other could be a team of translators comprising second-language missionaries and first-language converts. Recent work by Sylvia Brown and Arlette Zinck has taken up this challenge of examining translation practices. They focus on the 'biographies' of three translations of The Pilgrim's Progress in Canada (two into Cree and one into Inuktitut).[32] The two Cree translations were by Métis missionaries, John C. Sinclair and Archdeacon Thomas Vincent III; the Inuktitut by a white British missionary, Maurice Sidney Flint, a man with scholastic ambitions but an unfinished theological training.

Brown and Zinck examine the complex way in which the translations draw on and reflect oral forms of worship in the missionary community whilst also speaking to the personal trajectories of the translators and their struggle to use translation as a means of trying to gain status in the mission domain. In each case, the translator was met by a mission hierarchy unsympathetic to their translation ambitions, which were deemed inappropriate to their perceived standing. The three translators sought to use their work as 'a passport into a world to which he did not quite belong: the educated, Christian, and British missionary culture with which Bunyan's most famous narrative was for them associated'.[33]

Attention to questions of actual translation and circulation practices can also help throw more light on a persistent question in Bunyan scholarship, namely what made The Pilgrim's Progress so portable and 'universal'? For evangelicals, it was the text's Protestant message; for Marxists, his radical critique of social inequality; for those in English literature, his universal understanding of human nature. Another answer emerges from the way in which the text was translated and circulated. Episodic and hence friable, it could be translated serially as a sequence of freestanding instalments. The text has little realistic detail. Its topography is vague and Biblical in orientation and presents few impediments to translation. Also, the confetti of visual material that swirled around the text (wall charts, postcards, magic lantern shows, tableaux, dramatic re-enactments) spread knowledge of its episodes far and wide and created a field of participation in which everyone could apparently talk about the same text, even if in reality, different audiences dealt with vastly different texts.

While these new approaches will continue to gain momentum, the question that persists is what these various approaches might mean for 'mainstream' Bunyan scholarship with its focus on the seventeenth century. Can this new set of paradigms speak to these concerns?

Seventeenth-century postcolonial Bunyan?

The first obvious application of postcolonial approaches to Bunyan is to insert him into a seventeenth-century transnational field. As the discussion on Bunyan's readership and reception above indicates, this task is increasingly being undertaken from the eighteenth century onward. However, with regard to Bunyan in the seventeenth century, the postcolonial impulse has been weak. What might the seventeenth-century circulation of the text to Protestant Europe and the New World mean for understanding Bunyan in seventeenth-century Bedford? What might Bunyan's work mean if his lifetime is understood as unfolding in a transnational world, at a moment of nascent yet expanding imperialism? Bunyan himself grasped his world as a wide transnational one: he donated part of the meagre amount of money he made in prison from capping shoelaces to support Christians under Islamic imprisonment.[34]

Another function of Bunyan's transnational circulation is to direct closer attention to how he came to be canonised as a national, secular icon and figure of Englishness. This unpicking of Bunyan's making, particularly as a secular figure, has opened the way for a reconsideration of Bunyan as an evangelical writer. As Michael Davies argues, we need to move beyond a situation that segregates 'Bunyan the "Parnassian" creative writer and proto-novelist from Bunyan the harsh conventicling theologian'. This separation has been a pre-condition 'to redeem Bunyan from his own inhumane Calvinism and to render him readable still as "Literature" '.[35] Davies seeks to move beyond this division by formulating a mode of reading that integrates narrative and theology. From a different perspective, Galen K. Johnson provides an evangelical reading of Bunyan's thought that takes issue with interpretations of him as a nascent modern subject shaped by practices of rational individualism. Instead, Johnson argues for a view of Bunyan rooted in Christian community and scriptural authority.[36]

Johnson and Davies certainly do not write in response to postcolonial impulses. Their interest in Bunyan by and large unfolds in a national framework. Yet from a transnational perspective, their work is important insofar as it pushes us back towards Bunyan's evangelicalism. This promontory in turn could open up transnational vistas on Bunyan's thought in a seventeenth-century context.

One other type of transnational approach which deserves brief mention is Marxism, which has been an important plank in the Bunyan historiography. Marxism is of course a form of analysis that is committed to transnationalism, yet Marxist studies of Bunyan have taken the nation state as their focus, further testimony to the powerful national impetus in Bunyan historiography. Marxist analyses hence have had little to say on Bunyan's transnational reach. Hill includes a brief section in his final chapter in his biography of Bunyan, but this is of necessity based on speculation and draws on the idea that his wide appeal must reside in his radical social message. One interesting line of investigation would be to subject Bunyan to a transnational rather than national form of Marxist analysis.[37]

One recent attempt to think about Bunyan in a contemporary transnational world is Stuart Sim's reading of Bunyan's fundamentalism, an exercise prompted by the current state of international politics. Asking why Bunyan has tended to attract radical fundamentalist readers and interpreters, Sim concludes that much of his work is 'intolerant, repressive, authoritarian, and biblically literalist'.[38] In the context of the contemporary world with its battle of US imperialism and Islamist fundamentalism, these questions will continue to be pertinent. As the world itself becomes more globalised and integrated, questions of a postcolonial Bunyan will continue to loom larger. The field of postcolonial Bunyan studies seems set to expand.

NOTES

1. Tolu Ogunlesi, 'Pilgrim's Progress', nai-images@listserv.uu.se, 11 November 2008.
2. Isabel Hofmeyr, *The Portable Bunyan: A Transnational History of 'The Pilgrim's Progress'* (Princeton University Press, 2004), pp. 86–97, 65–8.
3. *Ibid.*, pp. 1–3.
4. *Ibid.*, pp. 217–27.
5. Augustine Birrell, 'John Bunyan Today', *The Bookman*, 73 (1927), 149–52 (at p. 152).
6. Susan Thorne, *Congregational Missions and the Making of an Imperial Culture in Nineteenth-Century England* (Stanford University Press, 1999).
7. Rudyard Kipling, *The Complete Verse*, ed. M. M. Kaye (London: Kyle Cathie, 1990), p. 266.
8. George Offor, *The Works of John Bunyan*, 3 vols. (1854; Edinburgh: The Banner of Truth Trust, 1991), I:lvii, 'Memoir of John Bunyan'.
9. Hofmeyr, *The Portable Bunyan*, pp. 137–50.
10. Report of Special Service at Westminster Abbey, 27 November 1928, unmarked newscutting in 'Newspaper Cuttings', Bunyan Collection, Bedford Library.
11. Alfred Noyes, 'Bunyan – A Re-evaluation' and 'Mr Alfred Noyes' Rejoinder', *The Bookman*, 445 (1928), 13–17, 104–6 (pp. 14, 16, 17, 106).
12. Hofmeyr, *The Portable Bunyan*, pp. 217–27.

13. Patricia Hurry and Alan Cirket (comps.), *Bunyan Meeting Museum Library Catalogue* (Bedford: Bunyan Meeting House, 1995).

14. Tamsin Spargo, *The Writing of John Bunyan* (Aldershot: Ashgate, 1997).

15. *Ibid.*, p. 1.

16. Margaret Olofson Thickstun, 'From Christiana to Stand-fast: Subsuming the Feminine in *The Pilgrim's Progress*', *SEL*, 26 (1986), 439–53; Margaret Soenser Breen, 'Christiana's Rudeness: Spiritual Authority in *The Pilgrim's Progress*', *BS*, 7 (1997), 96–111; Kathleen M. Swaim, 'Mercy and the Feminine Heroic in the Second Part of Pilgrim's Progress', *SEL*, 30 (1990), 387–409.

17. Spargo, *Writing of John Bunyan*, p. 105.

18. W. R. Owens and Stuart Sim (eds.), *Reception, Appropriation, Recollection: Bunyan's 'Pilgrim's Progress'* (Bern: Peter Lang, 2007).

19. Norman Vance, 'Pilgrim's Abounding: Bunyan and the Victorian Novel' and Vincent Newey, 'Bunyan's Afterlives: Case Studies', both in Owens and Sim (eds.), *Reception*, pp. 69–80 and 25–48.

20. J. A. Froude, *Bunyan* (London: Macmillan, 1880), p. 1.

21. Alice Law, 'Some Aspects of *The Pilgrim's Progress*', *The Empire Review*, 45 (1927), 48–55 (p. 55).

22. Richard L. Greaves, 'Bunyan through the Centuries: Some Reflections', *English Studies*, 64 (1983), 113–21 and Spargo, *Writing of John Bunyan*, pp. 96–112.

23. Ngũgĩ wa Thiong'o, *Devil on the Cross*, translated from Kikuyu by the author (Oxford: Heinemann, 1987); Tsitsi Dangarembga, *Nervous Conditions* (London: Women's Press, 1988).

24. Maxine Hancock, 'Bunyan as Reader: The Record of *Grace Abounding*', *BS*, 5 (1999), 68–86 (p. 69).

25. W. R. Owens, 'The Reception of The Pilgrim's Progress in England', in M. van Os and G. J. Schutte (eds.), *Bunyan in England and Abroad* (Amsterdam: Vrije University Press, 1990), pp. 91–104; Mary Hammond, '*The Pilgrim's Progress* and its Nineteenth-Century Publishers', in Owens and Sim (eds.), *Reception*, pp. 99–118.

26. Nathalie Collé-Bak, 'The Role of Illustrations in the Reception of *The Pilgrim's Progress*', in Owens and Sim (eds.), *Reception*, pp. 81–98.

27. David E. Smith, *John Bunyan in America* (Bloomington: Indiana University Press, 1966); Auguste Sann, *Bunyan in Deutschland* (Giessen: Wilhelm Schmitz, 1951); G. J. Schutte, *Bunyan in Nederland* (Houten: Den Hertog, 1989); Erik Esking, *John Bunyan i Sverige under 250 år* (Klippan: Skeab Verbum, 1980), English summary, pp. 197–203. See also, Brown, *Bunyan*, pp. 451–6.

28. Arjun Appadurai, *The Social Life of Things: Commodities in Cultural Perspective* (Cambridge University Press, 1986).

29. Fred Cooper and Ann Stoler (eds.), *Tensions of Empire: Colonial Cultures in a Bourgeois World* (Berkeley: University of California Press, 1997).

30. Isabel Hofmeyr, 'Evangelical Realism: The Transnational Making of Genre in *The Pilgrim's Progress*', in Owens and Sim (eds.), *Reception*, pp. 131–9.

31. 'Makowethu! Naantso incwadi, kha niyihlole. Ibalisa ngomHambi ohamba indlela abanga abaninzi benu bangayihamba. Kha nimphelekelele ke, nicotho-cothozise ngokufundana kwenu – nihambe nisima, ninqumama; nibe niphula-phula iinto azithethayo, nanibikela zona; nide nisuke niye kumngenisa apho waya wangena khona, ekupheleni kolo luhambo lwakhe.' Tiyo Soga, 'Intshayelelo'

(Introduction) to *Uhambo lo Mhambi (The Pilgrim's Progress*, Part 1), translated by Tiyo Soga (1868; Lovedale, South Africa: Lovedale Press, 1965), p. 7. My thanks to Monde Simelela for the translation.

32. Arlette Zinck and Sylvia Brown, '*The Pilgrim's Progress* among Aboriginal Canadians: Missionary Translation of Bunyan into Cree and Inuktitut', *1650–1850: Ideas, Aesthetics, and Inquiries in the Early Modern Era*, 13 (2006), 201–23.

33. *Ibid.*, 203.

34. Galen Johnson, 'Muhammad and Ideology in Medieval Christian Literature', *Islam and Christian–Muslim Relations*, 11.3 (2000), 334–46 (pp. 343–4), which discusses Bunyan's views on Islam.

35. Michael Davies, *Graceful Reading: Theology and Narrative in the Works of John Bunyan* (Oxford University Press, 2002), p. 4.

36. Galen K. Johnson, *Prisoner of Conscience: John Bunyan on Self, Community and Christian Faith* (Carlisle: Paternoster Press, 2003).

37. Hill, *Turbulent*, pp. 373–80; David Hawkes, 'Commodification and Subjectivity in John Bunyan's Fiction', *Eighteenth Century: Theory and Interpretation*, 41.1 (2000), 37–55.

38. Stuart Sim, 'Bunyan and his Fundamentalist Readers', in Owens and Sim (eds.), *Reception*, p. 225.

GUIDE TO FURTHER READING

Editions

The Minutes of the First Independent Church (now Bunyan Meeting) at Bedford, 1656–1766, ed. H. G. Tibbutt, Bedfordshire Historical Record Society, 1976.

Beaumont, Agnes, *The Narrative of the Persecution of Agnes Beaumont*, ed. Vera J. Camden, East Lansing: Colleagues Press, 1992; East Lansing: Michigan State University Press, 1998.

Bunyan, John, *Grace Abounding to the Chief of Sinners*, ed. W. R. Owens, Harmondsworth: Penguin, 1987.

Grace Abounding with Other Spiritual Autobiographies, ed. John Stachniewski with Anita Pacheco, The World's Classics, Oxford University Press, 1998.

The Miscellaneous Works of John Bunyan, gen. ed. Roger Sharrock, 13 vols., Oxford: Clarendon Press, 1976–94.

The Pilgrim's Progress, ed. N. H. Keeble, The World's Classics, Oxford University Press, 1984.

The Pilgrim's Progress, ed. W. R. Owens, The World's Classics, Oxford University Press, 2003.

The Pilgrim's Progress, ed. Roger Pooley, London: Penguin, 2008.

The Pilgrim's Progress, ed. Cynthia Wall, Norton Critical Editions, New York and London: Norton, 2009.

Reference and bibliography

Barnard, John, D. F. McKenzie and Maureen Bell, *The Cambridge History of the Book in Britain*, vol. IV, *1557–1695*, Cambridge University Press, 2002.

Forrest, James F. and Richard L. Greaves (comp.), *John Bunyan: A Reference Guide*, Boston: G. K. Hall, 1982.

Lemon, Rebecca, Emma Mason, Jonathan Roberts and Christopher Rowland (eds.), *The Blackwell Companion to the Bible in English Literature*, Oxford: Blackwell, 2009.

Sharrock, Roger (ed.), *'The Pilgrim's Progress': A Casebook*, London and Basingstoke: Macmillan, 1976.

Biographical studies

Brown, John, *John Bunyan, 1628–1688: His Life, Times, and Work*, 1885; 2nd edn, rev. Frank M. Harrison, London: The Hultbert Publishing Company, 1928.

Froude, James Anthony, *Bunyan*, London: Macmillan, 1880.

Greaves, Richard L., *Glimpses of Glory: John Bunyan and English Dissent*, Stanford University Press, 2002.

Hill, Christopher, *A Turbulent, Seditious, and Factious People: John Bunyan and his Church, 1628–1688*, 1988; Oxford University Press, 1989.

Lindsay, Jack, *John Bunyan: Maker of Myths*, London: Methuen, 1937.

Major Bunyan monographs and collections of essays

Backscheider, Paula R., *A Being More Intense: A Study of the Prose Works of Bunyan, Swift, and Defoe*, New York: AMS Press, 1984.

Batson, E. Beatrice, *John Bunyan: Allegory and Imagination*, London: Croom Helm; Totowa, N.J.: Barnes and Noble, 1984.

Camden, Vera J. (ed.), *Dissenting Women in John Bunyan's World and Work*, special issue of *BS*, 7 (1997).

Trauma and Transformation: The Political Progress of John Bunyan, Stanford University Press, 2008.

Camden, Vera J. and Kimberly Hill (eds.), *Identity, Agency and Gender in John Bunyan's England*, special issue of *BS*, 11 (2004).

Collmer, Robert G. (ed.), *Bunyan in Our Time*, Kent, Ohio: Kent State University Press, 1989.

Davies, Michael, *Graceful Reading: Theology and Narrative in the Works of John Bunyan*, Oxford University Press, 2002.

Dunan-Page, Anne, *Grace Overwhelming: John Bunyan, 'The Pilgrim's Progress' and the Extremes of the Baptist Mind*, Religions and Discourse 22, Bern: Peter Lang, 2006.

Furlong, Monica, *Puritan's Progress: A Study of John Bunyan*, London: Hodder and Stoughton, 1975.

Gay, David, James G. Randall and Arlette Zinck (eds.), *Awakening Words: John Bunyan and the Language of Community*, Newark: University of Delaware Press; London: Associated University Presses, 2000.

Greaves, Richard , *John Bunyan*, Grand Rapids, Mich.: Eerdmans, 1969.

John Bunyan and English Nonconformity, London: Hambledon Press, 1992.

Hancock, Maxine, *The Key in the Window: Marginal Notes in Bunyan's Narratives*, Vancouver: Regent College Publishing, 2000.

Hofmeyr, Isabel, *The Portable Bunyan: A Transcultural History of 'The Pilgrim's Progress'*, Princeton University Press, 2004.

Johnson, Barbara A., *Reading 'Piers Plowman' and 'The Pilgrim's Progress': Reception and the Protestant Reader*, Carbondale and Edwardsville: Southern Illinois University Press, 1992.

Johnson, Galen K., *Prisoner of Conscience: John Bunyan on Self, Community and Christian Faith*, Carlisle and Waynesboro, Va.: Paternoster Press, 2003.

Kaufmann, U. Milo, *'The Pilgrim's Progress' and Traditions in Puritan Meditation*, New Haven and London: Yale University Press, 1966.

Keeble, N. H. (ed.), *John Bunyan: Conventicle and Parnassus – Tercentenary Essays*, Oxford: Clarendon Press, 1988.

John Bunyan: Reading Dissenting Writing, Religions and Discourse 12, Bern: Peter Lang, 2002.

Laurence, Anne, W. R. Owens and Stuart Sim (eds.), *John Bunyan and His England, 1628–1688*, London and Ronceverte, W.Va.: Hambledon Press, 1990.

Lynch, Beth, *John Bunyan and the Language of Conviction*, Cambridge: D. S. Brewer, 2004.

Mullett, Michael, *John Bunyan in Context*, Keele University Press, 1996.

Newey, Vincent (ed.), *The Pilgrim's Progress: Critical and Historical Views*, Liverpool University Press, 1980.

Norvig, Gerda, *Dark Figures in the Desired Country: Blake's Illustrations to 'The Pilgrim's Progress'*, Berkeley: University of California Press, 1993.

Os, M. van, and G. J. Schutte (eds.), *Bunyan in England and Abroad*, Amsterdam: Vrije University Press, 1990.

Owens, W. R. and Stuart Sim (eds.), *Reception, Appropriation, Recollection: Bunyan's 'Pilgrim's Progress'*, Religions and Discourse 33, Bern: Peter Lang, 2007.

Runyon, Daniel Virgil, *John Bunyan's Master Story: The Holy War as Battle Allegory in Religious and Biblical Context*, Lewiston, N.Y.: Edwin Mellen Press, 2007.

Sharrock, Roger, *John Bunyan*, 1954; 2nd rev. edn, London: Macmillan; New York: St Martin's Press, 1968.

Sim, Stuart, *Negotiations with Paradox: Narrative Practice and Narrative Form in Bunyan and Defoe*, Savage, Md.: Barnes and Noble, 1990.

Sim, Stuart and David Walker, *Bunyan and Authority: The Rhetoric of Dissent and the Legitimation Crisis in Seventeenth-Century England*, Religions and Discourse 6, Bern: Peter Lang, 2000.

Spargo, Tamsin, *The Writing of John Bunyan*, Aldershot: Ashgate, 1997.

Swaim, Kathleen M., *Pilgrim's Progress, Puritan Progress: Discourses and Contexts*, Urbana: University of Illinois Press, 1993.

Talon, Henri, *John Bunyan: The Man and his Works*, 1948, trans. Barbara Wall, London: Rockliff, 1951.

Tindall, William York, *John Bunyan: Mechanick Preacher*, New York: Columbia University Press, 1934.

Vries, Pieter de, *John Bunyan on the Order of Salvation*, trans. C. van Haaften, Theology and Religion 176, Bern: Peter Lang, 1994.

Wakefield, Gordon S., *Bunyan the Christian*, London: HarperCollins, 1992.

Selected articles

Beal, Rebecca S., '*Grace Abounding to the Chief of Sinners*: John Bunyan's Pauline Epistle', *SEL*, 21 (1981), 147–60.

Breen, Margaret Soenser, 'The Sexed *Pilgrim's Progress*', *SEL*, 32 (1992), 443–60.

Camden, Vera J., 'Blasphemy and the Problem of the Self in *Grace Abounding*', *BS*, 1.2 (Spring 1989), 5–21.

'"Most Fit for a Wounded Conscience": The Place of Luther's "Commentary on Galatians" in *Grace Abounding*', *Renaissance Quarterly*, 50 (1997), 819–49.

Davies, Michael, 'Shaping Grace: The Spiritual Autobiographies of John Bunyan, William Cowper, and John Newton', *BS*, 12 (2007), 36–69.

Dunan-Page, Anne, '*The Life and Death of Mr Badman* as a "Compassionate Counsel to All Young Men": John Bunyan and the Nonconformist Writings on Youth', *BS*, 9 (1999–2000), 50–68.

'John Bunyan's *A Confession of my Faith* and Restoration Anabaptism', *Prose Studies*, 28.1 (April 2006), 19–40.

Dutton, A. Richard, ' "Interesting, but tough": Reading *The Pilgrim's Progress*', *SEL*, 18 (1978), 439–56.

Finley, C. Stephen, 'Bunyan among the Victorians: Macaulay, Froude, Ruskin', *Literature and Theology*, 3.1 (1989), 77–94.

Freeman, Thomas, 'A Library in Three Volumes: Foxe's "Book of Martyrs" in the Writings of John Bunyan', *BS*, 5 (1994), 47–57.

Hardin, Richard, 'Bunyan, Mr Ignorance, and the Quakers', *SP*, 69 (1972), 496–508.

Harrison, Frank M., 'Nathaniel Ponder: The Publisher of *The Pilgrim's Progress*', *The Library*, 4th ser., 15 (1934), 257–94.

Haskin, Dayton, 'Bunyan, Luther, and the Struggle with Belatedness in *Grace Abounding*', *University of Toronto Quarterly*, 50 (1981), 300–13.

'The Burden of Interpretation in *The Pilgrim's Progress*', *SP*, 79 (1982), 256–78.

'The Pilgrim's Progress in the Context of Bunyan's Dialogue with the Radicals', *Harvard Theological Review*, 77 (1984), 73–94.

Luxon, Thomas, 'The Pilgrim's Passive Progress: Luther and Bunyan on Talking and Doing, Word and Way', *ELH*, 53 (1986), 73–98.

'Calvin and Bunyan on Word and Image: Is There a Text in Interpreter's House?', *ELR*, 18 (1988), 438–59.

Lynch, Kathleen, ' "Her Name Agnes": The Verifications of Agnes Beaumont's Narrative Ventures', *ELH*, 67 (2000), 71–98.

Nussbaum, Felicity, ' "By These Words I was Sustained": Bunyan's *Grace Abounding*', *ELH*, 49 (1982), 18–34.

Pooley, Roger, 'The Wilderness of This World – Bunyan's *Pilgrim's Progress*', *BQ*, 27 (1978), 290–9.

'Language and Loyalty: Plain Style at the Restoration', *Literature and History*, 6.1 (Spring 1980), 2–18.

'Spiritual Experience and Spiritual Autobiography: Some Contexts for *Grace Abounding*', *BQ*, 32 (1988), 393–402.

Randall, James G., 'Against the Backdrop of Eternity: Narrative and the Negative Casuistry of John Bunyan's *The Life and Death of Mr Badman*', *BQ*, 37 (1994), 347–59.

Schellenberg, Betty A., 'Sociability and the Sequel: Rewriting Hero and Journey in *The Pilgrim's Progress*, Part II', *Studies in the Novel*, 23 (1991), 312–24.

Sharrock, Roger, 'Bunyan and the English Emblem Writers', *RES*, 21.82 (1945), 105–16.

'Spiritual Autobiography in *The Pilgrim's Progress*', *RES*, 24 (1948), 102–20.

Sills, Adam, 'Mr Bunyan's Neighborhood and the Geography of Dissent', *ELH*, 70 (2003), 67–87.

Sim, Stuart, 'Bunyan's *Holy War* and the Dialectics of Long-Drawn Outness', *Restoration*, 9.2 (Autumn 1985), 93–8.

'Isolating the Reprobate: Paradox as a Strategy for Social Critique in *The Life and Death of Mr Badman*', *BS*, 1.2 (1989), 30–41.

'Bunyan, Lyotard, and the Conflict of Narratives', *BS*, 8 (1998), 67–81.

Stranahan, Brainerd P., 'Bunyan's Special Talent: Biblical Texts as Events in *Grace Abounding* and *The Pilgrim's Progress*', *ELR*, 11 (1981), 329–43.

'Bunyan and the Epistle to the Hebrews: His Source for the Idea of Pilgrimage in *The Pilgrim's Progress*', *SP*, 79 (1982), 279–96.

Underwood, Ted L., ' "It pleased me much to contend": John Bunyan as Controversialist', *Church History*, 57 (1988), 456–69.

Walker, David, 'Bunyan and the Body and Kingdom of Christ, 1656–1663', *BS*, 8 (1998), 6–27.

' "Heaven is prepared for whosoever will accept of it": Politics of the Will in Bunyan's *Doctrine of the Law and Grace Unfolded*', *Prose Studies*, 21.3 (1998), 19–31.

Ward, Graham, 'To Be a Reader: Bunyan's Struggle with the Language of Scripture in *Grace Abounding to the Chief of Sinners*', *Journal of Literature and Theology*, 4 (1990), 29–49.

Zinck, Arlette M., ' "Doctrine by Ensample": Sanctification through Literature in Milton and Bunyan', *BS*, 6 (1995–6), 44–55.

Contextual and critical studies

Achinstein, Sharon, *Literature and Dissent in Milton's England*, Cambridge University Press, 2003.

Caldwell, Patricia, *The Puritan Conversion Narrative: The Beginnings of American Expression*, Cambridge University Press, 1983.

Cohen, Charles Lloyd, *God's Caress: The Psychology of Puritan Religious Experience*, Oxford University Press, 1986.

Corns, Thomas N., 'Bunyan's *Grace Abounding* and the Dynamic of Restoration Nonconformity', in Neil Rhodes (ed.), *English Renaissance Prose: History, Language and Politics*, Tempe: Arizona State University Press, 1997, pp. 259–70.

Cragg, G. R., *Puritanism in the Period of the Great Persecution, 1660–1688*, Cambridge University Press, 1957.

Cummings, Brian, *The Literary Culture of the Reformation: Grammar and Grace*, 2002; Oxford University Press, 2007.

Damrosch, Leopold, Jr., *God's Plot and Man's Stories: Studies in the Fictional Imagination from Milton to Fielding*, University of Chicago Press, 1985.

Davies, Michael, ' "Bawdy in Thoughts, precise in Words": Decadence, Divinity and Dissent in the Restoration', in Michael St John (ed.), *Romancing Decay: Ideas of Decadence in European Culture*, Aldershot: Ashgate, 1999, 39–63.

Delany, Paul, *British Autobiography in the Seventeenth Century*, London: Routledge and Kegan Paul, 1969.

Fish, Stanley E., *Self-Consuming Artifacts: The Experience of Seventeenth-Century Literature*, Berkeley: University of California Press, 1972.

Green, Ian, *Print and Protestantism in Early Modern England*, Oxford University Press, 2000.

Gribben, Crawford, *The Puritan Millennium: Literature and Theology, 1550–1682*, Dublin: Four Courts Press, 2000.

Hawkins, Anne Hunsaker, *Archetypes of Conversion: The Autobiographies of Augustine, Bunyan, and Merton*, Lewisburg, Pa.: Bucknell University Press; London and Toronto: Associated University Presses, 1985.

Hindmarsh, D. Bruce, *The Evangelical Conversion Narrative: Spiritual Autobiography in Early Modern England*, Oxford University Press, 2005.

Iser, Wolfgang, *The Implied Reader: Patterns of Communication in Prose Fiction from Bunyan to Beckett*, 2nd edn, Baltimore and London: Johns Hopkins University Press, 1974.

James, William, *The Varieties of Religious Experience*, 1902; London: Longmans, 1952.

Keeble, N. H., *The Literary Culture of Nonconformity in Later Seventeenth-Century England*, Leicester University Press, 1987.

'Puritanism and Literature', in John Coffey and Paul C. H. Lin (eds.), *The Cambridge Companion to Puritanism*, Cambridge University Press, 2008, pp. 309–24.

Keeble, N. H. (ed.), *The Cambridge Companion to the Writing of the English Revolution*, Cambridge University Press, 2001.

Knott, John R., Jr., *The Sword of the Spirit: Puritan Responses to the Bible*, University of Chicago Press, 1980.

Discourses of Martyrdom in English Literature, 1563–1694, Cambridge University Press, 1993.

Lamont, William M., *Richard Baxter and the Millennium: Protestant Imperialism and the English Revolution*, London: Croom Helm, 1979.

Luxon, Thomas H., *Literal Figures: Puritan Allegory and the Reformation Crisis in Representation*, University of Chicago Press, 1995.

Pooley, Roger, *English Prose of the Seventeenth Century, 1590–1700* (London: Longman, 1993).

Raymond, Joad, *Pamphlets and Pamphleteering in Early Modern Britain*, Cambridge University Press, 2003.

Rivers, Isabel, *Reason, Grace and Sentiment: A Study of the Language of Religion and Ethics in England, 1660–1780*, vol. I, *From Whichcote to Wesley*, Cambridge University Press, 1991.

Rosenfeld, Nancy, *The Human Satan in Seventeenth-Century Literature: From Milton to Rochester*, Aldershot: Ashgate, 2008.

Siebert, Frederick, *Freedom of the Press in England, 1476–1776*, Urbana: University of Illinois Press, 1952.

Smith, Nigel *Perfection Proclaimed: Language and Literature in English Radical Religion, 1640–1660*, Oxford: Clarendon Press, 1989.

Literature and Revolution in England, 1640–1660, New Haven and London: Yale University Press, 1994.

Stachniewski, John, *The Persecutory Imagination: English Puritanism and the Literature of Religious Despair*, Oxford: Clarendon Press, 1991.

Thickstun, Margaret Olofson, *Fictions of the Feminine: Puritan Doctrine and the Representation of Women*, Ithaca, N.Y.: Cornell University Press, 1988.

van Dyke, Carolynn, *The Fiction of Truth: Structures of Meaning in Narrative and Dramatic Allegory*, Ithaca, N.Y.: Cornell University Press, 1985.

Watkins, Owen C., *The Puritan Experience*, London: Routledge and Kegan Paul, 1972.

Watts, Michael R., *The Dissenters*, vol. I, *From the Reformation to the French Revolution*, Oxford: Clarendon Press, 1978.

Whiting, C. E., *Studies in English Puritanism from the Restoration to the Revolution, 1660–1688*, 1931; London: Frank Cass, 1968.

INDEX

Cambridge Companions To . . .

AUTHORS

Molière edited by David Bradby and Andrew Calder

Toni Morrison edited by Justine Tally

Nabokov edited by Julian W. Connolly

Eugene O'Neill edited by Michael Manheim

George Orwell edited by John Rodden

Ovid edited by Philip Hardie

Harold Pinter edited by Peter Raby (second edition)

Sylvia Plath edited by Jo Gill

Edgar Allan Poe edited by Kevin J. Hayes

Alexander Pope edited by Pat Rogers

Ezra Pound edited by Ira B. Nadel

Proust edited by Richard Bales

Pushkin edited by Andrew Kahn

Rabelais edited by John O'Brien

Rilke edited by Karen Leeder and Robert Vilain

Philip Roth edited by Timothy Parrish

Salman Rushdie edited by Abdulrazak Gurnah

Shakespeare edited by Margareta de Grazia and Stanley Wells (second edition)

Shakespearean Comedy edited by Alexander Leggatt

Shakespeare on Film edited by Russell Jackson (second edition)

Shakespeare's History Plays edited by Michael Hattaway

Shakespeare's Last Plays edited by Catherine M. S. Alexander

Shakespeare's Poetry edited by Patrick Cheney

Shakespeare and Popular Culture edited by Robert Shaughnessy

Shakespeare on Stage edited by Stanley Wells and Sarah Stanton

Shakespearean Tragedy edited by Claire McEachern

George Bernard Shaw edited by Christopher Innes

Shelley edited by Timothy Morton

Mary Shelley edited by Esther Schor

Sam Shepard edited by Matthew C. Roudané

Spenser edited by Andrew Hadfield

Laurence Sterne edited by Thomas Keymer

Wallace Stevens edited by John N. Serio

Tom Stoppard edited by Katherine E. Kelly

Harriet Beecher Stowe edited by Cindy Weinstein

August Strindberg edited by Michael Robinson

Jonathan Swift edited by Christopher Fox

J. M. Synge edited by P. J. Mathews

Tacitus edited by A. J. Woodman

Henry David Thoreau edited by Joel Myerson

Tolstoy edited by Donna Tussing Orwin

Anthony Trollope edited by Carolyn Dever and Lisa Niles

Mark Twain edited by Forrest G. Robinson

Virgil edited by Charles Martindale

Voltaire edited by Nicholas Cronk

Edith Wharton edited by Millicent Bell

Walt Whitman edited by Ezra Greenspan

Oscar Wilde edited by Peter Raby

Tennessee Williams edited by Matthew C. Roudané

August Wilson edited by Christopher Bigsby

Mary Wollstonecraft edited by Claudia L. Johnson

Virginia Woolf edited by Susan Sellers (second edition)

Wordsworth edited by Stephen Gill

W. B. Yeats edited by Marjorie Howes and John Kelly

Zola edited by Brian Nelson

TOPICS

The Actress edited by Maggie B. Gale and John Stokes

The African American Novel edited by Maryemma Graham

The African American Slave Narrative edited by Audrey A. Fisch

Allegory edited by Rita Copeland and Peter Struck

American Crime Fiction edited by Catherine Ross Nickerson

American Modernism edited by Walter Kalaidjian

American Realism and Naturalism edited by Donald Pizer

American Travel Writing edited by Alfred Bendixen and Judith Hamera

American Women Playwrights edited by Brenda Murphy

Ancient Rhetoric edited by Erik Gunderson